THE LOST WORLD OF
NICHOLAS AND ALEXANDRA

TSAR

THE LOST WORLD OF NICHOLAS AND ALEXANDRA

TSAR

BY PETER KURTH, PHOTOGRAPHS BY PETER CHRISTOPHER,
INTRODUCTION BY EDVARD RADZINSKY

A MADISON PRESS BOOK
Produced for
LITTLE, BROWN AND COMPANY
Boston New York Toronto London

First Edition

Library of Congress Cataloging-in-Publication Data

Kurth, Peter
Tsar : the lost world of Nicholas and Alexandra / by Peter Kurth.
p. cm.
Includes bibliographical references and index.
ISBN 0-316-50787-3
I. Nicholas II, Emperor of Russia, 1868–1918.
2. Alexandra, Empress, consort of Nicholas II, Emperor of Russia, 1872–1918.
3. Russia — Kings and rulers — Biography.
4. Russia — History — Nicholas II, 1894–1917.
I. Title
DK258.K84   1995
947.08'3'0922 — dc20
[B]   95–12820

10 9 8 7 6 5 4 3 2 1

Published simultaneously in Canada by
Little, Brown & Company (Canada) Limited and in Great Britain
by Little, Brown and Company (UK) Limited.

*Note: All dates in this book conform to the Western calendar, which was twelve days
ahead of the Russian calendar in the nineteenth century and thirteen days ahead in the twentieth.
In 1918 Russia adopted the Western calendar.*

Produced by
Madison Press Books
40 Madison Avenue, Toronto, Ontario
Canada M5R 2SI
Printed in Italy

Contents

For Nancy, Edward and Alexandra Wynkoop,
with twenty-five years of thanks
— Peter Kurth

For Patricia and Marina, who also left too early
— Peter Christopher

In March of 1917 a revolution took place in Russia. With frightening speed, in the space of only a few days, one of the world's greatest empires ceased to exist — the empire of the Romanov Tsars, the empire of Nicholas and Alexandra.

During those fateful days, the premiere of *Masquerade*, a play by the celebrated nineteenth-century Russian poet Mikhail Lermontov, took place at the Imperial Alexandrinsky Theater in Petrograd. The cream of the Russian intelligentsia assembled in the auditorium was stunned by the spectacle. On the stage there was unheard-of opulence: mirrors, cut glass, gilding. Neither before nor since has the Russian theater known such brilliance. This paean to the Palace proved to be a requiem for a world that, beyond the walls of the theater, was dying.

For in those few days, not only the monarchy perished; a unique civilization with its own religion, culture and traditions also came to an end.

The Russian aristocracy lived in magnificent palaces and obeyed a court etiquette that took the refinement of the last Bourbons and spiced it with the Asiatic traditions of the tsars of Muscovy. To the fabulous balls that dazzled Europe the women wore cascades of diamonds and the men resplendent dress uniforms. Sometimes they were serenaded by hundreds-strong gypsy choirs. Many a grand duke dissipated his life away in a fashionable club or lost his heart to one of the stunningly beautiful ballerinas of the Russian ballet.

In contrast to this stood the Orthodox faith, the bedrock on which everything else was

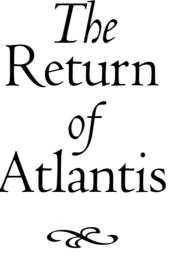

The Return of Atlantis

❧

founded. This was the Holy Russia of the tsars, with the golden cupolas of its countless churches, the unaccompanied singing of its church choirs and the solemn majesty of its worship.

"The Tsar is not God, but neither is he man. The Tsar is something between God and man," a contemporary wrote in his diary. There are many Russian folk sayings along similar lines: "Without God the world cannot be; without the Tsar the earth cannot hold."

And this entire world, the empire of Nicholas and Alexandra, perished in those few March days of 1917....

After the tsar's abdication, the last tsar and tsarina lived under house arrest in the Alexander Palace of Tsarskoe Selo, outside Petrograd. There, in a kind of Noah's ark, they tried to preserve a destroyed world.

The Socialist Sergei Mstislavski, an envoy of the revolution, visited Tsarskoe Selo during that period and described with amazement what he saw: "The servants continued to glide through the spacious rooms as noiselessly as ever in their immaculate livery. At the doors stood the blackamoors in their turbans and crimson gold-embroidered tunics, and *haiduks* well over six feet tall, who had only recently stood on the footboards of the vanished Imperial carriages, idled their time away around the Palace... And the Tsar himself, in the uniform of a Household Cavalry regiment now gone forever, walked along the corridor...."

Amid this fantastic scene stood Mstislavski in a dirty sheepskin coat, with a revolver protruding from his pocket, a representative of the new order that would soon kill off the old. In a dirty pit close to a wretched Ural hamlet, the

masters of the departed world, naked, their faces disfigured, were buried. And in the harrowing, impoverished, austere life that would descend on Russia, the vanished world of Nicholas and Alexandra was remembered like a strange, magical dream.

But the tsar, the tsarina and their children had adored photographing what they saw around them, unconsciously immortalizing their everyday life. As if sensing what was to come, they created a detailed chronicle of their way of life. In the evenings, the punctilious tsar would carefully glue these photographs into albums with paste sent specially from England. After their execution these albums were sent to gather dust in a secret archive. I remember the feeling when I first opened one of the morocco-bound volumes and experienced the sunken Atlantis, seeing it through *their* eyes.

As I turned the album pages, that world floated back from oblivion: the furniture of the imperial palaces was restored, the imperial regiments marched again, and the imperial hunt again took to the fields. Once again the lovely faces of Nicholas and Alexandra's four daughters shone with happiness, and the face of the heir, the blue-eyed prince from the fairy tale, grinned mischievously.

And once again, Nicky and Alix, two happy young people in love and rulers of one-sixth of the globe, dreamed of happiness in the century to come.

Now, at the end of that cruel century, their world has begun to come back to us. Inside this splendid illustrated book, photographs from many carefully preserved albums and from archives around the world are combined with color photographs of the palaces and places the last tsar's family knew to evoke this lost way of life.

Atlantis is rising again from oblivion.

— *Edvard Radzinsky*

CHAPTER ONE

Dancing on
the Precipice

The morning of March 6, 1913, was cloudy in St. Petersburg — leaden would be a better word to describe the heavy skies, the mist, the torrents of rain and occasional roll of thunder that broke over the city on what was meant to be a day of national rejoicing, the tercentenary of the Romanov dynasty. Three hundred years before, at a sixteenth-century monastery on the banks of the Volga River, a deputation of princes, warriors, boyars and clergy had hailed Michael Romanov, the teenage nephew-by-marriage of the late Ivan the Terrible, as the new tsar of Russia, thus putting to an end the twenty years of civil strife known as the Time of Troubles. Young Michael, regarded by these powerful Russian nobles as the most pliable candidate in a sea of rival claimants, was forced to accept a crown he didn't want, and greeted the

*The procession of the tsar and his family
(above) from the Winter Palace to the Cathedral of Our Lady of Kazan on March 6, 1913.
(Opposite) The Winter Palace today.*

news, according to his mother, with a mixture of "ire and tears."

Anger and sorrow had marked the reigns of most of Michael Romanov's successors; they would not have been out of place on this tercentenary day as the first Romanov's distant descendant, Tsar Nicholas II, accepted the honor and homage of the nation. The tsar's least pleasant duty that day was to preside over the afternoon reception for the several hundred members of the Duma, Russia's fledgling parliament. Nicholas stood passive and expressionless amidst the marble and gold of the vast Nicholas Hall of the Winter Palace while the president, Michael Rodzianko, paid tribute to his family.

Mouthing all the appropriate formulas, Rodzianko recalled the most glorious moments of the Romanov reign and the close, mystical connection that traditionally had existed between the tsar and his subjects. "During three centuries of glorious rule Holy Russia has survived all the trials sent upon her unshaken, and has attained her present might," he concluded. "The welfare of the Russian Tsars has always been the welfare of the Russian people; their cares have been the cares of the Russian people. As was the case 300 years ago, the Russian people today honors and loves its Tsar with boundless devotion."

But the tsar was unimpressed. The Emperor

*T*he crowning of Michael, the first Romanov tsar (top), in 1613. His Monomakh crown is depicted (above) in a gold and jeweled tercentenary brooch by Fabergé. (Right) Decorated for the celebrations, the People's Palace in St. Petersburg awaits a visit by the tsar.

and Autocrat of All the Russias was known to hold the Duma and its president in utter contempt. He had granted Russia a constitution and certain limited parliamentary democratic rights only eight years earlier during the revolutionary disturbances of 1905, and then only when he realized that his throne was in peril.

When the president had finished, Nicholas began his own tercentenary address to the elected representatives of his people. He spoke about his "crowned predecessors," about "the labor of all true sons of Russia" and those "tens of millions of ploughmen" — the "real people," whom he believed to be loyal, devoted and unconcerned with politics — "whose endurance and labor continues to better our nation's agriculture and increases the basic sources of national wealth." The speech was mechanical, cold and devoid of political significance, a major disappointment at a time when thinking people all over Russia had been hoping for concessions from the throne — some sign of generosity, compassion or even consciousness of the staggering problems that faced the empire.

Earlier in the day the tsar had ridden with his family through the rain and mud from the Winter Palace to the Cathedral of Our Lady of Kazan, the largest church in St. Petersburg, where a Te Deum mass was to be sung in their honor by the Orthodox patriarch of Antioch.

Twenty-one guns had sounded in salute from the Fortress of Peter and Paul, but the imperial banners that decked the route hung drenched and disconsolate amid crowds that were somewhat smaller (and whose cheering was far less enthusiastic) than Nicholas had a right to expect. Cossacks, lancers, cavalry, dragoons, scarlet-clad trumpeters and teams of prancing white horses did nothing to dispel the general gloom. Neither did the gravity of the tsar's expression nor the appearance of his son, Tsarevitch Alexei, the eight-year-old heir to the throne who had to be carried into the cathedral by a Cossack escort. During the solemn mass of thanksgiving for the life of the Romanov family, the boy did not kneel as was the custom of the Orthodox Church. The child's left leg was bent at the knee, crippled beyond any attempt to hide it. That the tsarevitch was ill was known, but the nature of his illness remained a mystery to all but the immediate family.

"Poor little fellow," a woman whispered as the tsarevitch was gingerly placed in his seat. His pinched, pale, anxious face worried and frightened the invited spectators: grand dukes and grand duchesses of the imperial family, ministers and delegates of the Russian court, high state functionaries, foreign royalty, senators, ambassadors, bishops and priests. In every corner of the cathedral stood chamberlains, cupbearers and *Chevaliers Gardes*, their medals and cuirasses glistening in the light of a thousand burning tapers, their faces turned toward the tsar and the altar where icons shone in a glory of diamonds, emeralds and precious stones. The women wore their finest attire: gowns of white silk cut low to the breast, with trains of red velvet and the imperial monogram — the Double Eagle framed in diamonds — pinned at the shoulder. Everywhere was the glint of gold: on the altar, on the icons and triptychs, on the vestments of the priests and the helmets of the

*In March, the tsarevitch
was carried into the Cathedral of Our Lady of Kazan
(opposite). He was borne by a Cossack again in May
during the Moscow celebrations (above),
which included (top) a procession down the Red Staircase
of the Kremlin. (Below) The heir and his parents
in an open carriage during the Moscow
festivities. (Right) Nicholas and his predecessors
adorn Fabergé's ornate tercentenary egg.*

guards. The court of the Romanovs was known far and wide as the wealthiest and most opulent in Europe.

"I shall long remember the dazzling display of jewels on the women's shoulders," wrote Maurice Paléologue, the French ambassador to St. Petersburg. "It was simply a fantastic shower of diamonds, pearls, rubies, sapphires, emeralds, topazes, beryls — a blaze of fire and flame."

But the splendor of the moment served only to accentuate the prevailing atmosphere of melancholy. Everyone in St. Petersburg knew that dozens, probably hundreds, of secret policemen had been placed in and around the cathedral that day to prevent an attempt on the life of the tsar. Everyone knew that his German-born wife, Empress Alexandra Feodorovna, suffered, like her son, from mysterious ailments (dizziness and palpitations of the heart) and that she was liable to faint at any moment, overcome with "nerves," or hysteria, or the simple pressure of a public appearance. She stood like an angry statue during the Te Deum mass, the Order of St. Andrew (the highest honor her husband could bestow) cutting a brilliant blue swath across her white-and-silver gown, pearls falling halfway to her knees and a diamond *kokoshnik*, the traditional headdress of all Russian women, taking the place of a crown on her head. Next to Alexandra was the tsar's mother, Dowager Empress Marie Feodorovna, the most popular member of the Romanov family, who made no secret of her dislike of her daughter-in-law.

Immediately behind the tsar, his wife and his mother stood his daughters, Olga, Tatiana, Marie and Anastasia, teenage girls of particular loveliness. They, too, wore orders — in their case the scarlet Order of St. Catherine — but they were politically insignificant because women could not inherit the Russian throne. There was hardly a soul in St. Petersburg who could have distinguished one of the girls from the other, so sheltered were their lives.

Throughout the service Nicholas stood erect, according to witnesses, "and with a glance that kept anxiously and furtively scanning the faces of the assembly as if afraid of meeting some secret danger." At one point both the tsar and tsarevitch were seen staring intently upward into the heights of the cathedral dome. Two doves had circled the rotunda at the moment of their benediction, and these, coupled with the unexpected ray of sunshine that cut through the murk and lit the tsar's face as he left the church, were the only encouraging notes on that frustrating day — signs from heaven, small as they were, to hearten a nation and a family obsessed with omens.

For the rest of that tercentenary spring, the sun saw fit to shine on the Romanovs, at least when it came to official appearances. In May the imperial family took a week-long boat trip along the Volga, retracing the journey of the first Romanov tsar from Kostroma, where he had been called to the throne, to Moscow, the ancient capital and spiritual heart of Russia. On the outskirts of Moscow, Tsar

Nicholas insisted on continuing by horseback to the gates of the Kremlin — an act of bravery, even rashness, given the turmoil of the times and the long history of assassinations that a few years earlier had cost the life of the governor of Moscow, the tsar's own uncle (and the husband of his wife's sister), Grand Duke Serge.

"He decided to ride into the city through the crowded streets in advance of all his escort and entirely unprotected," said a British observer, "followed by the Empress and their children in an open carriage. Between ten and twenty yards separated him from his guards. He rode at a foot's pace and with a set face. There was much more anxiety on those of many of the onlookers; and from many of them there came an audible sigh of relief when at last a great outburst of all the bells of the Kremlin told that he had reached the Iversky Chapel at its gate, which was always the first halting-place for prayer when the Russian Sovereign visited the Old Capital." Again Tsarevitch Alexei had to be carried, and again the empress looked fit to collapse. For many of the spectators it was their first and last glimpse of the imperial family — familiar faces, more or less attached to names, that hitherto had been known to them only through postcards.

The stiffness of the empress was a shock

to most observers. Only twice during the tercentenary celebrations did Alexandra seem at ease. In March, at a small reception in St. Petersburg, she had moved almost gaily from guest to guest, smiling and laughing, radiant in a dark blue velvet gown, which, in the words of one witness, "fell about her like midnight water." Then in May during the Volga cruise, the imperial travelers stopped at Kostroma to commemorate the election of the first Romanov in the Ipatiev monastery. There an ancient peasant woman, approaching on her knees, begged the empress for her blessing and received along with it a handsome silk shawl. This was the only occasion of the whole commemorative season when the population appeared to greet the imperial family with spontaneous good feeling, shouting "God save the Tsar!" and "Let your Sovereign Family live forever!" But it was enough to convince Alexandra that their mission had succeeded.

"Now you can see for yourself," she remarked, "what cowards those State Ministers are. They are constantly frightening the Emperor with threats of revolution, and here — you see it yourself — we need merely to show ourselves and at once their hearts are ours."

❧

The 1913 tercentenary celebrations marked Alexandra's first official appearance in St. Petersburg since the revolutionary upheavals of 1905. Since then the tsar and his family had lived almost permanently in the imperial enclave at Tsarskoe Selo, fifteen miles south of St. Petersburg, where they hoped to find refuge from the cares of state — as well as from terrorists' bombs — and where they managed eventually to isolate themselves completely.

The empress dreaded for her children the influence of the Russian aristocracy, "whose minds," she insisted, "even in the schoolroom, were fed with the foolish and often vicious gossip of a decadent society." She despised the

Russian glittering classes, and her hatred was returned in kind. "*Nemka,*" they called her, "the German Woman" — a particular insult in light of the fact that every Russian empress since the eighteenth century (with the technical exception of the tsar's mother, a "Danish" princess from the House of Schleswig-Holstein-Sonderburg-Glucksborg) had been drawn from the ranks of German royalty.

The year 1903 had seen the last great ball at the Winter Palace, when the Romanovs and the whole of their court had dressed in the style of Alexei the Mild, the "gentle" tsar of the seventeenth century who was Nicholas's personal favorite among his ancestors. The withdrawal of the imperial family from the capital, combined with the empress's open hostility, had left a regrettable gap in high society, where morale had never been lower and a competition seemed to be in progress as to who could whistle loudest in the dark. The 1913 social season was as brilliant as anyone remembered, but it went ahead as had become the custom without the tsar, without the empress, in an atmosphere of recklessness, restlessness, passion and what one commentator recognized as "plain insanity."

"That year they danced the tango," the tsar's cousin, Grand Duke Alexander Mikhailovitch, later recalled. "The languorous tempo of its exotic music sounded from one end of Russia to another. The gypsies cried, the glasses clinked.... Hysteria reigned supreme." St. Petersburg was "a city that ordered its champagne by the magnum, never by the quart," and nobody in it was immune to the charms of the twentieth century. At her palace on the Fontanka Canal, Countess Betsy Shouvalov gave a black-and-white ball where guests arrived in costumes by Leon Bakst, the stage and opera designer, and cocaine flew up a great many noses. Bridge was the upper-class craze of 1913, along with airplanes, motorcars, spiritualism and dope. Add

The procession through Red Square to the Kremlin (opposite top), in which Nicholas rode on horseback (opposite bottom), marked the climax of the 300th anniversary celebrations. The crowds were more enthusiastic, however, at Kostroma, where the first Romanov tsar had accepted the throne in 1613. There, his descendant was welcomed with bread and salt (above), and foundation stones for a Romanov memorial were laid (top).

Colored wigs for the ladies were the rule at this ball held at Countess Betsy Shouvalov's palace (above). "Fancy dress" was another source of amusement for the privileged (left), as were the ballet and opera seasons, for which Leon Bakst designed this program (right).

These views of St. Petersburg's factories provide a stark contrast to the gilded life of Russian high society. Industrial development had brought a flood of rural laborers into Russia's cities, where they lived and worked in miserable conditions.

to this an obsession with sex — "shocking scandal, extreme debauchery, frenzied searching" and pots of money — and the empress's fears for her children's purity seem amply justified.

While the aristocracy danced and the tsar and his family retreated into isolation, the empire fell apart. Political assassinations and other acts of terrorism had declined in the years following the near-revolution of 1905, but the signs of a society on the verge of collapse were unmistakable. Russian industrial output was rapidly increasing, but so were drunkenness, violence and premature death, and eight out of ten industrial workers in St. Petersburg lived on an income lower than the tsar's own government had determined was essential to survive. Strikes were a matter of everyday fact: in 1914, on the eve of the First World War, it was estimated that during the previous year, every second worker in Russia had taken part in some type of labor protest.

In the years following the emancipation of the serfs in 1861 there had been an exodus from the countryside by peasants in search of work. This exodus increased dramatically at the turn of the century after a series of disastrous crop failures led to widespread famine. Now in the overcrowded cities a vast disparity existed between the numberless poor and the privileged few. On Nevsky Prospekt, the largest and most fashionable avenue in St. Petersburg, elegant shops peddled candy and diamonds next to poverty so bleak it could scarcely be described. Cholera and tuberculosis were rampant. No wonder that in the wake of the political concessions of 1905 a swarm of political parties seeking radical or revolutionary change sprang up in the factories, the universities, the *zemstvos* (local councils): socialists, liberals, Bolsheviks, Mensheviks, anarchists, radicals, constitutionalists and more.

Conditions were somewhat better in the countryside. The illiterate peasants who formed

eighty percent of the Russian population remained very poor, but in recent years things had improved somewhat thanks to long-overdue land reform and a series of bountiful harvests. But the long-suffering peasantry, people to whom words like *constitution* and *Duma* meant nothing at all, had lost faith in the Russia of their ancestors. "God doesn't answer," the ancient proverb went, "and the Tsar is far away."

Even nature seemed filled with foreboding. In the years before the First World War, a series of natural disasters — floods and fires and shifts in the ground — lent themselves inevitably to apocalyptic predictions. In 1908 some kind of enormous blast, scientifically unexplained, was detected in the forests of Siberia, burning trees and flattening houses within a radius of twenty-five miles.

"The air is heavy with ominous things," said a sage in Voronezh. "Every day we see the glare of fires on the horizon; a bloody mist crawls over the ground; breathing and living have become difficult as before a storm." It was no different in the capital, where the occasional clear thinker still managed to exist. "No one expects or hopes anything," wrote a lady of the court. "Everyone grows indifferent ... waiting with apathy for the cataclysm that is bound to come."

It had been hoped that the tercentenary might herald a renewal of the ancient social contract between the tsar and his people, that the twentieth year of Nicholas's reign might witness the dawn of a new Golden Age, but such was not to be. In the winter of 1913 the dowager empress gave a brilliant ball at the Anichkov Palace for the tsar's two eldest daughters, the Grand Duchesses Olga and Tatiana, who danced till four in the morning. But when the proud father took his daughters home on the last train from town, he unknowingly brought down the curtain on their first and last appearance in St. Petersburg society.

A few days later, when Nicholas appeared with his wife at the Maryinsky Theater, during a state performance of Glinka's *A Life for the Tsar*, the empress's nerves caused her hands to shake violently.

"Not once did a smile break the immobile somberness of her expression," said Meriel Buchanan, the daughter of the British ambassador. "A dull, unbecoming flush was stealing over her pallor," and the crowd "could almost hear the belabored breathing which made the diamonds which covered the bodice of her gown rise and fall, flashing and trembling with a thousand uneasy sparks of light." Unable finally to endure the scrutiny of the public, the empress rose, whispered a few words to her husband and disappeared from view. The wave of resentment that greeted her withdrawal was almost palpable, remembered Miss Buchanan, and in the gold-and-white boxes of the Maryinsky sighs were heard, shoulders were shrugged and "men uttered despairingly below their breath. Was it not always the same story?" None of them knew that the empress was desperate, and that the year 1913 marked the last for their whole way of life.

Nicholas and Alexandra were often seen in formal portraits (above), but rarely in person. Public appearances were an ordeal for the empress (right), and her disappearance from view during a performance at the Maryinsky Theater (opposite) was resented by the audience.

The Imperial City

The city that Peter the Great had founded in 1703 as his "window through to Europe" was, by the time of the reign of the last of his successors, fast becoming a center of European-style political dissent and cultural ferment. New economic growth had created an industrial work force and a rising middle class, and had helped spur resistance to autocratic rule. It had also brought *art nouveau* commercial buildings into a city of baroque palaces, and encouraged trolley cars and automobiles to join carriages and sleighs on Nevsky Prospekt.

*N*evsky Prospekt circa 1900 (opposite), near the Gostiny Dvor, the main market building (at far left). Across the street is the entrance to the Passazh, a glass-roofed shopping arcade (right), once lined with expensive shops (inset). *The* style moderne exterior of the 1907 Singer Building, topped by the company's Atlas symbol (below), was one of the new architectural accents being introduced to a city more accustomed to details like the gilded griffins (above) on the footbridge over the Griboedova Canal.

*"On sunny days, especially
Sunday, all fashionable
St. Petersburg rode
along the 'Quai'...."*

— Grand Duchess Olga,
the tsar's sister

*The St. Petersburg depicted
in photographs taken before the Revolution can still be
found in the city of today. Petrovskaya Embankment,
for example, down which the empress led her four
daughters to embark on a boat in August 1912 (right),
has changed little in over eight decades (above).*

Jeweler to the Tsar

No name symbolizes the opulence of the twilight era of imperial Russia more than that of Peter Carl Fabergé. His elegant and often whimsical baubles were the gifts of choice for any fashionable occasion, but it is the imperial Easter eggs that have made the name Fabergé a legend. The first imperial egg, presented by Alexander III to his wife, Marie, in 1885, opened to reveal a "surprise," a tiny golden hen. Under Nicholas II ever more fabulous eggs were produced yearly with such "surprises" as a jeweled miniature of the coronation coach or the palace of Gatchina. Before the Revolution forced it to close, the Fabergé workshop in St. Petersburg employed over 500 craftsmen. Fabergé himself escaped to Switzerland in 1918 and died there in 1920.

The Fabergé Building in St. Petersburg (right), once housed display rooms, workshops and an apartment for Fabergé (top center). Nicholas poses with his near-identical cousin, the future George V, in a Fabergé frame (top left), while a miniature of him decorates a rocaille box (top right). When a pearl button is turned on the Lilies-of-the-Valley Egg (left), the tsar's Easter gift to Alexandra in 1898, miniatures of her husband and daughters Olga and Tatiana appear.

CHAPTER TWO

Nicholas and Alexandra

It was one of the great love matches of history — the union of the mild and gentle heir to the largest empire on the face of the earth and a beautiful, sorrowful, mystical princess, deeply religious and with a will of iron, whom tragedy marked with a special vengeance.

As a child, the future empress of Russia, Princess Alix of Hesse, was called "Sunny" by her family — Princess Sunshine — because she was always laughing and had a dimple in her cheek. But her mother died when Alix was six, and after that Princess Sunshine rarely smiled. She became obsessed at an early age with thoughts of God and the consolations of eternity. "All is in God's will," she wrote many years

later. "The deeper you look, the more you understand that this is so." In 1918, while a prisoner of the Bolsheviks in Siberia, she would explain her philosophy in a letter to a friend: "Life here is nothing — Eternity is everything, and what we are doing is preparing our souls for the Kingdom of Heaven.... It requires good food to make plants grow, and the gardener, walking through His garden, wants to be pleased with His flowers. If they do not grow properly, He takes his pruning knife, and cuts."

This gloomy person was not the "Alix H" with whom Nicholas fell in love, the girl he dreamed of marrying from the moment he began to think about brides. They first met in 1884, when he was sixteen and she a girl of

Nicholas and Alexandra (above)
first met as teenagers in 1884 at Peterhof, site of the Great Palace (right)
commissioned by Peter I in imitation of Versailles and Schönbrunn.

twelve. The occasion was the wedding of Alix's elder sister, Princess Elizabeth of Hesse (called "Ella" in the family), to Nicholas's uncle, Grand Duke Serge. Nicholas was by this time a handsome, blue-eyed, courteous youth who managed on first acquaintance to break through the wall of pathological shyness that already marked Princess Alix's character.

"I'm Nicky," he declared on the day they met in the Alexandria cottage at Peterhof, the Romanov family's summer retreat on the Gulf of Finland.

"I'm Sunny," she said.

"Yes, I know," he replied.

In fact, they were second cousins, closely related through the house of Hesse, and the question of a possible marriage between them may well have been raised in dynastic circles without either of them being the wiser. At Peterhof, they played and ran in the garden, according to Nicholas's diary, exchanged flowers, whispered secrets and scratched their names with a diamond on a window of the house.

"I like her awfully much," Nicholas observed with typical royal dryness. After four days of flirting he had become almost ardent: "We love each other." He gave Alix a diamond brooch, which she promptly gave back — worried, no doubt, about the reaction of her grandmother, Queen Victoria, to whom no simple gesture among royalty was without political significance. Alix was undoubtedly too young to fall in love with the tsarevitch as a result of this first acquaintance, but clearly she liked him very much. For Nicholas it seems to have been a case of love at first sight, and by the time Alix and

The Alexandria "cottage" at Peterhof was actually a large Victorian villa. Nicholas's parents and later his own family enjoyed this retreat and spent a part of every summer here.

her family returned home to Hesse, she seldom left his thoughts.

Alix's shyness no doubt stemmed from the tragic circumstances of her early childhood. She was less than a year old in 1873 when her three-year-old brother, "Frittie," accidentally fell from their mother's bedroom window and died within hours of internal bleeding — the first hemophiliac in the Hessian line. The gloom that enveloped the court at Darmstadt cannot have been lost even on an infant, even on the "sweet, merry little person" that Alix initially was.

Her mother, Alice, the grand duchess of Hesse, was a daughter of Queen Victoria, and had inherited from the queen and the century itself a morbid, almost erotic fascination with illness and the grave. Alice mourned little Frittie with a terrible grief, threw herself into charity work, talked about God and the reunion of souls, then died herself in 1878, felled by depression and an outbreak of diphtheria. In the general epidemic, Alix also lost her younger sister May. She was still called Sunshine, but her life had been covered by a cloud — she used the word herself — an aura of sadness and resignation that she wore like a cloak, or a shroud, till the day she died.

"Her attitude to the world was perpetually distrustful," said her cousin, Queen Marie of Romania, "strangely empty of tenderness and, in a way, hostile.... She held both great and small at a distance, as though they intended to steal something which was hers." Princess Marie Louise of Schleswig-Holstein, another cousin and one of her regular playmates in childhood, loved Alix like

Alix's family nickname of "Sunny" is belied by her expression in both of these childhood photographs (top and bottom). After the death of her mother, Alice (right), when Alix was six, solemnity became one of her distinguishing traits.

*T*he five surviving children of Hesse (above) after the deaths of their mother, their sister May, and their hemophiliac brother "Frittie." (Below) Still in mourning for their mother, Alix and her two older sisters, Victoria (left) and Ella pose with their grandmother, Queen Victoria, at Windsor in 1879.

a sister, but grew tired fairly early of the tragic look on her face. "Alix," she remarked, "you always play at being sorrowful; one day, the Almighty will send some real crushing sorrows and then what will you do?"

By the time Nicholas met Alix, these traits were firmly fixed, and he was one of the few people in later years who could bring a smile to her face. One wonders what first attracted him to this sad little princess from a German duchy. Perhaps she seemed about as far away as it was possible to get from his overbearing father, his glamorous mother and the tyranny of ritual and precedent that ruled the Russian court. Certainly her pedigree was spotless. As a granddaughter of Queen Victoria, and through her father's descent in the Hessian line, Alexandra could trace her lineage straight back to Charlemagne.

But Darmstadt, the capital of Hesse, was just another German town, a medieval merchants' center, all cobblestones and clocks, and Alix's father, Grand Duke Ludwig IV, reigned there as a virtual steward of the German emperor. Ludwig's wealth and style of living could not begin to match that of the tsar of all the Russias. The Hessian royal family owned a number of homes, among them the ghastly New Palace in Darmstadt, which Alix's mother had commissioned on her arrival in Germany in the 1860s and decorated in the "cozy," cluttered, suffocating style of Queen Victoria's estates at Osborne and Balmoral. The loveliest of the Hessian ducal residences was Wolfsgarten, a hunting lodge in the country between Darmstadt and Frankfurt, which Grand Duke Ludwig purchased only after the death of his wife and which became the favored residence of his family. It was and still is a heavenly place — wooded, peaceful and bursting with roses. But compared with the glory of imperial Russia, the manors and castles of Alix's childhood were like

so many bed-and-breakfasts stacked up against the Emerald City of Oz. The Winter Palace alone had more than a thousand rooms, and the tsar employed more than fifteen thousand personal servants. He was absolute ruler of one-sixth of the earth's land surface — 8.5 million square miles by the usual estimate.

But as far as intelligence and intellectual training went, Alix far outshone her future husband. She was well educated — extremely so by the standards of royalty at the time — and would have had difficulty finding anyone at the Russian court who had read, as she had while still in her teens, *Paradise Lost*, *The Life of Cromwell*, and a nine-volume history of the Hohenstaufens.

She had been raised to be more independent of thought than was the norm for the female representatives of European royalty. Her mother had been the most forward-thinking of Queen Victoria's daughters. At Darmstadt Alix's British governesses, handpicked by Queen Victoria, had trained her in the avoidance of gossip and "idle talk" — the lifeblood of the Russian court — and taught her to converse in public almost entirely on abstract themes. She read widely, embroidered for pleasure and as an adult — in conscious imitation of her mother — became devoted to the performance of charitable works.

The tsarevitch by contrast was an outdoorsman, not a man of ideas, never happier than when riding, shooting, walking or shoveling snow. His formal education, while carefully mapped out and rigorously supervised, was strictly *pro forma*. He was tutored in history, science, geography and mathematics. Special attention was paid to his religious instruction, and he grew up speaking five languages, three of them so fluently that he could have passed as a native of England or France as well as Russia. But the imperial schoolrooms were a place for

*T*he future emperor and empress of Russia, Alexander ("Sasha") and Marie Feodorovna ("Minnie"), photographed around the time of their marriage in 1866 (top) and with their first child, Nicholas, circa 1869 (above). An 1884 magazine illustration (opposite) shows Tsar Alexander III in full military dress.

memorizing, not thinking, and Nicholas, after finishing his studies in 1890, never again showed the slightest interest in anything intellectual.

In his defense it should be said that none of Europe's royal families had a reputation for intellectual prowess. Most of them had no conversation at all beyond the unchanging details of their daily activities and the latest news about one "dear" relation or another. Irony was lost on them, as were complexity and the merest suggestion that their opinions might not be infallible. "Once a prejudice gets into a royal head," warned a lady-in-waiting to Queen Victoria, "it can never be got out again till the end of time." The Romanovs (eccentrically, in view of their oppressive form of government) often behaved like merry little children in whom practical joking never gave way to a more mature sense of humor. It was not uncommon to see a Russian grand duke tossing oranges at his sisters or tripping a footman who was carrying a tray into the formal dining room.

Such was the lighter side of the world in which the future Russian emperor grew to manhood. He was born at the imperial retreat of Tsarskoe Selo on May 19, 1868, the first child of the man who would, much sooner than expected, ascend to the Russian throne. Alexander III was a gigantic, imposing, hot-tempered titan, built like the bears of Russian legend and notorious for his enormous strength and spartan habits. "He tried to be Russian down to the smallest details of his personal life," said General A. A. Mossolov, who became head of chancellery under Nicholas II. "He claimed, perhaps without reasoning it out, that a true Russian should not be too highly polished in his manners, that he should have a touch of something like brutality."

Nicky's mother, Marie Feodorovna, the petite former Princess Dagmar of Denmark and daughter of King Christian IX, may have appeared an unlikely match for Alexander, but she proved an ideal consort, and their marriage was a happy one. It could never be said of Empress Marie that she lacked personality, but like her sister in England, the Princess of Wales (later Queen Alexandra), she preferred parties to politics, card games to books, and fashion, gossip and dancing to everything else. She bore Alexander six children, five of whom survived to adulthood (Nicholas, George, Xenia, Michael and Olga) and raised them at the palace of Gatchina, south of St. Petersburg, where they lived on the mezzanine floor in simple rooms that had been originally intended for servants.

This rugged choice was Alexander's, not his wife's. He was determined that his children — above all Nicholas — should not be coddled. As a child Nicholas II slept on an army cot without a pillow and took a cold bath every morning, but the toughness so prized by his father failed to take root in his character. In fact it was Nicholas's gentleness that impressed itself on everyone who met him — particularly the depth of kindness in his eyes, which no one ever forgot. Sydney Gibbes, who later became the English tutor to Nicholas's children, described him in terms that were by no means unusual in their ardor: "He had a 'presence' that was second to none, so full of quiet and assured self-possession and dignity. But it never inspired fear. The deepest sentiment that it invoked was *awe*, not fear. I think the reason for this was his eyes. Yes, I am sure that it was his eyes, so wonderful were they. Of the most delicate shade of blue, they looked you straight in the face with the kindest, tenderest, the most loving expression.... His eyes were so clear that it seemed as if he opened the whole of his soul to your gaze, a soul that was so simple and pure that it did not fear your scrutiny.... This was his great charm and this was politically his great weakness."

If truth be told, the young Nicholas had no political strengths or weaknesses at all. He was not trained in politics; he did not like it, and he did not understand it. At the age of thirteen he saw his grandfather, Alexander II, die in agony in the Winter Palace after a terrorist's bomb literally blew him to pieces. The most liberal of the nineteenth-century tsars, Alexander was the man who freed the serfs and started Russia on the road to modernity; that he of all the Romanovs should be murdered so cruelly appeared to his family to be not an irony but a sign that Russia was on the wrong course.

The result was a wave of repression under Alexander III and a disastrous recommitment in the Romanov family to the principle of absolute rule. No other idea of a political nature ever entered Nicholas's head, and when he came to the throne in 1894 he was completely unprepared for the task.

*T*he palace of
*Gatchina (opposite), where outdoor activities such as
boating (right) could be enjoyed in the extensive
park, was the preferred residence of Alexander III.
A twelve-year-old Nicholas (below) poses in the
uniform of a Cossack regiment.*

"It was my father's fault," Nicholas's youngest sister, Grand Duchess Olga Alexandrovna, later admitted. "He would not even have Nicky sit in Council of State until 1893. I can't tell you why. The mistake was there." When Nicholas was already twenty-five and it was suggested to his father that he head up a committee to supervise the completion of the Trans-Siberian railway, Alexander was incredulous. "Have you ever tried to discuss anything of consequence with him?" the tsar inquired about his son and heir. "He is still absolutely a child; he has only infantile judgments. How would he be able to become president of a committee?"

A
*family photo from about 1888 (above)
shows (left to right) George, Xenia, the emperor holding Olga, Michael, Nicholas and the empress.*

33

Grand Duchess Olga remembered that her father "disliked the mere idea of state matters encroaching on our family life," and Nicholas himself was in no hurry to enter the world of edicts, manifestos, ministers and wars. ("When my father died," Nicholas would later complain, "I was simply the commander of the Escort Squadron of the Hussars and for the first [years] of my reign was just taking the measure of how the country was run.")

At the age of fourteen, Nicholas began to keep a diary, which he maintained faithfully on a daily basis until just before his death. It is the record of almost nothing but hunts, walks, shoots, the weather, birthdays, parades and the occasional calamitous event in his empire, invariably described as "horrible" or "dreadful" and put down to the will of God. Ordinary psychology, not to mention the literary standards of the age, can provide no explanation for the unrelieved vapidity of Nicholas's observations. His was a mind untroubled by deep thought or difficult questions.

The friends he chose reflected his simple tastes and enjoyment of the outdoors. His closest childhood confidants were his brother Grand Duke George ("darling Georgie") — a sensitive, sweet-tempered boy whose delicate health kept the entire family on tenterhooks — and the so-called Mikhailovitchi, grandsons of Tsar Nicholas I through Grand Duke Michael Nicholaievitch. For many years Grand Duke Alexander ("Sandro") and his brother, another George, were Nicholas's boon companions. Sandro developed into a clever, cynical, sensual bon vivant. George, more reserved but closer to the tsar, married Nicky's favorite cousin, Princess Marie of Greece and Denmark.

Nicholas had grown up handsome. In spite of his small stature, he was attractive to women and not above some youthful carousing in the darker reaches of St. Petersburg. At nineteen, in the family tradition, he entered military service, earning a command in the Hussar Guards and ultimately attaining the rank of colonel. He adored the military life, the drilling and parading, the camaraderie of the barracks and the extended debaucheries of the evening hours, where he found he could drink with the best of them. But even if there were passing affairs for the young officer, he did not forget the lovely Alix.

Early in 1889, with the tsarevitch now twenty-one and the princess a blooming seventeen, what had begun as a teenage infatuation turned into an adult passion. Nicholas had not set eyes on Alix since their first meeting five years earlier. Now she arrived in St. Petersburg with her father and brother to visit her sister Ella and brother-in-law Serge for the winter social season that would end when Lent began. During this sojourn Nicky and Alix saw each other at every opportunity — at the endless succession of grand balls, lavish dinners and evenings at the ballet or the opera (inevitably followed by a champagne supper lasting almost till dawn). In the afternoons they went on jaunts to skate on

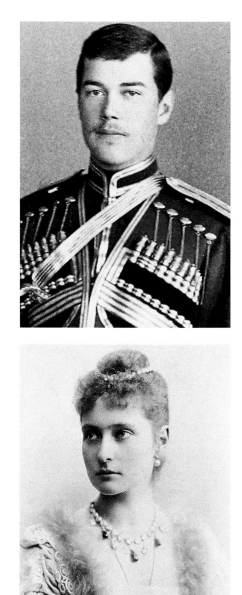

In December 1890, Nicholas (top) wrote in his diary, "My dream is to marry Alix H some day. It's ages I have loved her, but still deeper and stronger since 1889 when she spent 6 weeks in Petersburg."

The Belosselsky-Belossersky Palace in St. Petersburg was the town residence of Grand Duke Serge and Alix's sister Ella. It was here that Alix stayed during her visit in 1889. (Opposite, center) This portrait of Serge and Ella was taken one year before his assassination by terrorists in Moscow.

the frozen Neva or to toboggan on specially built artificial hills in the countryside.

On the eve of Lent, Nicholas hosted an intimate ball in Alix's honor in the Alexander Palace at Tsarskoe Selo. Knowing how shy she was, he invited only close relatives and a few of his officer friends. The ballroom was perfumed with a profusion of fresh flowers — roses and orchids — and the young couple danced until

the stroke of midnight, when the festivities came to an abrupt end. When Alix returned home to Darmstadt at the end of her family's six-week stay in the Russian capital, she had fallen deeply in love with her Russian cousin, and Nicholas with her. Shortly after her departure for home, he pasted Alix's photograph on the first page of his diary for 1889.

The Russian court was not so enthralled.

"Devoid of charm, wooden, cold eyes, holds herself as if she'd swallowed a yardstick" was one unkind verdict on Alix from aristocratic circles. But the courtiers were only speaking what they believed their sovereigns wanted to hear. In fact the only people who seem to have been enthusiastic about the prospect of marriage between the future tsar and this German "ramrod" were Serge and Ella.

Alix's 1889 visit to Russia also left Queen Victoria exceedingly displeased. Her granddaughter's affection for the tsarevitch was leading to "every sort of report," and the British monarch had reason to believe that Ella was "encouraging and even urging" Alix to marry him. She was already amazed that Ella had managed to survive the Russian winters, which had "ruined the health of almost all the German princesses who went there."

Since the death of Alix's mother in 1878, the old queen had kept a watchful eye on her surviving grandchildren in Darmstadt — Victoria, Ella, Irene, Ernie, and "sweet darling Alicky." She had practically raised them herself in a stream of directive letters and on their long summer holidays in England. When the time came for them all to marry, she hoped to "place" them where she pleased.

"Russia I could not wish for any of you," the queen confessed to Alix's sister Victoria, just before Ella married Grand Duke Serge and was "carried away" to that "dreadful country." Russia was a "horrid" place, in the queen's opinion — "so bad, so rotten, that at any moment something dreadful might happen."

Nicholas's own parents were no less leery of the match. In the first place the tsar of Russia despised the queen of England, whom he regarded as "a pampered, sentimental, selfish old woman." He worried about the possibility of her "meddling," through Alix, in Russian affairs, and in any case was firmly committed to the recently concluded alliance between Russia and France (in Paris the Pont Alexandre III still grandly straddles the Seine). For a time there was talk of a marriage between Nicholas and Hélène d'Orléans, the daughter of the pretender to the French throne. But the plan can't have been taken too seriously by anyone, given that Hélène was a Catholic who would not convert to Orthodoxy and that she was really a princess of Nowhere, there being no sign that the French people had any intention of restoring the Bourbon monarchy.

The idea that Nicholas's parents objected to his marrying Alix because she was a German princess, while constantly repeated, is transparently false, since the first serious target for imperial matchmaking was Margaret of Prussia, the sister of Kaiser Wilhelm and another granddaughter of Queen Victoria. The queen never got a chance to register her objections to the match; on hearing about the proposed alliance, Nicholas declared that he would rather become a monk than marry Margaret. It would be Alix or no one, he vowed. His determination to stay the course of his "desperate quest" was the first, and arguably the only, sign of steel in his character. He would wait, he said, "calmly and meekly" placing his trust in the will of God and "looking to the future."

In what seems to have been a deliberate attempt by the tsar to make his son forget the Hessian princess, in the spring of 1890 Alexander III engineered a liaison with the ballerina Mathilde Kschessinska, the tiny seventeen-year-old rising star of the Russian Imperial Ballet.

"Where is Kschessinska?" Alexander bellowed after a performance of the state ballet school's graduating class. When she quiveringly appeared, he pronounced a benediction: "Be the glory and adornment of our ballet." All of the tsars were devoted to the ballet — indeed, they

Memorabilia from the life and career of Mathilde Kschessinska, prima ballerina assoluta of the Russian Imperial Ballet and mistress, briefly, of the future Nicholas II. At right is a studio portrait of her in stage costume. (Far right) Also shown are an 1892 poster for a masquerade ball at which she performed (top) and a 1902 program (bottom) for a ballet called Mikado's Daughter. Below is a letter to Nicholas from her and photos of them both in fancy dress, he as Eugene Onegin. After the Revolution Kschessinska immigrated to Paris, where she married the tsar's cousin Grand Duke Andrei Vladimirovitch. A distinguished ballet teacher, she counted Dame Margot Fonteyn among her pupils. She died in 1971 at the age of 99.

"I adored the tsarevitch and wanted only one thing ... my happiness, however brief it might be."

— Mathilde Kschessinska

owned and maintained it — provided the dances they saw were familiar and pretty and didn't depart from the fluttery traditions of the eighteenth century.

In 1890 Fokine, Diaghilev and Nijinsky had yet to make their mark with the Ballets Russes. It would be fifteen years before Isadora Duncan came to St. Petersburg and, with her revolutionary concepts of "free" movement, permanently transformed the world of dance. Mathilde Kschessinska was the undisputed heiress to the old school, a brilliant dancer but emphatically not a creative genius. In her willingness to please the emperor, she was also completely mainstream. When Alexander sat her next to Nicholas at a post-performance supper with the admonition that they not "flirt too much," we may assume that a certain amount of nudging and winking went on until Nicholas got the point.

The tsarevitch's diary announces that he "liked" Kschessinska "very much," though there is some question about when their relationship became physical. Kschessinska later mentioned a quarrel they had over Nicholas's reluctance to sleep with her. He didn't want to be "the first," he explained, as otherwise he would be "forever in her debt." But he saw a great deal of her as time went by and ultimately bought her a house — actually, a palace — in St. Petersburg, where "we led a quiet, retiring life," according to Kschessinska, and where Nicholas was often seen galloping up on his charger in the middle of the night.

"Spent all night with MK," his diary reports, "— wonderful. Left as the sun was coming up." Kschessinska, in the meantime, was madly in love with her "Niki," while realizing that by no conceivable stretch of the rules could she ever become his wife. He never concealed from her his love for Alix of Hesse, and she was content to remain, as he told her when they finally parted, "the happiest memory of his youth."

During the summer of 1890 Alix returned to Russia to visit her sister at Ella and Serge's country estate of Ilinskoe just outside Moscow, but this time Nicholas was forbidden to see her. His affair with Kschessinska continued, but the close proximity of his beloved Alix, combined with her continued unavailability, was pure agony for him. In his diary of August 20 Nicholas wrote, "Lord! Am dying to go to Ilinskoe.... Otherwise, if not now, then I might have to wait an entire year to see her. And that is hard!!!"

That autumn, Nicholas was dispatched by his parents on a nine-month tour of the Far East. Whether the trip was meant to broaden his mind or simply to remove thoughts of Princess Alix, it did nothing to dampen his ardor. The tsarevitch traveled in the company of his brother Grand Duke George and their cousin Prince George of Greece through Egypt, India, Thailand and Japan. For most of the journey Nicholas was bored to distraction.

"All palaces look the same," he grumbled. "I might as well have stayed at home." The palm trees were boring, the potentates dull; nothing, said Nicholas, was really "worth talking about." Belly dancers in Egypt provided some small relief — "They undressed themselves" — and in Japan Nicholas suddenly came alive. "My eyes didn't know where to look first," he wrote, "such were the wonders" of the architecture and the costumes, the teahouses and the "hundreds of

*K*schessinska's St. Petersburg palace (left) was a gift from Nicholas who often used this rear entrance (inset). The mansion was sacked in March of 1917 and later became Lenin's headquarters.

geishas." "Japanese erotica is more refined and subtle than the crude proffers of love on European streets," he observed. "The tea ceremony ends.... All that follows remains a secret." Whether he actually took advantage of any of the geishas' artful charms is a question not answered in his diary.

This diverting Japanese interlude almost ended in disaster, however. On April 29, after visiting Nagasaki and Kyoto, Nicholas and his companions were passing through the town of Otsu. As they walked along a crowded street, a crazed policeman attacked the tsarevitch with a sword, delivering a glancing blow to his forehead.

"What! *What* do you want?" cried Nicholas as blood poured from the gash.

He was saved from assassination by the quick thinking of his cousin George, who lunged at the attacker with a bamboo cane — a souvenir bought earlier in the morning — and, swinging it wildly, warded off what might have been a fatal second attempt. But the first blow left a permanent scar ("the Otsu mark") on Nicholas's forehead.

"What I don't understand," said Nicholas later, "was how Georgie, that fanatic and I had ended up alone in the middle of the street [i.e., without attendants or police protection], why no one from the crowd rushed to my aid." The only plausible explanation is that the tsarevitch's own guards had failed miserably at their watchdog duties.

Horror gripped the Russian court when news of the Otsu incident finally reached St. Petersburg. Gossip spread like wildfire, since both of the Georges in Nicholas's company, his brother and his cousin, were homosexual. There was talk of male brothels and "unspeakable acts," and the rumor even got around that George of Greece had played a role in provoking the attack by insulting the honor of a Japanese boy. This story, unfounded, was favored

by Queen Victoria, more worried than ever that Nicholas might marry her granddaughter and still wondering how to prevent it.

After his return, Nicholas picked up his affair with Kschessinska. Although they both realized they could never marry, their mutual affection was genuine. For a time they virtually cohabited in a small house she had rented from the composer Rimsky-Korsakov. But Nicholas yearned for Alix as deeply as ever. Since his father would not permit the match, he chose simply to wait, refusing to consider any other. Meanwhile, Alix remained firm in her reluctance to convert to Russian Orthodoxy. She loved Nicky and had never concealed it, but she was a Lutheran, confirmed at the age of sixteen in a solemn ceremony in Darmstadt; religion, she said, was not a thing to be slipped on and off "like a glove." Then, in 1892, when her father died and her brother Ernie succeeded him as grand duke, she became the first lady of Hesse. Until Ernie married, Alix was his hostess, mistress of the court of Darmstadt, and apparently content to remain so. Her relatives, indeed, were almost convinced that she would remain a spinster.

Early in 1894 the situation changed. Nicholas's seemingly superhuman father was ailing — losing weight, his complexion growing sallow, his feet swelling. The first ball of the St. Petersburg season was postponed because of the tsar's ill health, and when it was finally held, the fine clothes hung loosely on his gaunt frame and everyone could see that he was not himself. Suddenly concerned with an orderly succession, Tsar Alexander relented in his opposition to a marriage between Nicholas and Alix of Hesse.

Now only one major obstacle remained: Alix's attachment to her Lutheran religion. But this, too, was beginning to weaken. In 1892 her beloved older sister Ella had voluntarily converted to Russian Orthodoxy. That opened a crack in Alix's resolve. The crack grew into a

A gathering of royalty at Coburg in 1894 for the wedding of Alix's brother Ernie and her cousin "Ducky," Princess Victoria of Edinburgh. The bridal pair are not depicted here, but among the guests are Nicholas (top row, center) with Kaiser Wilhelm's hand on his shoulder, and Alix (middle row, third from the right), with a rare smile on her face. Serge and Ella sit with the children in front, and the future King Edward VII of England stands at the far right.

chasm with the impending marriage of her brother to Princess Victoria of Edinburgh and Coburg ("Ducky"), probably Alix's least favorite cousin and a woman disastrously unsuited, in her opinion, to her brother's sensitive and "artistic" nature. Ernie was yet another homosexual ("Footmen, stableboys — he slept quite openly with them all," one of his cousins recalled), though this fact was never mentioned, even hinted at, in the vast archives of European royal correspondence. Some have said that Alix changed her mind about marrying Nicholas once she realized that the much-loathed Ducky would be taking her place as Darmstadt's *grande dame*. More likely this was simply the final straw,

and it provided Nicholas with the opportunity for which he had waited so long.

When the tsarevitch and his entourage traveled to Coburg in mid-April 1894, he had only one thought: that he would propose to Alix and that she would accept. (Before leaving St. Petersburg he said good-bye to Kschessinska for the last time.) While the cream of European royalty — Romanovs, Hohenzollerns, Saxe-Coburgs and Guelphs — gathered in this German backwater to celebrate the nuptials of two minor members of the nobility, a separate and far more riveting drama was being played out in the drawing rooms and private chambers of the Coburg Schloss.

At the earliest opportunity, the morning of his second day in Coburg, Nicholas arranged to be alone with Alix. For two hours he pleaded his suit. The princess was torn. On the one hand she loved Nicky; on the other she still could not bear the thought of giving up her religion. As Nicky talked she wept continuously and repeatedly whispered, "No, I cannot." When the interview was over, both were exhausted, and Nicholas went away without the answer he so desired.

For the next two days Alix wept and fretted and prayed and moped. She attended her brother's wedding in a troubled trance, clearly tormented by Nicholas's proposal. The wedding

itself became almost a footnote to the real question of the day: would Alix of Hesse marry the future tsar? Queen Victoria continued to oppose the match, but other powerful voices now urged Alix to say yes. First came Kaiser Wilhelm II, "Cousin Willy," who visited Alix that night and told her it was her "bounden duty" to marry Nicholas. (Wilhelm saw his own political advantage in the union, which would inevitably move Russia away from France and closer to an alliance with Germany.)

But the most potent voice of all was surely Ella's, who could speak not only with a sister's love but from her personal experience of conversion to the Russian religion. In her new faith, she assured Alix, she had found at least as much comfort as in the old. By the time Ella left Alix's room, the princess had decided to accept her prince. She needed only a second proposal, which came the following day, April 20.

They met in a room overlooking the palace gardens while a thunderstorm raged outside. Nicholas carried a bunch of flowers snatched from a table and wore a ceremonial sword that Kaiser Wilhelm had hastily strapped on while urging the tsarevitch to get on with it. Once again there were tears from Alix, but this time they were happy tears of acceptance, acceptance of the young man who soon would rule an empire and of whatever fate held in store. Now at last she could receive "those sweet kisses," as she later told her husband, "which I had dreamed of and yearned after so many years."

"Oh God, what happened to me then," Nicholas wrote his parents. "I cried like a child, and she did too, but her expression had changed at once: her face was lit with a tranquil pleasure." There was great rejoicing among Alix's family, and in Russia the news was received with unexpected pleasure. From St. Petersburg Nicholas's mother wrote to inquire what "stones" "dear Alix" preferred — "sapphires or emeralds? I would like to know for the future" — while Queen Victoria, ever the sentimentalist, blessed the couple and warned Alix after the jewels arrived not to get "too proud." Only in private did the queen confess that her "blood ran cold" when she thought about her granddaughter's future.

Nicholas and Alexandra (above) on the day of their engagement. Also taken that day was this famous portrait (left). Queen Victoria sits at center, between her eldest grandchild, Kaiser Wilhelm, and his mother — Victoria's daughter — the Empress Frederick. Nicholas and Alexandra are to the left of Victoria. To the right of Alix are her sisters Victoria of Battenberg and Irene of Prussia, and Albert, the Prince of Wales, stands behind Nicholas.

CHAPTER THREE

A New Tsar

For Nicholas and Alix there were just six months of quiet happiness — "heavenly bliss," as Nicholas said — before destiny propelled them onto the throne of Russia. No date had yet been set for their wedding when Nicholas returned to St. Petersburg, but they were not apart long. In June the tsarevitch traveled to England to meet his betrothed at Walton-on-Thames, where Alix's eldest sister, Princess Victoria of Battenberg, kept a holiday cottage. There they enjoyed "a veritable idyll ... boating up and down the river, picnicking on the shore." Alix embroidered and Nicholas read, and "everything," he remembered, " — nature, people, places, all seem[ed] nice, dear and lovable." It was at this time, immediately after their engagement, that Alix got into the habit of reading Nicholas's diary and inscribing in the margins different entries of her own. One morning she drew a heart next to her promise of undying fidelity: "*Toi, toi, toi, toi....*" Her love for Nicholas was literally ecstatic, based in large measure on a passionate sexuality that, given the stiffness of her

This painting of a peasant procession by Ilya Repin is a realistic depiction of both the country and the religion that Alix of Hesse would soon make her own.

44

demeanor in public, most people never guessed she had. ("I press you to my yearning breast," she wrote when they had already been married for more than twenty years, "I kiss all the dear places I so tenderly love — Ever Nicky, my Angel, my own treasure, my Sunshine, my life.") Nicholas had told her about his love affair with Mathilde Kschessinska, and she had forgiven him with a great rush of appreciation. "I want you to be quite sure of my love for you," Alix explained, "and that I love you even more since you told me that little story, your confidence in me touched me, oh, so deeply, and I pray to God that I may always show myself worthy of it."

From Walton, the lovers went to Windsor as the guests of Queen Victoria, who invited Nicholas to call her Granny and pronounced him "good," "dear" and even "liberal-minded" — a sign, if not of clear thinking, at least of her hopes, with the marriage inevitable, that it might not lead to disaster. From Russia two emissaries arrived: a language teacher, Catherine Schneider ("Trina"), who became Alix's *lectrice* in Russia, her court reader and one of her most trusted servants and friends, and Father John Yanishev, the Romanov family's private confessor, who was much impressed with Alix's piety and her "thoroughness" in the matter of conversion. Having made the leap, she did not look back. She took to Orthodoxy with an ardent thirst, learning the rites and the names of the saints, poring over volumes of advanced theology and refusing only to follow that part of the conversion ceremony that required her to spit three times on the ground in defiance of her old religion. When the formal moment came in Russia, the spitting ritual was dropped.

That occasion came sooner than anyone expected, despite Alexander's III's failing health. In the summer of 1894 the forty-nine-year-old tsar was diagnosed with nephritis, an acute inflammation of the kidneys. The disease supposedly owed its origin to an almost unbelievable physical exertion six years before. In 1888 the tsar and his family had been riding toward Kharkov in the imperial train when it crashed near the town of Borki, jumping the rails and causing the roof to collapse into the dining car where the family was eating lunch. Though unhurt, they were pinned to the ground,

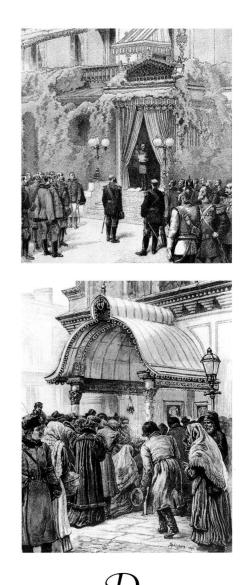

*D*uring their courtship, Nicky and Alix wrote to each other nearly every day. (Left) In this letter from Windsor Castle, Alix describes the arrival of her Russian teacher, Fraulein Catherine Schneider, who would remain her trusted servant until the end. (Opposite) The ailing tsar gives final counsel to his son and heir while crowds (top and above) wait outside the palace at Livadia for bulletins on the emperor's health.

and Alexander, struggling through a narrow space on the floor of the carriage, lifted the iron roof on his shoulders and held it there until everyone had crawled to safety. The strain was thought to have permanently damaged his vital organs. Now he was desperately ill, shrunken, sleepless and spitting up blood. By October it became obvious that his condition was fatal, and Alix was hurriedly summoned from Darmstadt, where she had returned following her English summer idyll, to join the imperial family at the deathbed of the tsar.

The family gathered at Livadia, their Crimean retreat on the shores of the Black Sea, where the tsar's doctors had hoped he might benefit from the sunshine and air. But neither rest nor medicine made any difference, and he died quietly, sitting upright in his chair, on the afternoon of November I. Alexander lived long enough to welcome Alix, whom he insisted on receiving in full dress uniform as befitted a future empress. Alix in turn assured the dying tsar that her conversion to Orthodoxy would take place immediately; until her wedding she would be known as "the Truly Believing Grand Duchess Alexandra Feodorovna." She was present with the whole family when the emperor finally died, conducting herself "like a little Angel of comfort," as her sister Ella remembered. After that she was completely ignored. The emperor's widow, Marie Feodorovna, disappeared into her private apartments where she sat huddled for days with her sister, the Princess of Wales, while twenty-six-year-old Nicholas, overwhelmed with grief and mute with terror at the prospect of becoming tsar, was further distracted by plans for his father's funeral and by the inevitable rituals and ceremonies that attended his accession to the throne.

"My God, my God, what a day!" he wrote in his diary. "The Lord has called to Him our adored, dear, fondly loved Papa." It was "the worst thing" that Nicholas could imagine, "the moment he had dreaded all of his life." When "the horrible reality" began to sink in, he turned to his cousin Sandro, Grand Duke Alexander Mikhailovitch, for reassurance.

"Sandro, what am I going to do?" Nicholas cried. "What is going to happen to me, to you... to Alix, to Mother, to all Russia? I am not prepared to be Tsar. I never wanted to become one. I know nothing of the business of ruling. I have no idea of even how to talk to the ministers."

Sandro tried to calm him, but saw no purpose in disputing the obvious: Alexander III had held Russia together singlehandedly and with a proverbial iron fist. Everyone knew it; everyone at Livadia had cause to fear for the future of the empire. "I cannot describe the sense of desolation we all felt," said Marie of Greece, "as we adored [Alexander III] and considered him our best friend. Our only comfort was to behold the marvelous expression of peace and serenity on his dear face."

Nicholas stands beside the Prince of Wales (below left) during the funeral of Alexander III. Each member of the family was given a gold leaf from a royal funerary wreath as a memento. This one (below) belonged to Nicholas's sister, Grand Duchess Olga.

The interment of Alexander III (opposite) in the Cathedral of Peter and Paul in St. Petersburg. Nicholas and his mother, now the dowager empress, wept copiously as the coffin was lowered into the floor. Alix (at bottom right) stood quietly and discreetly at the back of the family group.

In the time it took to bury the body, that beloved face began to rot. A number of the emperor's grief-stricken relations, gathered for the funeral from the courts of Europe, were not above mentioning the stench of the open coffin as Alexander lay in state, first at Livadia, then in Moscow and finally, after a two-week journey through the heart of Russia to allow his subjects a glimpse of the corpse, in St. Petersburg, where the Romanovs had all been buried since the days of Peter the Great. For another whole week the imperial family was obliged to attend twice-daily masses for the soul of the tsar, which also meant, according to custom, that they were obliged to kiss his decaying face on entering and leaving the church. By the time the emperor was finally laid to rest in the Cathedral of Peter and Paul, Nicholas, Alix and most of the family were on the verge of collapse.

"Come ye all that love me and kiss me with the final kiss," read the Metropolitan of Petersburg as the coffin was lowered into its vault, "for I depart unto the judge where no respect of persons is." Nicholas and his mother both burst into tears at the moment of interment while Alix — she was Alexandra now — stood slightly to the side, pale and grave and giving no sign of the intense emotions that must have been whirling within. This grievous loss to her fiancé's family, which was also a political disaster for their unsteady empire, was her introduction to Russia. When she married her beloved Nicky on November 26, 1894, in the

chapel of the Winter Palace in St. Petersburg, she noticed very little difference between one ceremony and the other.

"Our marriage seemed to me a mere continuation of the masses for the dead," Alexandra admitted, "with this difference, that now I wore a white dress instead of a black." Nicholas had wanted to be married immediately, while still at Livadia, but a consortium of Romanov uncles and cousins had persuaded him to wait and do it "properly" in St. Petersburg. In different circumstances Alexandra would probably have gone back to Darmstadt to wait out the official period of mourning before marrying the tsar, but Nicholas wouldn't hear of her leaving St. Petersburg when he needed her so badly, and it took no persuasion to induce her to stay.

"My poor Nicky's cross is heavy," she wrote later, "all the more so as he has nobody on whom he can thoroughly rely and who can be a real help to him.... He tries so hard, works with such perseverance, but the lack of what I call 'real' men is great. Of course, they must exist somewhere, but it is difficult to get at them." She would be man and woman both in the meantime, if the circumstances required it. She reminded her husband that beneath her flowing gowns she wore a pair of "invisible trousers." She would "be all, know all, and share all" with him. "Beloved," she wrote in any number of letters, *"listen to me."*

She rode to her wedding in white, sitting with Nicholas's mother in a golden coach and waving stiffly to the crowds on Nevsky Prospekt as a twenty-one-gun salute was fired from the

Fortress of Peter and Paul. A "small" wedding had been planned in deference to the family's grief. There would be no reception, no wedding breakfast and no honeymoon, but black, at least, had been banished for the day. Nicholas wore his hussar's uniform (and fumbled his responses until prompted by the priest), and Alexandra appeared in the ravishing garb of Russian imperial brides: a low-cut gown of silver brocade, a cape of cloth-of-gold, a diamond *kokoshnik* adorning her hair, and ribbons, orders, pendants and pearls to complete her majestic attire. It took four pages to carry her train, and in a moment of panic just before the ceremony she muttered nervously, "I don't think I can move. I'm pinned to the ground." Her future mother-in-law, the dowager empress, had been helping her with her hair.

"Yes, I know how heavy it all is," she said. "But I'm afraid it's only one of the lesser weights that need to be borne by a Russian empress."

Given the unusual circumstances of Alexandra's arrival in Russia and her very private personality, these weights were heavy indeed. Her future subjects had first seen her draped in mourning, a somber and mysterious figure at the endless rites and ceremonies that attended the death of the emperor. "She has entered our land behind a coffin," the peasant seers proclaimed. "She brings misfortune with her."

To make matters worse, the young princess of Hesse was simply overwhelmed by the transition from sleepy Darmstadt to the glittering center of a huge empire. The unexpected death

*G*uests at the tsar's wedding (above) ascend the Jordan Staircase of the Winter Palace (opposite). Of the imperial couple (below) their cousin, the future King George V, said that he "never saw two people more in love." (Left) This wedding postcard was one of many commemorative items distributed throughout Russia.

of Alexander III had hurled her, at the age of twenty-two, into the loftiest (or at any rate the most imposing) royal station in the world. "To the Emperor of All the Russias belongs the supreme and unlimited power," read Article I of the Fundamental Laws of the Russian Empire, the document that took the place of a meaningful constitution during Nicholas II's reign. "Not only fear, but also conscience commanded by God Himself, is the basis of obedience to this power." As Nicholas's consort, Alexandra would bear the same titles and descriptives as her husband: "Sacred," "Most Holy," "All Powerful," "August." It was a gigantic leap for a young woman who, only weeks before her marriage, had stayed at a boardinghouse in Harrogate and bicycled with her sister through the English countryside, something no Russian empress would have dreamed of doing (much less been allowed to do by the police who were on guard day and night). She barely had time to catch her breath, let alone adjust to the unique combination of unbending protocol and reckless frivolity that set the tone of the Russian court. She was homesick, unsure of herself, surrounded by strangers and, simply, bewildered.

"I wish you would *tell* me something about these people," Alexandra complained to Princess Maria Galitzine, whom the dowager empress, without asking, had appointed as her daughter-in-law's first mistress of the household. "Then I would *know* what to talk to them about."

"What does it matter what you say to them?" the princess replied. "It is honor enough that they are meeting the Empress!"

"The wife of Alexander III had lived in [Russia] for seventeen consecutive years preceding her coronation," said Nicholas's cousin, Sandro, in Alexandra's defense, "but Princess Alix was given exactly ninety-six hours to study the language and get acquainted with the national customs." It took her years to master the Russian language. She spoke in an Anglo-German housewifely trill, and at public ceremonies, which she dreaded to the depth of her soul, her discomfort expressed itself in sweating, tremors and an eruption of ugly red blotches on her face. Her natural beauty was almost completely obscured by her terror of social occasions, and only when she was alone with her husband, her children and a handful of worshipful friends could the Princess Sunny of childhood emerge. When she smiled, people remembered, "It lit up her face, it turned her mouth into a flower, it did something unforgettable to her beautiful eyes. It was a smile which, in the language of Russian peasants, 'was like the gift of a big silver coin.'" And it was a smile her people never saw.

Alexandra's charms, public and private, were completely lost on her mother-in-law. From the very beginning, to the tsar's discomfort and the undisguised glee of the Russian court, relations between Alexandra and the dowager empress were, if not hostile, distinctly strained, awkward, often grudging and reduced before long to mere shows of politeness. The tsar's sister Olga believed the two women "had tried to understand each other," but they were so "utterly different in character, habits, and outlook" as to seem like creatures of a different species.

"She never tells me what she does," the dowager empress complained, "or what she intends to do; when we are together she speaks of everything in the world except herself. I would be happy if she would throw off this reserve for once." Alexandra, for her part, had no use for her mother-in-law's unceasing frivolity, her passion for dancing, flirting, fashion and gossip.

Matters were not helped by the fact that Nicholas and Alexandra, finding themselves so suddenly married, also found themselves homeless. They had had no time to select and prepare their own apartments, and for the first months

The Anichkov Palace (opposite top) was the permanent city residence of the dowager empress (above), and where the new tsar and his bride (below) lived after their marriage. The tsar's mother liked having her family and their attendants under one roof, but it made the palace rather crowded and tensions simmered between members of "the old court" and "the young court" of Nicholas and Alexandra. (Opposite bottom) Away from "Motherdear," the new tsar busses his wife on the stairs in the garden at Peterhof while his sister Xenia sits in the lap of her husband, Sandro, and his youngest sister, Olga, seems prepared to take flight.

of their marriage they lived with the dowager empress in Nicholas's boyhood rooms at the Anichkov Palace in St. Petersburg. It was not the time, Nicholas said, for "Motherdear" to be "left with another empty place at her dinner table." Alexandra was prepared to shoulder this unforeseen connubial burden, but with her husband "all day occupied," as she wrote in a letter to Germany, and his mother ignoring her at every meal, she began to feel that she had come to Russia "on a visit" and wasn't married to the tsar at all. When she realized, however, that the protocol of the dowager empress's household would also extend into public life, Alexandra was deeply resentful. Eventually, she rebelled.

The issue that brought the two empresses to war involved a matter of precedent — the order in which the members of the tsar's family could file into rooms and leave them, which of their names was mentioned first in ritual prayers for their health, and who sat next to whom at dinner. Under the Romanov house law, the mother of an emperor ranked higher than his wife, but in previous reigns this point had never been pressed — indeed, it had never come up. The dowager empress had been lucky enough to enjoy her years on the throne in the absence of a mother-in-law, which is the only conceivable legitimate excuse for her unfeeling behavior toward Alexandra. She could not have known how humiliating it was to be shunted aside in public. Nevertheless, she refused to give way, and for the whole of Nicholas's reign, at every state and family function, she walked arm in arm at the head of the line with him, leaving Alexandra to take second place in the company of one of her husband's brothers or some senior grand duke or visiting dignitary.

Alexandra quickly learned that not a single detail of Russian imperial etiquette could be altered without a struggle; even the tsar was powerless against his mother when it came to points of protocol. But when Marie Feodorovna also refused to relinquish the crown jewels, which belonged to the state and by right were worn by the reigning empress, Alexandra struck back. If Motherdear desired the jewels, she said, then Motherdear should have them. Her disingenuously noble gesture threatened a minor scandal, and the dowager empress, bound no less by pride, was obliged to dispatch the Romanov hoard directly to her daughter-in-law.

In the end the Russian court under Nicholas II divided into camps: those who followed the dowager empress and, by extension, the glittering traditions and sensuous pleasures of old St. Petersburg, and those, much smaller in number, who adhered to Alexandra and her "puritan" ways. She was despised from the outset by St. Petersburg society, which judged her to be haughty, prudish, snobbish, awkward and empty of charm.

A famous story of her first days in Russia presents Alexandra as "deeply shocked" during a ball at the Winter Palace, when she sent a lady-in-waiting to reprimand a female guest whose dress she thought was cut too low.

The new empress in court dress (below). Not long after their wedding, Alexandra and her husband visited the Alexander Palace (opposite) and decided to make it their principal residence.

"Madame," the message went, "Her Majesty wants me to tell you that in Hesse-Darmstadt we don't wear our dresses that way."

"Really?" came the answer. "Pray tell Her Majesty that in Russia we *do* wear our dresses this way."

Nor did the wellborn of St. Petersburg appreciate the simple, homely activities Alexandra favored. "The Russian aristocracy could not understand why on all the earth their

Empress knitted scarves and shawls as presents for her friends," said Julia ("Lili") Dehn, one of the very few women of Russian high society whom Alexandra took to her heart. "Their conception of an Imperial gift was entirely different, and they were oblivious of the love which had been crocheted into the despised scarf or the useful shawl." One of Alexandra's first projects in St. Petersburg was a charity knitting circle, a society of handwork whose noble members were supposed to knit three garments a year for the poor. The idea was dismissed as provincial, and the empress as hopelessly Teutonic. She spent her first days in Russia in a nightmare of misdirected effort, "lost in a thicket of thorns," as one of her biographers said — lonely, increasingly resentful and taking comfort only in the arms of her husband, her "Sweetheart," her "darling boysy dear."

The split between the empress and her mother-in-law was not formal or even openly acknowledged, but after 1895, when Nicholas and Alexandra left his mother's household, the rivalry was fact.

They moved not to the Winter Palace, the official St. Petersburg residence of the reigning tsar, but to Tsarskoe Selo (the Tsar's Village) the Romanov family's fairy-tale compound south of St. Petersburg. Since the murder of Alexander II in 1881, none of the Romanovs had cared to live in the heart of the capital. The threat of assassination was something Alexandra got used to only slowly. Wherever she went she was followed by guards. Anyone who spoke to her was afterward interrogated by the secret police: "What was the subject of your conversation with Her Imperial Majesty?" Alix yearned for the simple joys of her childhood in Darmstadt, and she found them — better said, she built them from scratch.

Ten days after their wedding, Nicholas and Alexandra had paid a visit to the Alexander

Palace in Tsarskoe Selo, where they had danced the night away during Alix's winter visit to Russia in 1889. Now they decided on the spot that they would make it their home. The Alexander was the smaller of two eighteenth-century palaces at Tsarskoe, an unpretentious two-winged structure with a central hall and a scanty (by imperial standards) one hundred rooms. Nicholas had been born there — "that charming, dear, precious place" — though recently the palace had been used mainly for small receptions and as a kind of hostel for the imperial family's innumerable relations and guests. Not far away, presiding like a blue-and-white battleship over Tsarskoe Selo's elaborate artificial park, was the Catherine or so-called Big Palace, Bartolomeo Rastrelli's rococo master-piece named in honor of Catherine I.

Alexandra's choice of the modest Alexander when she might have had the Catherine, Gatchina (also within easy reach of St. Petersburg) or the Winter Palace itself bolstered society's opinion of her questionable taste. When she finished her renovations, there were no questions left. She had made the place over in the style of an English gentlewoman, stuffing it with knickknacks and drowning it in chintz. Her furniture came from Maples in London (mail-ordered, to the horror of the court), and her famous Mauve Boudoir, every

The official portrait of Nicholas and Alexandra with Olga, their firstborn child. Queen Victoria pronounced the baby girl "splendid" in spite of her "immense head."

inch and surface of which she had decorated in that color, was a horror to almost everyone who saw it. The empress of Russia was a *Hausfrau* at heart: she moved heaven and earth to secure for her family a cozy island in a sea of gold.

By 1895 she was pregnant. Her primary function as empress, of course, was to produce an heir to the throne, and since women, by edict of Catherine the Great's son, Tsar Paul I, were barred from the line of succession, Nicholas and Alexandra were praying for a son.

"It has become very big and kicks about and fights a great deal inside," Nicholas observed in a letter to his mother, but it was a girl for all of that — a "splendid" child, fat and rosy with a full head of hair, which the Russian midwives declared was an omen of her future happiness. The baby was named Olga, and though her sex carried with it a whiff of disappointment, her parents were not yet alarmed about the future of the dynasty. On the contrary they were "radiantly happy" with their "precious little one," the senior grand duchess of imperial Russia, and eager to present her to the Russian people when they traveled to Moscow for their coronation.

❧

When Nicholas II came to the throne in the middle of the last decade of the nineteenth century, he inherited not only an empire but a form of government — autocracy — that gave him literal authority over every aspect his subjects' lives, from the central issues of war and peace to the quarrels of peasants over who owned a cow. The tsar of Russia *was* Russia: no distinction was made in law between the will of the sovereign and the good of the nation. An enormous bureaucracy, estimated at ten percent of the urban male population and backed by the power of the army, the church and the secret police, had the task of enforcing the tsar's commands. Their authority derived directly from him, and his, of course, came from God. "I have the firm and absolute faith," Nicholas once said, "that the destiny of Russia, my own fate and that of my family are in the hands of Almighty God, who has placed me where I am. Whatever may happen, I shall bow to his will, conscious that I have never had any other thought but that of serving the country he has entrusted to me."

In January 1895, in a speech before a powerless delegation of provincial councilmen in St. Petersburg, Nicholas baldly reasserted the theory of absolute rule. He summarily dismissed the widespread call for constitutional reform — even a limited system of representative government — as a "senseless dream." "I shall maintain the principle of autocracy," he declared, "just as firmly and unflinchingly as it was preserved by my unforgettable late father."

Nicholas's speech shattered the hopes of the Russian people that the new tsar would be more liberal than his father, and it caused an uproar all over the country. It did not matter that his words were no more than a restatement of his father's well-established policy, which was all Nicholas had to guide him at the outset of his reign. From exile, revolutionaries and political dissidents smuggled pamphlets into Russia, warning the tsar that they would "fight to the bitter end." His speech was actually credited as the specific provocation, the final insult that led to the founding of the Russian Social Democratic Workers' party — later divided into Bolsheviks and Mensheviks — that would become the driving force behind the Revolution that would erupt in 1917.

Even Nicholas's family and the high nobility were offended by his choice of words, regarding his reference to senseless dreams as tactless and unnecessary at a time when terrorism had substantially declined and the nation was at peace. They blamed Alexandra, imagining that she, after only three months in Russia, had already become more tsarist than the tsar and was prodding her husband relentlessly to "be a man" and assert himself. The suspicion had a certain degree of truth, but in his effort to be a strong ruler — "Be Peter the Great," Alexandra later advised, "be Ivan the Terrible" — Nicholas would only move from blunder to blunder, half-conscious at best of the disparate forces that pressed in upon him. The January 1895 speech restating his belief in absolute autocracy was the first in a series of avoidable errors that became the hallmark of Nicholas's reign — terrible mistakes of judgment perceived by his people as acts of heartlessness that ultimately earned him the epithet Nicholas the Bloody.

A more disastrous event in every respect took place at the tsar's coronation in May 1896. It was the custom at the crowning of a Russian tsar for the sovereign to provide a feast for his subjects, offering them unlimited free food and barrels of beer in conjunction with the granting of amnesties and pardons, the lifting of minor fines and distribution of gifts: cups, mugs, medallions and so forth, all emblazoned with the imperial monogram, the new tsar's initial, and the date. Hundreds of thousands of

Crowds gather in Moscow for the coronation procession.
It was estimated that more than a million Russians flooded the city to catch a glimpse of their new tsar and tsarina.

people, most of them peasants, had traveled the length and breadth of Russia in order to catch a glimpse of the tsar as he rode in triumph to the Kremlin. Half a million, at least, were herded onto Khodynka Field, a scrubby tract of land used for military drills on the outskirts of Moscow, where tables and tents were hastily installed on top of a series of ditches in preparation for the feast — and incidentally to contain the crowd and keep the riffraff well away from the emperor, his family and their guests. "A gang of princes" had arrived from Europe, according to the tsar's diary, but by tradition, no reigning monarch whose rank might rival his own was at the coronation service.

For the tsar and his wife, their crowning at Assumption Cathedral in the Kremlin on May 26 was the occasion of their formal marriage to Russia. It was the moment of Nicholas's divine anointing and, from a religious point of view, the most significant event of his reign. In regard to the ceremony itself, no expense had been spared, no detail overlooked. Nicholas swore his oath as "Lord and Judge" of the Russian nation and crowned Alexandra with his own hand — "so carefully," in the memory of his sister, Grand Duchess Olga Alexandrovna, and "so tenderly" that it brought tears to the eyes of the gathered assembly.

They kissed each other, then sat on their gold-and-ivory thrones for the remainder of the five-hour service, staring straight and solemnly ahead while a deacon read their titles in full: "Nicholas Alexandrovitch, Emperor and Autocrat of All the Russias, Tsar of Moscow, Kiev, Vladimir, Novgorod" — and on through a list of provinces and fiefs claimed by Russia as the tsar's by right: "Poland, Finland, Bulgaria,

The Coronation Easter egg by Fabergé (above) echoes the pattern of the tsar's mantle and opens to reveal a miniature of the coronation coach, perfectly modeled in gold from the original that appeared in the procession (above left) to Assumption Cathedral (opposite).

"The weather, happily, was marvelous.... It all took place in Assumption Cathedral, though it seems a dream. I shall not forget it my whole life long."

— Nicholas II's diary, May 26, 1896

Tver...Semigalia, Samogotia, Armenia and the Mountain Princes." Outside, from the banks of the Moscow River, guns were fired; bells rang out, and cries of "Hurrah!" "Many Years!" and "God Save the Tsar" were heard from one end of the city to another.

That night, following the inevitable performance of the opera *A Life for the Tsar*, the emperor and empress greeted the crowd from the balcony of the Kremlin Palace, its ancient facade ablaze with the light of thousands of tiny bulbs. Fetes, theatricals, fireworks and a series of brilliant balls decorated the coronation from beginning to end. No one could have guessed that the splendor of the event, the last of its kind in imperial Russia, was about to be erased from popular memory.

"The crowd who spent the night in

Nicholas and Alexandra (above) in their coronation regalia. (Above left) The tsar takes communion before his holy anointing, and later kisses the empress after placing the crown of Catherine the Great on her head (top). At the end of the five-hour ceremony, the new tsar and tsarina receive the homage of the church, the government and a variety of popular delegations (above middle).

*N*icholas II,
anointed and crowned, proceeds from the
cathedral (above) under a feathered baldachin
held aloft by nobles. The empress rode behind
him in a coach. That evening the Kremlin
complex was lit up by thousands of tiny
bulbs (right), a display of electrical wonder
that amazed ordinary Russians.

"Till this day, thank God,
all has gone smoothly, but today
a grave sin has befallen..."

— Nicholas II's diary,
May 30, 1896

Khodynka Field," Nicholas wrote in his diary four days later, "pending the giving out of a dinner and a mug, pressed upon the wooden constructions, and there was a terrible jam, and it's dreadful to add, about 1300 people were trampled down!" The cause of the mass stampede was never precisely determined. The most common explanation was the impatience of the crowd, many of them already drunk, who heard a rumor that the supply of beer was about to run out and surged forward in an effort to claim their share. Hundreds of people fell into ditches and were crushed by the crowds behind them or suffocated slowly under the weight of others who fell on top of them. The throng moved as "a single body," according to reports, unable to stop or reverse direction, "surging and billowing" toward the police barricades at the far end of the field. The police, of course, had their own methods for dealing with unruly Russian crowds, and further contributed to the slaughter by blocking passage at the front of the line. When it was over, bent and twisted legs and arms rose in grisly profusion from the series of ditches that crossed the field.

The tsar and the empress were scheduled to

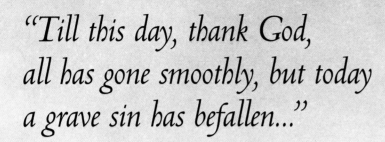

Nicholas II drinking a glass of vodka (above) on Khodynka Field. During a coronation celebration held here for the public, the distribution of commemorative mugs (opposite top) and other treats caused a stampede in the crowd, and hundreds, if not thousands, were trampled (opposite middle and bottom).

make an appearance at Khodynka that day, and in order to spare their sensibilities, the bodies were hastily covered with tarpaulins and tossed onto trucks, which drove through Moscow in search of cemeteries and morgues. They took the same roads in the same direction as the coronation guests who were making their way in gilded carriages to a party, a ball, or a dinner of duckling and crème brûlée. The contrast could not have been more stark, and to ordinary people the fact that the parties went on was a scandal in itself.

The death by trampling of a thousand people (or two thousand, or three — no one ever knew the precise number) would have been horrible enough under any circumstances. As the unexpected climax of a state celebration whose central premise was authentic knowledge of the will of God, horror combined with a mystic tradition and emerged as a vision of apocalypse, a terrible omen for the future of Russia and a blight on the reign of Nicholas II. The tsar remarked in his diary that everything at the coronation had gone smoothly "till this day," when "a grave sin" befell the country.

The situation might have been salvageable had the man responsible for security at the coronation not been Nicholas's uncle, Grand Duke Serge, the fierce and much-despised governor of Moscow, and had Nicholas and Alexandra, on the night of the disaster, not given in to the wretched advice to appear as planned at a ball in the French embassy. France was Russia's only ally in Europe, and the ambassador had spent more than half a million rubles in preparation for the dance.

Observers unanimously agreed that the imperial couple were devastated by the tragedy, that their eyes were red and their faces swollen from weeping when they led the Polonaise that opened the ball. For the next several weeks the tsar and the empress made a sincere display of their grief and concern for the Khodynka victims, visiting the hundreds of wounded in hospitals and generously providing for the families of the dead. But the first impression was the one that stuck. They danced while Russians died. They mocked the suffering of the people.

To complicate matters Grand Duke Serge subsequently escaped punishment or even meaningful censure for his failure to provide appropriate security on Khodynka Field. In the wake of the tragedy Nicholas found himself buffeted by the conflicting ambitions and stupid squabbling in his family. His mother, in the interest of containing the disaster and because she had no love for Serge (her late husband's brother), wanted him dismissed from his position as governor of Moscow. Serge's sister-in-law, Empress Alexandra, understandably did not. An official investigation refused to fix blame on anybody, and Nicholas, giving the first formal notice of his style of government, simply listened to the last voice he heard. In this case, unfortunately, it was the voice of confusion, and so he did nothing, confirming the worst suspicions of his people. The tsar was against them; another tyrant had mounted the throne.

Thus the reign of Nicholas II began in disaster, disorder and negative feeling all around. For its first decade the tsar would stumble and grope and call on God to guide him in his heavy task, taking counsel first from his mother, then from his uncles and finally from his wife who, in her efforts to protect him from what she called the "bad men" of government and the "vipers" of St. Petersburg society, eventually managed to remove him from reality altogether, cocooning him in their cozy apartments at the Alexander Palace in Tsarskoe Selo, alienating his family, outraging his ministers and turning inexorably — indeed, fanatically — toward a view of his sovereignty as a holy crusade, infallible in its purpose and not to be judged or interfered with by ordinary mortals.

The Last Ball

Scenes from the great imperial costume ball held at the Winter Palace in February 1903. The theme was Old Russia during the reign of Alexei I, the second Romanov tsar and the ancestor Nicholas most admired. In their bejeweled traditional robes, the guests posed for a photograph in the Hermitage Theater (right), which has recently been restored to its former elegance (opposite). This legendary evening proved to be a glittering swan song. The following year brought war and unrest, and Alexandra distanced herself from St. Petersburg society. The Winter Palace had seen its last ball.

The imperial couple appeared as Tsar Alexei and his consort (above, left and second from left). Alexandra's headdress and earrings were so heavy that she could not move her head. Unlike her daughter-in-law, the still-youthful dowager empress (third from left) reveled in grand occasions. Her daughter Xenia (fourth from left) carried a Fabergé ostrich fan (left) that is today in the Forbes Collection. She was accompanied by her husband, Sandro (third from right). Also elaborately costumed were Alexandra's sister Ella and her husband, Serge (second from right and far right).

CHAPTER FOUR

The Heir

Between 1897 and 1901, in a series of difficult pregnancies that ruined her health and left her a semi-invalid, Alexandra bore Nicholas three more daughters — Tatiana, Marie and Anastasia — but no son, no heir to continue an imperial line whose future depended on her. Securing that future became her obsession.

No evidence suggests that the empress ever entertained political ambitions in the ordinary sense. Her active involvement in affairs of state may be traced to the autumn of 1900, when the tsar fell ill and nearly died of typhus while vacationing in the Crimea. Suddenly the question of succession rose in a terrifying form. She was pregnant at the time with Anastasia, later to become the most famous figure in the Romanov family, and she was not alone in thinking that her time was running out. Until recently Nicholas's brother George had been tsarevitch and heir to the throne, but George died of tuberculosis in 1899, making the tsar's second brother, Michael, the heir.

A much-beloved but empty-headed character known variously as "Misha" and "Flopsy," Grand Duke Michael now became the object of the empress's intense suspicion.

The crib of the last tsarevitch (above) has recently been brought out of storage. (Opposite) An imperial family portrait taken shortly after the birth of Anastasia in 1901. The empress is wearing black in mourning for her grandmother, Queen Victoria, who died in January of that year.

She believed, not without reason, that the dowager empress hoped to see Michael on the throne one day. With Nicholas seemingly near death, Alexandra persuaded the tsar to deny Michael the formal title of tsarevitch, pointedly leaving him in the position of temporary heir — next in line, but soon to be replaced.

During Nicholas's illness Alexandra kept everyone, including his ministers, away from his bedside and made it clear that she expected to be appointed regent of Russia in the event of his death. Her child might be a boy, she explained, and if so she would reign in his place until he reached his majority. The proposal met with howls of protest from everyone who heard it, and in the end, because Nicholas recovered, it never came to the test. But Alexandra had reached new heights of agitation in her desire to produce a son.

In retrospect, it is difficult not to sympathize with the empress in her plight. Her sisters (with the exception of the childless Ella, whose husband, Serge, had left her untouched on account of his "curious tastes") had each given birth to boys, while Nicholas's sister Xenia had borne six of them by the time she was through — strapping lads who must have been a constant affront to Alexandra in her misery.

Following the birth of Alexandra's third daughter, Marie, in 1899, the empress began to consult a series of mystics, witches, seers and spiritual healers who she thought might help her, "through God," to become pregnant with a boy. She was aided in her quest by the so-called Black Sisters, daughters of the king of Montenegro, who had married a pair of Russian grand dukes and led the aristocratic craze for table rapping and Orthodox voodoo in Russia at the time. In contrast to most of the rest of the imperial family, the Montenegrin sisters, Anastasia and Militsa, treated Alexandra with a gooey respect, bowing and scraping and flattering her at every turn.

In 1901, when Alexandra was well into her fourth pregnancy, the sisters introduced her to Philippe Nizier-Vachod — "Monsieur Philippe" — a French "soul doctor" and one-time butcher's assistant who led the empress down many a blind path with his prayers, chants and supplications to the Almighty. Philippe could make himself invisible, the Montenegrins affirmed, and like all psychics, he "could tell you in a few words what was troubling you, and what you did not dare confess to him." He predicted that the child Alexandra was carrying would be a boy; a girl was born. He convinced the empress that she was pregnant again in 1903; she was not, but she walked around in maternity clothes for a number of months and canceled her engagements, taking the opportunity to withdraw from court life in St. Petersburg.

The false pregnancy, medically designated as "hysterical," later led to astonishing claims about the birth of a *fifth* daughter to Nicholas and Alexandra, smuggled out of Russia, ostensibly, on the emperor's order in an effort to save the dynasty. Philippe was sent back to France, but not before he told Alexandra that she would shortly "have another friend who, like me, will speak to you of God." Thus the way was paved for the coming of Rasputin — the *starets*, the "Holy Devil," the "Mad Monk of Russia," whose influence on Nicholas and Alexandra would prove fatal to the monarchy.

After Philippe's departure, Alexandra turned for help to a ghost, a religious hermit named Serafim of Sarov who had died in 1833 after living for years in the Sarov wilderness as a local apocalyptic seer. Despite his failing some of the usual tests of sainthood — Serafim's corpse, for instance, had badly decomposed — Alexandra bulldozed his canonization through the Orthodox Church with the argument that "everything is within the Tsar's power, even to the making of saints." In the summer of 1903 she led the entire imperial family on a pilgrimage to Serafim's retreat, where she bathed naked in a pool by moonlight, praying to the saint for a son. A year later Alexandra's prayer was answered, sealing forever her belief in the mercy — and mysterious methods — of God.

So it was that on August 12, 1904, three hundred shots rang out from the Fortress of Peter and Paul to announce the arrival of the

After giving birth to four daughters (shown above circa 1904), Alexandra prayed for a son. She was advised that the spirit of the holy man Serafim of Sarov could help her, and so she arranged for his canonization. The 1903 ceremony is depicted by Fabergé on the jeweled egg commemorating the fifteenth anniversary of the coronation (left). (Opposite top) Olga and Tatiana shown as toddlers, were known as "the Big Pair" after the birth of their younger sisters, Marie and Anastasia (opposite lower left). (Opposite lower right) One of the grand duchesses' dolls, preserved for over seven decades.

heir, Tsarevitch Alexei. It was "a great, never-to-be-forgotten day," Nicholas wrote in his diary from Peterhof, where the family had repaired as usual to escape the summer heat. He and the empress had just sat down to lunch when Alix's labor began. Only an hour later an apparently perfect eight-pound boy was born.

"I don't think you have yet seen my dear little Tsarevitch," the tsar grew fond of saying to his ministers and staff, apparently to his wife's annoyance. Alexandra herself was "transfused with the delirious joy of a mother who had at last seen her dearest wish fulfilled," according to Pierre Gilliard, the Swiss professor who taught French to the tsar's daughters. But her notions of privacy and propriety did not relax, and she hated to see Alexei, naked from his bath, bounced in his father's arms in front of anyone who happened by.

The bouncing ceased just six weeks later when the infant began to bleed from the navel, a worrisome situation that continued on and off for the next two days. This initial incident, the parents told themselves, could have been the result of a too-sharp cut to the umbilical cord at birth. Later, when each tiny bruise grew into an ugly dark blue swelling, there could be no denying the nature of the problem. Their son had hemophilia, a genetic disease of the blood affecting only males but transmitted by their mothers and fatal in every case. The empress knew the symptoms all too well. Several of her nephews suffered from the disease and her own brother had died from it, as had one of her uncles, Queen Victoria's youngest son, Leopold, the duke of Albany. Victoria, on hearing about Leopold's condition, had simply denied that matter in her own brisk way by declaring that "this disease is not in our family."

But the queen had four sons and Alexandra had only one. Her despair was indescribable.

Alexandra knew that her son's "shining" appearance would prove no shield in his battle with the illness. More

"At 1:15 this afternoon, Alix gave birth to a son.... There are not words to thank God properly for the comfort he has sent us...."

— Nicholas II's diary,
August 12, 1904

The imperial family after Alexei's birth (above). In a September diary entry (left) Nicholas included the first photos of the tsarevitch and wrote "...our 'sonny' has visibly grown and is healthy, thank God." (Opposite) The proud father poses with his baby son.

than forty doctors and physicians were accredited to the Russian court, but it would be many years before medicine would develop an effective treatment for hemophilia. For most of his life Alexei was cared for by three of the medical staff, S. P. Fedorov, Vladimir Derevenko and Eugene Sergeievitch Botkin (who became physician-in-ordinary to the tsar and empress—that is to say, their family doctor—in 1908). These medical men could do nothing for Alexei beyond ordering him to be careful and trying to make him comfortable during the worst of his attacks. Mudbaths for his stiffened limbs and sedatives for his pain were their chief modes of treatment.

Apart from tending to the imperial family in a general capacity, Dr. Botkin also had the daily task of monitoring the empress's mounting array of physical complaints. After Alexei's birth, Alexandra had trouble breathing, walking or standing for any length of time. She suffered from exhaustion, poor circulation and what she called "an enlarged heart," an angina that may or may not have been psychosomatic. "Hiding one's sorrow," she said, "swallowing all, makes it so bad." Botkin was the man who soothed her and assured her that her sufferings were real. He came from the most famous medical family in Russia, and while he was not himself a monarchist, his devotion to Nicholas and Alexandra was such as to transcend any question of politics. Much of what we know about the private life of the last Romanovs comes from the memoirs of Dr. Botkin's children, Tatiana and Gleb.

In the end, after the Revolution had decimated what was already a very small number, there were only a handful of people who could speak with any authority about the nature of that life: the Botkins, one or two of the empress's ladies-in-waiting, the tsar's sister Olga (who spent nearly every weekend before the First World War with her brother's family at Tsarskoe Selo), the children's tutors, servants and maids

— and Anna Viroubova, the "Ania" of Alexandra's letters.

Ania, a dumpy, doll-faced, excitable spinster, virgin though having been briefly married, was Alexandra's one and only intimate friend. She occupied no official position at court, and Alexandra never meant to give her one. "She is my *friend*," the empress repeated. "I mean to keep her as such." Her closeness to the imperial family and unimpeded access to the Alexander Palace earned Ania the deep resentment of St. Petersburg society (they called her *La Vache* — The Cow), the more so after it became known that she also served as Alexandra's chief liaison with Rasputin.

The tragedy that was about to unfold might not have been so poignant, the final cat-astrophe not quite so heart-rending, had the tsar's family not loved each other so much; had their "happy home life" (as the empress called it) been run along stricter and sterner lines, with the emphasis on formality and the outward display of pomp that characterized other European courts at the time; had blond, curly-haired, blue-eyed Alexei not been such a winning child and his sisters not looked so innocent and assured in their white summer dresses and Edwardian flowered hats. While still a child, the eldest daughter, Olga, once told her governess how glad she was to be living in a time when "people were good," when "evil men" had been "put away" and no one went about executing people or chopping off their heads. The shock these children were due to experience in the Russian

*T*he cottage in the imperial park (below left), given by Alexandra to her devoted friend Anna Viroubova, was the scene of many meetings with Rasputin. (Bottom) Ania entertains the empress in the cottage circa 1914, and (below) relaxes with Alexandra, Olga and Marie on an outing some years earlier. In the 1906 photograph of the imperial family at Peterhof (opposite), the empress appears "tall and slender like a willow-wand," as described by another friend, Lili Dehn.

Revolution can scarcely be imagined.

From the moment of the tsarevitch's birth, he was the undisputed center of his family's existence — their pride and joy, their "dear one," "wee one," "Sunbeam," the focus of all their attention and all their concern. His naturally lively and rambunctious nature was especially remarkable in view of his precarious health. He wanted more than anything else to be like other boys. He was defiant in the face of his illness and sometimes seemed to be tempting fate. Any cut, any fall, any bruise might lead Alexei to a fatal hemorrhage — and if not fatal, then assuredly agonizing — as his blood, unable to clot, welled up inside his body and pressed against his muscles and bones until it could find no further place to go. The boy's sufferings

during his hemophilic attacks were a horror to witness, and his screams of pain a horror to hear. Many times he asked to die, to be poisoned or smothered out of his misery, crying, "Lord, have mercy on me!" and "Mama help me! Won't you help me?"

It took months for Alexei to recover after each crisis had passed, which was the given explanation for both his slow growth and the enormous gaps in his education. His tutors found him bright and affectionate, but chronically inattentive and not really interested in learning anything that didn't concern soldiers, sailors or trains. He was stubborn and headstrong. For instance, he refused to speak English with his family as they invariably did when alone, and he insisted on adopting his father's preference

for "Russian" clothes and habits — peasant trousers and collarless shirts. But to all of these he preferred a naval uniform, and for many years he was dressed (and repeatedly photographed) as a *matelot* of the imperial yacht, his sailor's suits and caps with the legend *Standart* made expressly for him.

That Alexei was spoiled and willful, no one doubted. Sydney Gibbes, the Yorkshireman whom the empress appointed to teach English to her children, decided immediately that the tsarevitch needed to be cured of some "piggish" habits. (Gibbes owed his appointment to Alix's Uncle Bertie, by now Britain's King Edward VII, who had told the empress how badly her children spoke English.) Alexei's lapses of conduct included "eating in company" and interrupting

The tsarevitch (left) with a toy drum on the Standart circa 1908. A few years later, Derevenko keeps a close watch (top far left) while Alexei explores the Finnish shore. At Mogilev in 1917 (bottom far left), Nagorny stands with a teenaged Alexei, his two companions and the old Russian tutor, Petrov. (Below) A younger Derevenko with his two-year-old charge.

The Sailor Nannies

With the revelation of his hemophilia, the tsar and the empress took special care that Alexei should never be left unattended. Two sailors from the imperial navy, Andrei Derevenko and Clementy Nagorny, were assigned the task of caring for the heir. When the tsarevitch was ill they acted as nurses. "Derevenko was so patient and resourceful that he often did wonders in alleviating pain," Anna Viroubova recalled. "I can still hear the plaintive voice of Alexei begging the big sailor, 'Lift my arm.' 'Put up my leg.' 'Warm my hands.'" Derevenko's two young sons were often Alexei's playmates at Tsarskoe Selo, although their father always made sure that the play never got too rough.

Tutors were assigned to the tsarevitch when he reached school age, and one of them, Pierre Gilliard, took issue with the presence of the sailor nannies. "I considered that the perpetual presence of the sailor Derevenko and his assistant Nagorny were harmful to the child," he recalled in his memoirs. "The external power which intervened whenever danger threatened seemed to me to hinder the development of will-power and the faculty of observation. What the child gained possibly in safety, he lost in real discipline."

Although Derevenko was the heir's principal attendant (and the one most often photographed), it was Nagorny who was faithful to the end. After the abdication of the tsar, Derevenko took his revenge on the boy he had served for ten years, bawling insults and commands at him before deserting the palace. Nagorny accompanied the family to exile in Siberia and was shot in an Ekaterinburg prison after preventing a Bolshevik guard from stealing a gold chain from Alexei.

his lessons by ringing for the servants whenever he wanted something — a snack or some chocolate, which he would greedily devour as if he were just another of his own peasant companions, those "simple" boys, the sons of sailors and servants, whom his mother selected as his only regular playmates apart from his sisters. According to Princess Elizabeth Naryshkin ("Madame Zizi," Alexandra's mistress of the robes), all five of the tsar's children "generally behaved like young savages," and Gibbes had very little success in taming Alexei's more defiant impulses. The boy was not above pulling rank when it pleased him, and he once ordered a band of sentries to march out to sea — on foot. The tsar joked that he "trembled for Russia" under the future rule of his son, "Alexei the Terrible."

For the first few years of his life Alexei was healthy more often than not, although his hemophilia hung like a threatening cloud over all their sunny days. The real danger to the tsar's regime lay elsewhere, in the gathering storm of social unrest brewing over his vast and unwieldy empire.

Alexei's birth in August 1904 provided a brief but splendid counterbalance to Russia's disastrous war with Japan, which had begun six months earlier. It was supposed to have been "a small victorious war," fought in the land-grabbing spirit of nineteenth-century imperialism and, in Russia's case, in a cynical attempt to divert attention from mounting unrest at home.

In the years leading up to Nicholas's Far Eastern adventure, Russia's social fabric had begun to tear. There were crop failures in 1897 and 1898, followed by famine and a mass migration of peasants to the cities. There were bank failures and wild fluctuations in the value of the ruble brought on by the rapid industrialization of a country with no foundation to support the change. Meanwhile Nicholas II

The tsarevitch's teddy bear and small Cossack uniform are today on display in the palace of Pavlovsk.

went doggedly on with the official program of "Russification" ("Russia for the Russians"), the odious policy of racial purification begun under his father, by which the Russian government hoped to eliminate ethnic distinctions in the reaches of the empire and annihilate any culture but its own. As a result pogroms against the Jews increased (no one knows the precise number of Jewish victims slaughtered with the tacit approval of Nicholas II, but they were certainly in the thousands), while the traditional nationalism of the imperial provinces — Poland, Ukraine and the eastern and Islamic lands — assumed a bitter and vengeful dimension, for which Russia, at the end of the twentieth century, is still paying the price.

In all matters of domestic policy Nicholas listened to one adviser or another but seldom heeded anyone for long. That a vacuum, essentially, sat on the Russian throne was no secret to anyone in the tsar's government. "God preserve you," said his minister of communications, "from relying on the Emperor even for a second on any matter; he is incapable of supporting anyone over anything."

In foreign policy Nicholas's government was equally rudderless. It followed no particular strategy, guided only by the desire to preserve Russia's established territorial interests and by an amorphous ambition for expansion that focused first on Turkey, then on Persia and finally on China and the Far East, where the tsar had "grandiose plans," according to one of his generals, for the annexation of Manchuria, Korea, Tibet or anything else that presented itself to be swallowed.

In 1895 Russia had acquired Port Arthur, its first ice-free Pacific port, and had subsequently expanded its Far East holdings to include much of Manchuria, "temporarily" occupied during the turmoil of the Boxer Rebellion in 1900. Next on the list was Korea, into which Russia had made serious inroads by 1903. Unfortunately the Japanese emphatically regarded the Korean peninsula as part of their sphere of interest. After repeated warnings to Russia to withdraw, the Japanese finally acted.

In February 1904 the Japanese attacked the Russian naval base at Port Arthur, and the tsar went to war on the bad advice of his interior minister, Vyacheslav Plehve, a despicable anti-Semite and officer of the secret police whom Nicholas had appointed to the top domestic post after the murder of its previous occupant. Plehve himself died that July as a result of a terrorist bomb before the Japanese war was over. No one imagined that Japan could defeat the massive Russian army. But at the eastern end of the southern spur of the not-quite-complete Trans-Siberian Railway, the Russians were at a terrible disadvantage.

Caught by surprise at Port Arthur, the Russian Far East fleet was crippled before the war began, and Japan gained immediate mastery of the sea. The Japanese army could now land at will. And on the Asian mainland the Russian forces were both outnumbered by the Japanese and subject to far more tenuous lines of supply. The result was a humiliating rout for Tsar Nicholas's legions. But the worst news came in January 1905, when Port Arthur finally fell to the besieging Japanese forces.

The loss of Port Arthur was the match that

A Cossack breakfasting on a Japanese soldier (opposite) reflected Russia's mood at the beginning of the "small victorious war." (Below) The dowager empress looks on as her son gives his blessing to troops leaving for the east in 1904. (Bottom) Scenes from a disastrous venture (from left): conscripts are mobilized in St. Petersburg; a Russian battery during the fall of Port Arthur; a Cossack cavalry charge; a few of the more than 30,000 Russian casualties.

lit the powder keg of Russian social upheaval. The loudest explosion came in St. Petersburg, where a minor strike at a steel mill rapidly grew into a massive labor protest. All these protestors needed was a leader, and he emerged in the person of Father Gregory George Gapon, a young activist priest who had actually been secretly working for the interior ministry but who now became a dedicated revolutionary. It was he who formed the idea of leading a huge march to the

Winter Palace to present a petition to the tsar — the people appealing directly to their sovereign. The petition called for fundamental reforms, including the founding of a constituent assembly and the granting of universal suffrage.

Unfortunately for Nicholas, he was not told of the impending march until the night of Saturday, January 21, the eve of the protest, and no one seems to have considered the possibility that the tsar might actually have met the protestors

A winter's day in Palace Square evokes memories of the massacre of Bloody Sunday (right).

and listened to their grievances. Instead the Russian interior minister, Prince Peter Sviatopolk-Mirsky, ordered additional troops into the city, creating a situation ripe for bloodshed.

The march began peacefully as more than 100,000 striking workers from the poor parts of the city began to converge on the Winter Palace. The marchers carried icons and portraits of Nicholas II, and their mood was happy, expectant. Some sang hymns and the imperial anthem, "God Save the Tsar." But before the converging columns of protestors could reach the Winter Palace, they were met by ranks of heavily armed troops. Still the marchers moved forward. Then the soldiers opened fire. Hundreds of people were killed in the slaughter, among them a significant number of the workers' wives and children who had joined the march in a demonstration of solidarity and as a sign of their good faith. This was the event that came

Scenes from the revolutionary disturbances of 1905. For several months following the Japanese military disasters, most of Russia was effectively on strike. A full-blown revolution was avoided only because the tsar reluctantly agreed to grant political concessions and constitutional government to his people.

A contemporary depiction of the widespread peasant rebellions of 1905-1906. Most of the violence was directed against property and involved seizing land and setting fire to buildings on the landlords' estates. It took two years to calm the countryside, and hundreds of peasants were hanged in the wave of repression that followed.

to be known as Bloody Sunday, the catalyst for the revolution of 1905.

Nicholas, who was at Tsarskoe Selo when the shooting occurred, learned of the tragedy only when it was over. His only known comment on the matter was a note in his diary that it was "painful and sad." The empress, too, had an urge to minimize the appalling nature of the massacre. "Don't believe all the horrors the foreign papers say," she wrote her sister Victoria in England. "They make one's hair stand on end — foul exaggeration. Yes, the troops, alas, were obliged to fire. Repeatedly the crowd was told to retreat and that Nicky was not in town ... and

that one would be forced to shoot, but they would not heed and so blood was shed." The Russian people were "devoted to their Sovereign," Alexandra continued to insist. In numerous letters over many years she expressed the opinion that Russians were "childlike," docile and "good," but "utterly unbalanced" and accustomed to "the whip."

The furor over Bloody Sunday could not be dismissed, much less allayed, by Alexandra's wholehearted conversion to autocracy or her deluded faith in the "holy inwardness" of Russian peasants. "We have no tsar anymore," said Father Gapon. "Rivers of blood separate

the Emperor from the people."

For several months more Nicholas refused to relent — or perhaps he did not know how — as the revolt in St. Petersburg spread throughout the country, cresting into a ferocious wave of riots, strikes, mutinies, murders, the cutting of power lines and blowing-up of rails, and a rebellion among the peasants — not childlike at all — that eventually reached into every corner of Russia. Thousands of the rebels were killed without trial in the repression that followed, but the strikes continued and the insurrection spread — "like a horse," said the empress in her bewilderment, "that has been held very tight in hand, and then suddenly one lets the reins go."

The domestic crisis deepened in May, when the "Japanese monkeys" annihilated the Russian Baltic fleet, which had sailed all the way from Europe to the Far East in a desperate attempt to reverse the fortunes of war. The battle of Tsushima humiliated the tsarist empire past the point of endurance. This final calamity convinced the tsar that his only option was to sue for peace, but the damage was done. The defeat at Tsushima only further fanned the flames of revolution at home.

Through it all the imperial family remained sequestered at Peterhof on the Gulf of Finland where, Nicholas's ministers reasoned, the tsar could make a speedy escape from Russia if the need arose. That summer there would be no cruise through the Finnish skerries on their yacht, *Standart*, out of fear that the boat might be torpedoed or sunk. "It makes me sick to read the news," said Nicholas from his enforced retreat, "strikes in schools and factories, murdered policemen, Cossacks, riots. But

The destruction of the Russian Baltic fleet at Tsushima (opposite top) forced the tsar to dispatch Serge Witte (above) to a peace conference with the Japanese (opposite bottom) set up by President Theodore Roosevelt in Portsmouth, New Hampshire. Unrest in Russia following the war prompted this cartoon (above right) in a British magazine, which was captioned, "Do I smell something burning?"

the ministers instead of acting with quick decision only assemble in council like a lot of frightened hens and cackle about providing united ministerial action."

By September even the cackling had stopped. The ministers were paralyzed; the government ceased to function. Finally in October, with the outbreak of a nationwide railway strike, the tsar was faced with the choice of surrendering his power to a military dictatorship — the dictator of his choice being his father's cousin, the grand duke and commander in chief of the army, Nicholas Nicholaievitch — or of bowing to reality by granting Russia a constitution. This he finally did on October 17, but only after Nicholas Nicholaievitch reportedly pulled a gun from his pocket and threatened to shoot himself on the spot if the tsar did not relent.

"There was no other way out but to cross oneself and give what everyone was asking for," the tsar explained in a letter to his mother. That the revolution failed on its first attempt may be credited to the wisdom of those two or three ministers in Nicholas's cabinet who were able to think with anything like clarity on any political subject. Most notable among these few was Serge Witte, the only man approaching statesmanlike status in Russia at the time. The tsar rewarded this architect of the October Manifesto, the man who saved the monarchy, with the title of count. Not long afterward, however, Witte fell out of favor and was dismissed from office.

On paper the October Manifesto provided for all the traditional freedoms of liberal democracy — of press, religion, assembly and so on — and guaranteed that no law would be established in Russia "without the consent of the

State Duma," the newly constituted parliament. Since the tsar retained the right to dissolve the Duma at will, however (provided he set a date immediately for new elections), and since he still controlled the army, the bureaucracy, the police, the succession, foreign policy and almost half of the national budget, the new system was almost guaranteed to fail.

The first two assemblies, in fact, heavily leftist in composition and clamoring for radical action, were both dismissed within weeks of their initial sittings. It was not until the electoral laws were reformed in 1907 under Prime Minister Peter Stolypin, limiting the franchise of the workers and peasants in favor of the upper classes, that a stable body could be assembled, defusing the call for violent revolution while fooling no one.

With the Duma in place, Russia was the only country in the world that could describe itself as a constitutional monarchy under an autocratic tsar. It is said that Nicholas burst into tears upon actually signing the constitution. Certainly his wife and mother were both weeping at the opening of the first Duma in the spring of 1906. Alexandra spied evil all around

The exhibition of a painting depicting Nicholas reading the address from the throne during the 1906 opening of the first State Duma at the Winter Palace. To the left of the throne stand members of the imperial family, defiant in all their finery. The rest of the assembled crowd consisted of court officials and the recently elected members of the first authentic "parliament" in Russian history. (Opposite) Although photographed here in the robes of a monk, Rasputin was in fact a starets — an unordained, wandering holy man with an eye toward his own advancement.

her, and Marie Feodorovna, as jealous as the rest when it came to her prerogatives, was "crushed for several days afterward" by the "indescribable emotions" she had suffered at the scene.

"Let us hope something good will come out of this," she wrote her childhood governess in Denmark, "though it doesn't look like it.... What a misfortune, and how sad to have to witness such a downfall." The dowager's words did not understate the case. Her son had temporarily managed to salvage his crown, but by granting a constitution, however restricted, and rights to the people, however limited, the tsar had betrayed the very essence of his power. The Romanovs ruled Russia by dint of superstition disguised as religious faith. As democrats, they made no sense at all.

∽

"We have got to know a man of God, Grigory, from Tobolsk province," wrote the tsar in his diary in the autumn of 1905. The agony of granting a constitution and compromising his autocratic power was behind him, but his son's health remained as precarious as ever. Rasputin's introduction to the imperial family was engineered by the same Montenegrin sisters who had introduced the empress to the French psychic Philippe Nizier-Vachod.

After their first quiet meeting in St. Petersburg, Nicholas and Alexandra invited Rasputin to Tsarskoe Selo, where he met their children and presented the whole family

with gifts — holy icons and consecrated bread. No one knows the date of his first return to the palace in his "healing" capacity — that is, on a mission to rescue the ailing tsarevitch — but Alexei apparently "bubbled with laughter" when he saw Rasputin at his bedside. "Rasputin laughed too," according to a contemporary account. "He laid his hand on the boy's leg and the bleeding stopped at once. 'There's a good boy,' said Rasputin. 'You'll be all right. But only God can tell what will happen tomorrow.'" By 1907 Rasputin was firmly ensconced in the empress's mind as her son's only hope and, by extension, the savior of Russia.

Rasputin was not, in fact, a monk, or a priest, or in any way officially connected with the Orthodox Church. He was a *mouzhik*, a Siberian peasant, a drunkard, a lecher and a self-proclaimed "Man of God" who, having had visions of Christ and the Virgin Mary, wandered through Russia with a message about sin and salvation not normally heard in ecclesiastical circles. Sin was essential, Rasputin maintained, if renouncing it were to mean anything. There could be no forgiveness without dereliction, no redemption without a fall from grace. Rasputin's "theology" was actually a hodgepodge, grab-bag compilation of obscure religious traditions in Russia, tolerated (but not endorsed) by the Orthodox Church in the interest of peasant loyalty. Properly speaking,

Rasputin was a *starets*, an unordained holy man, and a *strannik*, or religious vagabond, and his "holiness" was not doubted by anyone who knew him, including most of his enemies.

His powers of hypnosis and healing were real. Time and again the record confirms that he soothed the sick, healed the wounded, even raised the dying out of comas with his prayers and laying on of hands. Countless volumes have been published since his death in an effort to explain how he did it, but the mystery remains.

"In Rasputin's presence one immediately sensed the wisdom, gravity, deep comprehension of life and majesty of thought which he possessed to such a remarkable degree," said Elizabeth Judas, one of the *starets'* lifelong adherents and defenders whose little-known book, *Rasputin: Neither Devil Nor Saint*, provides one of the truest pictures of his character. Those who knew him best insisted that his "greatest talent [was] his ability to calm and comfort troubled souls," which would have its own bearing on the healing of the body. He rescued Alexei, he rescued the son of the empress's friend Lili Dehn, when her child was thought to be dying from diphtheria, and he rescued Anna Viroubova shortly before his own death, when she was permanently crippled (and nearly killed) in a train accident in 1915. A lady of the court whose daughter was dying and who called in Rasputin as a desperate measure was unable to explain exactly what he had done to revive the girl.

"I don't know what happened," she said. "He took my hand. His face changed and he looked like a corpse, yellowy, waxy, and dreadfully still. He rolled his eyes till the whites alone were visible ... and said in a dull voice, 'She won't die, she won't die.' Then he let my hand go and the blood flowed back into his cheeks again. He continued talking as if nothing had happened."

In the early days, before scandal made his visits to the palace impossible, Rasputin normally saw the empress in the evening after Nicholas had finished working and could join them in the drawing room. "They would kiss three times in the Russian fashion, and then would start to talk," recalled Major-General Alexander Spiridovitch, the head of the tsar's personal security services. "[Rasputin] would speak to them of Siberia, of the needs of the peasants, of his pilgrimages. Their Majesties would always discuss the health of the Tsarevitch and their current worries about him. When he withdrew after an hour's conversation with the Imperial family he always left Their Majesties cheerful, their souls filled with joyous hope."

Whatever the source of Rasputin's healing power, Alexandra's motives in embracing him were pure. The sole basis for the empress's devotion to Rasputin was her belief that he could save the life of her hemophiliac son, that his powers were a gift of God and that his advice, which he offered more and more frequently as time went by, represented the embodied will of the Russian people — the "true" people, as Alexandra reasoned. Politically, however, the situation was such that from the first even Alexandra understood the need for discretion. When she met Rasputin she normally did so not at the palace but at Anna Viroubova's grace-and-favor cottage at the edge of Alexander Park.

At first, very few people knew how often Rasputin and the empress met or to what specific purpose. But soon the rumors began to fly and multiply. Orgies, black masses, cryptic communications with the kaiser or the pope — all, at one time or another, were advanced as explanations for the mysterious pairing of the empress and the *mouzhik*. It never occurred to Nicholas and Alexandra — it would not have occurred to any monarch of the time — to make the true situation known, to announce the fact of Alexei's illness and appeal to the public

*A*nna Viroubova *with Rasputin in his home village of Pokrovskoe circa 1913. She was widely thought to be his mistress (one of many), but after the tsar's abdication and her imprisonment, the provisional government exonerated her of all charges of "depravity" and issued medical certification of her virginity.*

for sympathy and understanding. Instead, they turned inward to each other, to their children and the sweet illusions of Tsarskoe with its parks and ponds, its familiar corridors and homey rooms, its walks, its drives and bowers of lilac. Here, in their "enchanted fairyland," as Gleb Botkin described it, the reality could be hidden, the fantasy maintained, the autocracy preserved.

Rasputin's rise coincided with imperial Russia's short-lived and ill-fated experiment with constitutional monarchy. Peter Stolypin became prime minister in the spring of 1906 following the issue of the October Manifesto. In the general atmosphere of optimism that attended the creation of the Duma, he is generally regarded to have been Russia's last hope for intelligent government, the man who might have transformed an ancient autocracy into a modern democratic state. Indeed, the country briefly prospered under his guidance.

Once in office Stolypin moved swiftly to restore order in the wake of the insurrections of 1905, ruling by decree and ruthlessly imposing his authority. He realized that before there could be reform, he needed to "pacify" the population (an undertaking that led to the most brutal police action Russia had ever seen). Only then could Stolypin hope to preside over the empire's headlong plunge into the twentieth century. His tenure saw major advances in industry, education and agriculture. A massive redistribution of arable land replaced the old communal system of peasant landholding with a *pro forma* private ownership: by the time of the Revolution of 1917, about a million of these new "consolidated farms" existed in Russia.

In the cities, after 1905, the press was suddenly "free," subject still to fines and major crackdowns, but flourishing in comparison to anything Russia had known before. Political parties had sprung into life; trade unions were legalized, and history can only guess what kind of social advances might have been made were it not for the series of disasters that were soon to follow.

Inevitably Stolypin's efforts at reform made him a target for assassination. (Only a month after taking office, he narrowly escaped a bomb explosion at his country house, where one of his daughters was severely wounded.) The radical nature of his land reforms left many Russian revolutionaries in despair. From his wandering exile in Europe, the failed revolutionary Vladimir Ilyich Lenin wrote, "If this should continue, it might force us to renounce any agricultural program at all."

Others, however, were not so fatalistic. On an imperial visit to Kiev in September 1911, the tsar and his prime minister attended a performance of Rimsky-Korsakov's opera *Tsar Sultan* at the Kiev Opera House. During the second intermission, the assassin struck.

"We had just left the [imperial] box as it was so hot," Nicholas reported to his mother, "when we heard two sounds as if something was dropped. I thought an opera glass might have fallen on somebody's head and ran back into the box to look.... Women were shrieking and directly in front of me in the stalls Stolypin was standing.... He slowly sank into his chair and began to unbutton his tunic.... Olga and Tatiana saw what happened." Stolypin's last gesture before he fell was to raise his hand in a sign of benediction toward his sovereign.

The prime minister lingered for five days. The tsar visited the nursing home where the dying man lay — though Stolypin's wife refused to let Nicholas actually see her husband — and presided over a memorial service in his honor, but he did not seem to mourn the loss to his government when this great man finally died. The day after the shooting at the opera house, the tsar wrote in his diary only that Stolypin

*P*eter Arkdeyvitch Stolypin, the last best hope of imperial Russian government. Prime minister from 1906, he was assassinated in 1911, following a series of radical political and agricultural reforms and a reconstruction of the Duma so that it represented predominantly the interests of the upper classes.

"had a bad night." In fact the coolness and equanimity with which both he and the empress greeted Stolypin's demise was so pointed as to scandalize even their close relations. The prime minister's "role in the world was ended," Alexandra maintained, "his destiny was fulfilled.... Believe me, one must not feel sorry for those who are no more." There was one reason above all others for Alexandra's unfeeling dismissal of the man who had done so much to preserve her husband's reign: Stolypin had had the courage to take on Rasputin.

≈

During the four years that Peter Stolypin sought to guide Russia peacefully into the twentieth century, the imperial family continued their life

of splendid isolation centered around the health of the heir, Alexei. It is not known how early or with what degree of precision the young grand duchesses — Olga, Tatiana, Marie and Anastasia — were told about their brother's illness, but they knew it was a secret and they kept it faithfully to the end of their lives. They adored Alexei; they refused him nothing and never showed the slightest resentment over all the extra attention he received. The girls functioned as a unit, sometimes signing their cards and letters jointly with the acronym of their names: "OTMA."

Tatiana was the empress's favorite, tall and stately like her mother, the most classically beautiful of the sisters and their designated leader:

This hauntingly beautiful official portrait of the young grand duchesses (left to right) Olga, Tatiana, Marie and Anastasia dates from 1906. That summer (opposite left) they posed less formally in sailor suits aboard the royal yacht, Standart, with their young brother, Alexei. On a visit ashore from the yacht in 1908 (opposite right), Tatiana (top), Marie and Anastasia (left) play on an improvised swing.

she was nicknamed the Governess. Olga, though older, more thoughtful and more intelligent, was also more difficult, brooding and sulky. A certain antagonism rose up between her and her mother when she reached adolescence, though nothing so strong as to be considered rebellion or open conflict. "The children with all their love have quite other ideas and rarely understand my way of looking at things," Alexandra sighed. "The smallest, even — they are always right and when I say how I was brought up and how one must be, they can't understand, find it dull. Only when I speak quietly with Tatiana she grasps it. Olga is always most unamiable about every proposition, though she may end by doing what I wish. And when I am severe — sulks me."

But the two youngest daughters did not live long enough — or did not live long enough outside captivity — for their characters to fully emerge. By common agreement Marie was "an angel," plump and pretty with "eyes like saucers," a warm and loving girl who wanted to marry a Russian soldier and have twenty children. Once, when Marie had been caught in some mischief or other, her father joked how glad he was to discover she was only human: "I was always afraid of the wings growing." Marie was *so* good that the other girls referred to her as their stepsister.

Anastasia, the youngest, was a legend in the Romanov family almost from the moment of her birth. Short, mercurial, and "a very monkey for jokes," she was a natural comedienne, and the *enfant terrible* of the last tsar's family. Russian court memoirs are filled with anecdotes about Anastasia's pranks, her wit, her leaps of thought and lively imagination. Privately, among her surviving cousins, she was remembered as "a nasty little girl," "wild and rough," a hair-puller, a leg-biter and a tripper-up of servants. Small for her age, she was pained to see anyone taller to whom she held superior rank. Her cousin Nina, the daughter of Grand Duke George Mikhailovitch and Princess Marie of Greece, suffered torments at Anastasia's hands because, exactly two days younger than Anastasia, she was also a good head taller, a situation that struck the emperor's daughter as a form of *lèse majesté.*

*O*n the beach at Peterhof with her sisters, Anastasia (above, at left) holds her camera. Each of the girls had a Kodak box camera and sometimes they developed the photographs themselves. Their albums were decorated with watercolors and pressed flowers. Here the pages depict scenes on the Standart and trips ashore to their favorite Finnish island.

But the young grand duchesses seldom played with their Romanov cousins or with anyone at all besides each other, and then only under close supervision. The empress kept them strictly isolated from outside influences. She directed every aspect of their daily lives, chose their clothes and dressed them identically, supervised their extremely narrow education (far more circumscribed than her own) and caused them to grow up, in many ways, retarded — not mentally but socially — in the way they saw the world and related to other people.

As young women they spoke disconcertingly like ten-year-old girls. They giggled, poked each other, ran into corners and were incapable of writing any but the simplest correspondence in any one of the four languages they were taught: Russian, English, French and German. Never once in their lives did they go anywhere unescorted or without each other, except to the extent that they were split into pairs, "Big" and "Little."

The girls must have been lonely though their devotion to their parents was not artificial. The grand duchesses were perfectly happy to sit in the evenings *en famille* while their father read aloud or the empress and Ania played duets at the piano; everyone, without exception, pasted innumerable family snapshots into green leather photograph albums stamped with the imperial seal. This routine never varied, whether the family was at Tsarskoe, Peterhof, Livadia (where a splendid new Renaissance-style palace of white marble was erected in 1911 to replace the gloomy mansion where Alexander III had died), or Spala, the tsar's rustic, timbered hunting lodge in the forests of Russian Poland, where the family went only in the autumn for a shoot. Here, in the sylvan depths, the world invariably looked dark, foreboding.

Appropriately enough, it was during a visit to Spala in October 1912 that the link between

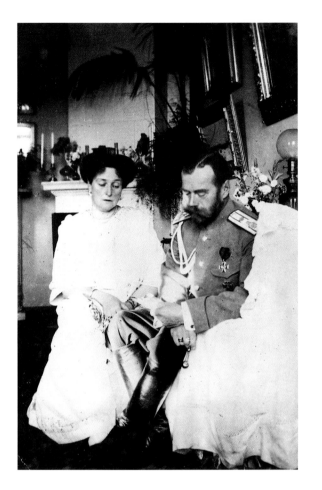

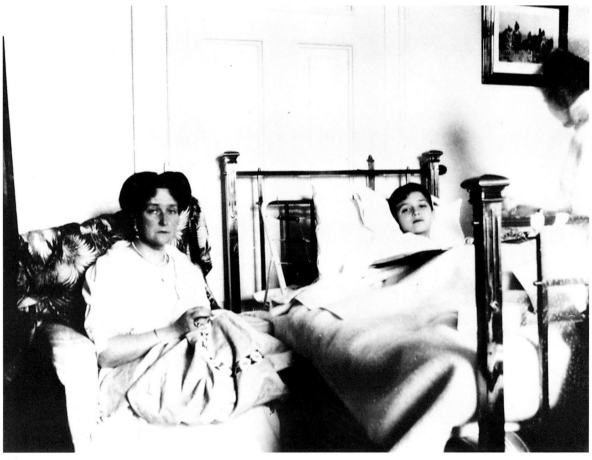

Nicholas and Alexandra read letters and telegrams of prayer and support (above) during the tsarevitch's near-fatal illness at Spala. (Above right) Alexandra sits at her son's bedside shortly after his recovery, visibly aged by the ordeal. At the far right, partially hidden, is Alexandra Tegleva, Anastasia's nurse and nanny to all the tsar's children.

the empress and Rasputin was permanently forged. A few weeks earlier Alexei had bruised his groin after falling on the side of a bathtub. At Spala the injury from which he seemed to be recovering suddenly grew worse. Day after day the blood filled his groin, lower abdomen and leg, causing the leg to bend until the knee was pressed against his chest.

Alexandra spent ten days without sleep at her son's bedside, listening to his shrieks and moans while the doctors stood helplessly by. When the pain became unbearable, Alexei begged to die. During this agonizing vigil, the empress's blond hair began to streak with gray. After eleven days the boy was so weakened that both parents believed the end was near. A bulletin was drawn up announcing the death of the heir. On the night of October 9, when all hope seemed lost, a priest

administered the last sacraments.

Only now did Alexandra turn to the man who had helped her son in the past. It may be that she had agreed not to consult the *starets* in view of the mounting opposition to his influence on her family. In any case, Rasputin was at home in Siberia, which is where Anna Viroubova's telegram reached him.

"God has seen your tears and heard your prayers," he wired back immediately. "Do not grieve. The Little One will not die. Do not allow the doctors to bother him too much." It is said that Alexandra never even waited for her son to recover before appearing in the drawing room, radiant and completely relaxed.

"The doctors notice no improvement," she announced, "but I am not a bit anxious." By morning, indeed, the boy was on the mend.

Crisis at Spala

"One of the dampest, gloomiest palaces I have ever seen," is how Anna Viroubova described the imperial hunting lodge at Spala, near Warsaw. Its dark rooms were an apt setting for the vigil at the bedside of the suffering tsarevitch in October of 1912. Viroubova recalled that the boy's "constant cries of pain" meant that those present "had often to stop [their] ears with [their] hands." During this ordeal the empress was unable to sleep or even lie down, although she sometimes retired to the curtained balcony (opposite left) that stood at one end of the lodge (opposite top right). Since there was no church on the estate, a large green tent was erected in the garden as a temporary chapel (opposite bottom right). Just as the death of the tsarevitch seemed imminent, the empress received a reassuring telegram from Rasputin. Within hours, the bleeding had subsided and Alexei began a slow recovery. Before long, the tsar again found time for a little shooting (right).

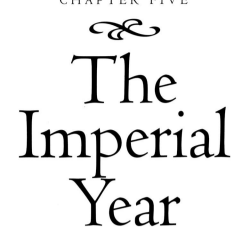

CHAPTER FIVE

The Imperial Year

From 1905, when they moved permanently to the Alexander Palace at Tsarskoe Selo, until 1914, with the outbreak of the First World War, the daily life of Nicholas II's family followed an unchanging routine. The emperor rose at eight, had breakfast with his wife and children — normally in Alexandra's bedroom or the Mauve Boudoir, since the empress rarely left her bed before noon —

then swam for half an hour before taking a walk in the garden. For an hour in the morning, from nine-thirty to ten-thirty, Nicholas dealt with the business of the court; from ten-thirty to one he turned to the business of government, receiving his ministers and their reports in his green, walnut-lined study. Lunch was brief, and served in any room where their majesties felt like having it. In the afternoon, until five, the tsar received ambassadors and petitions, visiting dignitaries and

*S*cenes from a
family's life: (opposite) Alexei boards a sleigh
circa 1915, as his wheelchair rests in the background;
(right) Olga in the uniform of her Hussars' regiment;
(below right) the empress in the Mauve Boudoir
circa 1912 with three of her daughters and
(below) with Anastasia, Alexei and Marie on the
Baltic coast in 1910; (bottom) the tsar and Alexei
in dress uniform in 1913.

military commanders. There were more "reports"
from six to eight, then dinner with all the family
followed by slow, cozy evenings of reading, sewing
and pasting photos into albums. Everyone was in
bed by eleven except the tsar and the empress, who
may have retired to their private chambers but
often kept working long into the night.

Tea was served at five o'clock sharp each day.
A central occasion in any Russian household, tea
at Tsarskoe, as Anna Viroubova remembered, was

a meal without the slightest variation: "Always appeared the same little white-draped table with its silver service, the glasses in their silver standards, and for the rest simply plates of hot bread and butter and a few English biscuits. Never anything new, never any surprises.... The Empress often used gently to complain, saying that other people had much more interesting teas, but she, who was supposed to have almost unlimited power, was in reality quite unable to change a single deadly detail of the routine of the Russian Court, where things had been going on almost exactly the same for generations. The same arrangement of furniture in the state rooms, the same braziers of incense carried by footmen in the long corridors, the same house messengers in archaic costumes of red and gold with ostrich-feathered caps, and for all I know the same plates for hot bread and butter on the same tea table, were traditions going back to Catherine the Great, or Peter, or farther still perhaps."

It was no different "on the road," when the imperial family left Tsarskoe Selo for one of their other homes. The imperial train was a palace in microcosm. Its seven deep blue salon cars provided a mauve-and-gray sitting room for the empress, a study with green leather furniture for the emperor, a paneled lounge car for members of the imperial suite and a dining room that could seat twenty. The car for the children was outfitted with the familiar white-painted furniture. An identical train, a decoy to fool terrorists, traveled a few miles away from the one bearing the imperial party.

With the March thaw, St. Petersburg, which had been built on a swamp, became one again, whereupon the tsar took his family on the long train trip to the Crimea. By common agreement Livadia, near Yalta, was their favorite place and its palace their favorite residence, and they normally stayed there at least through Easter. In May or early June they headed north again to take up residence at Peterhof. There, they never stayed at Peter the Great's magnificent castle on the shores of the Baltic, but always in the Tuscan-style villa in the Alexandria Park where Nicholas and Alexandra had first been attracted to each other as adolescents in the summer of 1884. Peterhof was home base for the summer cruises that followed on the *Standart*, the 4,000-ton Danish-built yacht that was the envy of all other sovereigns in the world. Several weeks each summer were spent offshore, sailing among the Finnish skerries and frequently stopping for picnics or huge Russian meals on the beach or in the woods.

In August the family went to Poland, then part of the Russian empire, for "the shoot." There were several imperial hunting lodges in the forest of Bielovezh, but Spala was the preferred residence. Alexandra never liked it, and never went again after Alexei's near-fatal illness there in 1912. In September it was Livadia again, then back to Tsarskoe in November to sit out the long Russian winter.

Anna Viroubova was often a part of the "royal progress" and she documented her experiences in photo albums and later, after the Revolution, in her memoirs. "How far," she wrote in the 1920s from her Finnish exile, "how unbelievably far away now seem those peaceful days."

"Monotonous though it may have been, the private life of the Emperor and his family was one of cloudless happiness."

— Anna Viroubova

The young emperor (left) circa 1898. His two eldest daughters, Olga and Tatiana (opposite top), pose in a window of the imperial train in 1903. Nicholas II and Kaiser Wilhelm inspect the day's kill after a hunt in Oranienburg, Germany (opposite bottom right), in November 1910. The tsar stands with his family (opposite bottom left) by the empress's driving carriage at Tsarskoe Selo circa 1913.

Tsarskoe Selo

"A world apart, an enchanted fairyland," was the description given to Tsarskoe Selo by Gleb Botkin, son of the court physician. This 800-acre compound, fifteen miles south of the capital, included the enormous Catherine Palace (below), used by the last imperial family only on formal occasions, and the smaller Alexander Palace (at top right), which was their principal residence. The two palaces were surrounded by groomed lawns and gardens dotted with fountains, obelisks and follies, an artificial lake and a Chinese village. On the extensive grounds, Nicholas II and his children pursued the outdoor activities that provided a welcome break from their carefully scheduled daily routine.

The Alexander Palace

With only one hundred rooms, the Alexander Palace was a relatively small and simple home for a Russian tsar. The ocher Palladian-style building had two wings that stretched out from a domed semicircular hall. In front of the courtyard stood a colonnade of Corinthian columns (right). The imperial family lived in the west wing in rooms that Alexandra furnished in a cozy, cluttered, chintz-and-potted-palm style that was a marked contrast to the gilt-and-marble splendor of the state apartments. The empress's Mauve Boudoir is the palace's most famous room, but across the hall was Nicholas's study, his dressing rooms and a large indoor saltwater swimming pool.

The empress (top left) in the Mauve Boudoir, surrounded by vases of fresh flowers. The matching chintzes she favored can be seen in the photograph of Tatiana and Olga (middle left) circa 1906. (Bottom left) Chief tutor Petrov gives lessons to Alexei in the palace's schoolroom.

The Feodorovsky Gorodok (above left)
was built in the park by Nicholas II in a style
reminiscent of traditional Russian villages. (Top)
The family's pet cemetery on the children's island
near the Alexander Palace. (Above) Snow
shrouds an abandoned sled on the palace grounds.

The first snow comes to St. Petersburg in late October
and the winter days are short. But like most Russians, the imperial family enjoyed the pastimes the season
brought — sledding, skiing, skating and even shoveling. At Tsarskoe Selo (below from left): Olga and Alexei
help Anastasia climb a snow tower; Nicholas stands with Alexei and Tatiana and his sister Xenia's son
Nikita; Alexei rests outdoors in a wheelchair; the empress, in an uncharacteristic moment, sleds on the park's
man-made hill, which is still in use today (far right).

*I*n the eighteenth century, Empress Elizabeth began
construction of a canal (left) from Tsarkoe Selo to St. Petersburg. Although never completed, the canal and the park's lakes
provided her successors (top) with ideal places for boating. (Above) Accompanied by Derevenko, Alexei feeds an
elephant, a gift from the king of Siam. (Above right) Under house arrest in May of 1917, Tatiana and Anastasia row
past the playhouse on the children's island, which still stands today (right). Many family photographs were taken on the
empress's balcony (below right), including (below left) Anastasia awaiting morning tea and (below middle) Olga and
Marie dressed up in furs.

Livadia

❦

"We drove through the dazzling sunshine and under the fresh green trees of springtime until the white palace, set in gardens of blooming flowers and vines, burst on our delighted eyes," wrote Anna Viroubova of the imperial family's first visit to the newly completed palace at Livadia in 1911. The splendid white marble complex replaced the gloomy wooden palace in which Alexander III had died in 1894. Its rooms were decorated with white furniture and flowered chintzes, and often the scent of roses wafted in from the gardens. Idyllic days here were filled with walks, swimming, tennis, and wild berry and mushroom gathering.

The Livadia Palace (right) today. (Above) A hand-tinted photo from the family album. (Opposite, from left) The tsar sea bathing with his sister Olga, at left, and Tatiana; Alexei wading; the empress comforts her son during a mud bath treatment.

The Italian Renaissance–style balconies of the palace (left) still offer splendid views of the Black Sea and the surrounding hills. The inner courtyard (right) was a favorite meeting place after lunch. (Below) The empress confers with Count Benckendorff while Alexei rests by a pillar.

Following afternoon tennis, tea was served (above) in the little Tudor-style house in the garden. Anna Viroubova sits at left. (Right) Olga and Tatiana perch on the balustrade as Pierre Gilliard gives a lesson on the terrace. (Far right) Marie happily poses with young officers in 1913.

The Standart

❧

Black and sleek and 420 feet long, the *Standart* was the most splendid of all royal yachts. Below its gleaming teak decks were staterooms for the family (decorated with the empress's signature chintz), rooms for members of the imperial suite, a chapel, quarters for servants, the crew and a platoon of the *Garde Equipage*, and sometimes, a brass band and balalaika orchestra. For two weeks each June, the imperial family cruised the coast of Finland, often going ashore to explore rocky shores and pine-covered islands.

*A relaxed informality prevailed on board the Standart.
The family knew many of the crew by name and shipboard flirtations blossomed between the grand duchesses
and dashing young officers. (Below, from left) Each of the girls chose her partner for a dance on the
dowager empress's name day on July 22, 1912; Nicholas reads and Alexandra embroiders
during a tranquil moment on deck; the tsar and the heir in naval whites; an officer gazes
from afar at the tsar's four daughters, seated next to their mother.*

Trips Ashore

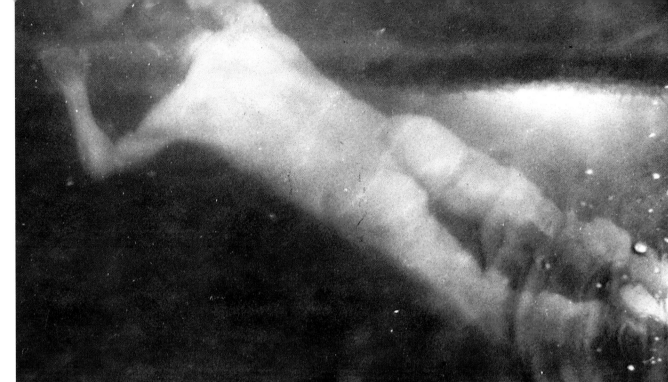

During the imperial family's annual cruise through the Gulf of Finland, a frequent anchoring spot was a sheltered bay surrounded by small islands, dubbed "the Bay of *Standart*" by the tsar's children. Each morning the launch went ashore to their favorite island for hikes, picnics and tennis on a court built by the tsar. Because of her sciatica, the empress usually remained on board, reading, writing letters and embroidering.

Nicholas, with his ever-present cigarette (opposite), sits on a fence on the island with Anastasia. (Above, from left) Officers and grand duchesses in a high-spirited melee; Alexei drills the ship's boys on the sandy shore; the tsar takes an icy plunge in the Baltic; a close-up shot (top right) reveals the imperial posterior; Nicholas stands by the island's court in tennis clothes. (Bottom right) Anna Viroubova joins the empress on a rare excursion ashore.

CHAPTER SIX

The Holy Devil

Rasputin's miracle-working telegram to Spala restored him immediately to the state of full imperial favor that he had lost the previous year. That year, 1911, was the closest his enemies came to destroying his influence on Empress Alexandra, until his violent murder finished it once and for all.

From the moment Rasputin began to visit the imperial family in 1905, he was under surveillance by the secret police, and soon reports of his outrageous behavior were being dutifully forwarded to Tsarskoe Selo. It is not known whether the tsar read them or simply put them aside, but he certainly ignored them. He knew that his wife's equilibrium, no less than his son's precarious health, depended on the continued well being of "Father Grigory," "Grishka," "Our Friend."

In the early years at least, Nicholas seems to have taken Rasputin at face value. "This is merely a simple Russian man," Nicholas remarked soon after he first met him, "very religious and believing. The Empress likes his sincerity, she believes in the power of his prayers for our Family and Alexei, but after all this is our own business, completely private."

"He would be surrounded by his admirers," testified one of Rasputin's servants in St. Petersburg, after his star had risen and he enjoyed what amounted to diplomatic immunity, "with whom he also slept. He would do his thing with them quite openly and without shame. He would caress them ... and when he or they felt like it he would simply take them into his study and do his business." That Rasputin had a wife at home in his native Siberian village of Pokrovskoe caused neither of them any distress for, as Madame Rasputin once remarked when asked, "He has enough for all." The number of Rasputin's female conquests is incalculable —

At Rasputin's St. Petersburg apartment (opposite, the windows directly below the balcony), there was always a steady stream of visitors seeking guidance and favors from the starets (right). Among the devotees in the photograph at left are Anna Viroubova (second row standing, third from left) and Lili Dehn (back row in hat, on left of doorway).

"You think that I am polluting you," he explained to recalcitrant partners, "but I am not. I am purifying you."

Three or four hundred people might call on him at his St. Petersburg apartment on any given day — "professional political intriguers, unscrupulous senior officials ... society women as well as many of his own class ... who hoped to get some material assistance from him. They were never disappointed, for Rasputin never once refused to help anyone who needed money. Whenever a well-to-do caller left a pile of money behind him, Rasputin distributed some of it to the next needy petitioner waiting to see him." Not even the police informers who hung around his flat were immune to Rasputin's mesmeric charm.

"Above all I noticed his eyes," wrote one. "With a fixed steady gaze his eyes blazed with a kind of phosphorescent flame. It was as if he were feeling out his listeners with his eyes.... I noticed that his stare had an extraordinary effect, especially on women, who found it dreadfully embarrassing, would grow disturbed and begin to look at him timidly, and were often drawn to come up and start talking or listening to him. After staring at someone like that he would begin to talk to somebody else, and then suddenly turn back to the one he had stared at twenty minutes before, and breaking off his conversation would say: 'It's bad, mother, bad, yes, you cannot live like that, look, try to make amends, it's a business, love, yes ... well.' Changing the subject again he would start moving round the room while people would whisper that he had divined something, spoken the truth, that he had second sight, and a nervous *exalté* mood would descend, the kind of mood you find in the proximity of holy men in monasteries."

Rasputin was untouchable as long as the empress remained his devout patron and refused to hear any accusation against him. He used his special status to carve out for himself an unheard-of position of wealth and privilege — unheard-of for someone who was, after all, a mere peasant. Among the Russian peasantry, in fact, Rasputin's unprecedented prosperity in the capital became a subject of increasing pride.

As his influence grew, so did his daring. He was heard referring to the tsar and the empress in public as "Papa" and "the Old Lady." He insisted that Nicholas regarded him as Christ incarnate and that with Alexandra "he could do what he wanted." But the empress would hear nothing against him.

"He is hated because we love him," said Alexandra in a brisk summation of her life's philosophy. She did not deny that the *starets* had "faults" — she simply refused to discuss them. As early as 1908 Rasputin found himself in serious conflict with the tsar's government. After reading a condemnatory report handed to him personally by Prime Minister Stolypin, Nicholas supposedly agreed that he and the empress would "no longer see him." An order was drawn up banishing the *starets* from St. Petersburg, but it never went into effect and was ultimately rescinded, presumably under pressure from the palace. By 1911, in any case, hardly anyone but the empress, Anna Viroubova and a few of their own devoted friends had any illusions about the dual nature of Rasputin's character.

His former mentors in the Orthodox Church, who had done more than anyone else in the early years to ensure his rise to prominence, renounced him now in an effort to rescue their own reputations, but even Bishop Theophan, formerly Alexandra's confessor and a prelate of unimpeachable character, could not break the *starets'* grip. It was Theophan who first went to the tsar with formal complaints about Rasputin's licentious lifestyle. But when the empress confronted the wily peasant with the charges, he appeared genuinely shocked and denied them all.

This popular but repeatedly suppressed lampoon (above) shows the imperial couple as puppets in Raputin's hands. Cartoons of a more salacious nature were also circulated, and their sentiments are echoed in this Bolshevik poster from 1920 (opposite). In the parade of horrors from the previous regime is a blood-drinking Rasputin clutched by a naked tsarina and followed by an emasculated tsar.

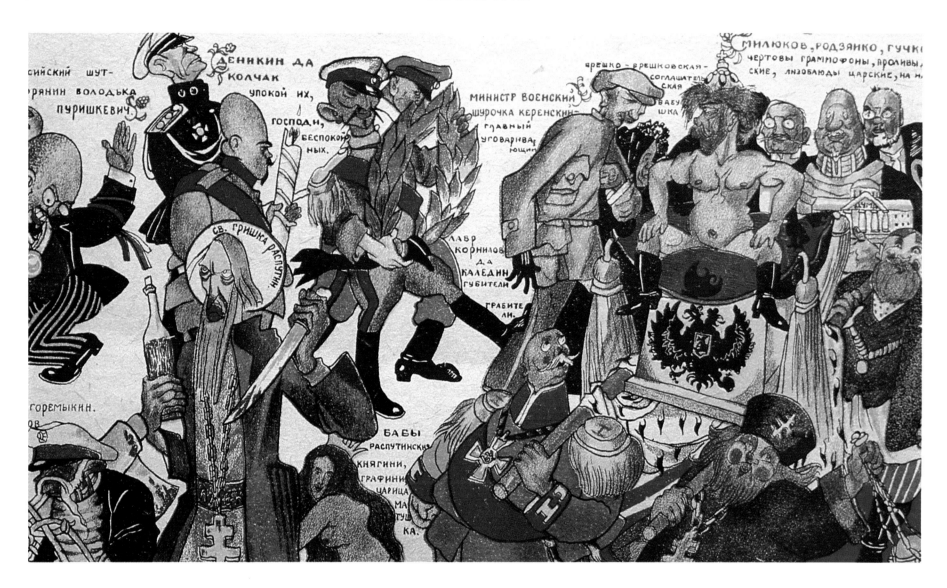

As a result Theophan, not Rasputin, was banished from St. Petersburg.

Beginning around 1911, however, copies of letters Rasputin had received from the empress and her daughters began to circulate all over Russia. It was later claimed that they had been "stolen" from Rasputin's apartment in St. Petersburg, but in fact he had released them himself several years before in an effort to prove his "close connections" at Tsarskoe Selo. The letters appeared to reveal a connection between Rasputin and the women of the tsar's family far more intimate and much less religious than was hitherto supposed. "I only wish one thing," Alexandra had written her mentor, "to fall asleep, forever on your shoulders and in your arms.... Where are you? Where have you gone? Oh, I am so sad and my heart is longing.... Will you soon be again close to me? Come quickly.... I love you forever. Mama." Letters from the grand duchesses, though less ardent, were equally compromising and more of a shock since the eldest of the girls was only sixteen at that time.

A scandal could not be avoided. Pornographic lampoons of Rasputin and the empress, with her daughters and Anna Viroubova cavorting naked in the background, quickly made the rounds of St. Petersburg, along with photographs that purported to show the *starets* in lusty debauch with several ladies of high society. Few were in a position to know that the women of the imperial family addressed all of their intimates as "darling," "yearned" for their presence, "longed" for their kisses and so on. Nor was Alexandra ashamed to be called Mama by a simple peasant. She wanted to be thought of as the mother of Russia, having an almost mystical connection to her husband's people. In short, there is no shred of historical evidence that Alexandra was ever Rasputin's mistress.

But the scandal had run out of control. Hoping to convince the tsar at last about the "true nature" of the empress's mentor, Stolypin had commissioned yet another police investigation of the *starets'* activities. "The report was largely concerned with Rasputin's private life," said one of the tsar's senior security officers, "a series of drunken and sometimes scandalous and riotous celebrations, a number of sexual liaisons and, recently, dealings with dubious entrepreneurs and backers trying to turn his influence to advantage." In typically passive fashion, Nicholas read the document and said nothing — either to Stolypin or his wife. So the prime minister again took the initiative and ordered Rasputin to leave St. Petersburg.

Alexandra was outraged. She stamped and fumed and insisted that "saints are always calumniated" in their lifetime, but the tsar would not overrule the man on whom his government so depended. According to one report, Rasputin himself appeared to plead his case before the tsar, who agreed with him that the time might be right for a pilgrimage to the Holy Land, and in the spring of 1911, Rasputin departed on a mission to Jerusalem, keeping in touch with Alexandra by letter. She never forgave Stolypin. According to one account, Nicholas commanded his prime minister "never again" to speak to him about Rasputin, and a coolness developed between them that was never dispelled.

What the tsar really thought about Rasputin belongs on the long list of imponderables that made up his character. A witty remark, bearing no relation to anything we know of Nicholas's mental or verbal capacities, has found its way into history books. "Better one Rasputin," he is supposed to have said, "than ten fits of hysterics a day." The tsar's preternatural passivity, described as "fatalism" by his defenders and endowed by them with a spiritual hue, is probably the best explanation for his refusal to face the truth about the dangerous

nature of his wife's obsession. Even Dr. Botkin, whose own air of religious exaltation mounted along with his importance at the palace, confessed to his daughter before the Revolution, "As a doctor, I can no longer certify the Empress as being fully normal."

After Stolypin's assassination, according to Count Vladimir Kokovstsov, his successor as prime minister, "the concept of a government, of its significance, dwindled," to be replaced by a notion of "the purely personal nature" of autocratic rule. At Tsarskoe Selo, "the government increasingly came to be considered as a wall cutting the ruler off from his people."

Rasputin's banishment in any case was brief. He was back in St. Petersburg in March 1912 — well before the miraculous telegram to Spala restored him to favor — although for a while he kept out of the public eye. But he secretly joined the imperial family on their annual Crimean holiday in Livadia.

With Stolypin dead there seemed to be no one capable of challenging the *starets*, except in meaningless ways. In March 1913, as the congregation of Kazan cathedral waited for the tercentenary Te Deum to begin, Michael Rodzianko was astonished to find Rasputin sitting in a seat reserved for one of his fellow Duma members. "He was dressed in a magnificent Russian tunic of crimson silk," the president of the Duma reported, "patent-leather top-boots, black cloth full trousers" and a sable-lined coat. "Over his dress he wore a pectoral cross on a finely wrought gold chain."

"Clear out at once, you vile heretic," Rodzianko ordered. "There is no place for you in this sacred house!"

"Oh, Lord, forgive him such sin!" Rasputin replied before stomping out of the cathedral and riding off in a shiny automobile — a gift from the empress.

Perhaps nothing could have halted the slide

of the monarchy into chaos and dissolution apart from Rasputin's or Alexandra's "annihilation" — the word used by a senior grand duchess, Marie Pavlovna, in advance of the Revolution. Most of the Romanovs had clearly had enough of Alexandra and her mystical ways. And certainly, as 1913 drew to a close, rumors of plots — against Rasputin, against the empress — swirled through the elegant salons of St. Petersburg.

Superficially the social life of the aristocracy continued as before, while a whole new class of rising entrepreneurs and artists made their mark. It was Russia's literary Silver Age and the era of the Ballets Russes — but the music was dissonant, the painting abstract and the morals of artists more alarming than not. At the Maryinsky Theater, Vaslav Nijinsky danced *Le Spectre de la Rose* in tights that were tighter than the audience was used to, one night causing the tsar's mother to sweep in horror from the imperial box at the sight of his bulging groin. Her open disapproval had no effect whatever on the pleasures of the town. The tsarist capital was a vast "cabaret," said Princess Catherine Radziwill, who wrote muckraking books about the imperial family under the pseudonym Count Paul Vassili, where society lived from thrill to thrill, "eager only for enjoyment and pleasure, seeking always new subjects of excitement, devoid of serious thought and hating serious pursuits."

If the judgment was harsh, the spectacle was fantastic — furs and jewels and troikas in winter, carnivals, opera, *bals blancs* and *bals roses*. In the past this world had been open only to the most prestigious Russian families (the Orlovs and Sheremetievs, the Yussupovs and Cantacuzenes) but money suddenly had arrived in Russia — Western market capitalism — and with it the ancient barriers fell. Financial adventures, investments and schemes sprang into being almost overnight. It was the talk of every salon,

The empress with her children and a nurse (above) in a rare photograph with Rasputin, taken at Anna Viroubova's cottage. (Below) Rasputin in Siberia in 1914, recovering from stab wounds sustained during an attempt on his life. At bottom is a handwritten prayerful message from him.

the goal of every Russian on the make: more cash, more deals, more bonds and bank accounts. In the 1913 city census, forty thousand persons in St. Petersburg registered as stock exchange speculators, and a wave of suicides joined a passion for gambling and a return to violent murder as a means of settling scores.

And through it all, society danced. It danced from New Year's to Lent, and after that it ate till Easter — great plates of salmon, *blinis*, mushrooms, caviar, cucumbers, sturgeon, partridge and dessert. At the St. Petersburg Yacht Club, the most exclusive private refuge in the city, grand dukes and generals dined and drank and smoked cigars that were handed to them by servants in resplendent livery — emerald frock coats, scarlet collars, gold braid and tricornered hats. It was gaiety gone mad; a high society no less out of touch with reality than the pious rulers at Tsarskoe Selo.

Sequestered at Tsarskoe, that suffocating hothouse of misguided intentions, the imperial family was, if possible, more isolated from their empire than ever before as 1914 began. Once again the tsar and tsarina shunned the winter social season in St. Petersburg, but beyond the aristocratic pale, the danger signs were everywhere. Labor unrest mounted inexorably. At the beginning of the year more than a million men were on strike, by June a million and a half — and the number continued to grow. Since Stolypin's murder, the tsar's ministers had been mostly a sorry lot. Increasingly his was a government aimlessly adrift in a world it did not understand.

Not every member of the tsar's family was oblivious to the tide rising against them. Dr. Botkin's daughter Tatiana remembered that the two eldest, Olga and Tatiana, were "well aware" of the danger of their parents' myopic course. Nor is it entirely clear that these two — now on the verge of womanhood — still appreciated

the kisses, pats and smacks of Rasputin, who came to the palace with increasing rarity. A governess, Sophie Tiutcheva, had already been dismissed from the Alexander Palace when she dared to object to Rasputin's familiarity with the girls. Olga, as she grew older, became frankly morose — "grumpy," said her mother — and was apparently cheered only by the antics of the young Anastasia, whose high spirits (and distinctly scatological sense of humor) seemed immune to tension and gloom. All the tsar's daughters were beside themselves with delight in June 1914, a summer already noted for its glorious weather, when the British Royal Navy's First Battle Cruiser Squadron arrived on a ceremonial visit to Russia. They boarded Admiral Beatty's flagship, *Lion,* and were given a tour by a group of handsome young midshipmen. "Never have I seen happier faces," reported the British ambassador, Sir George Buchanan.

To Nicholas II the incident that triggered a world war did not at first seem cause for particular concern. The news of the assassination of Archduke Ferdinand, heir to the throne of the Austro-Hungarian Empire, reached the Russian ruler aboard the imperial yacht *Standart* only four days into the family's annual summer Baltic cruise. Archduke Ferdinand's death, while serious, did not cause undue alarm. Far more immediate and at least as upsetting to Nicholas and Alexandra was the news, received only the next day, of the attempted assassination of Rasputin. (The assassin, a crazed ex-prostitute acting on behalf of another "mad monk," the charlatan Serge Iliodor, one of the *starets'* most ferocious religious enemies, had plunged a knife several times into Rasputin's stomach and screamed out, "I have killed the Antichrist!" The fact that Rasputin survived the attack only burnished the legend of his superhuman durability.) But events in Vienna soon brought the Balkan crisis to the fore.

Emperor Franz Josef and his generals concluded that the archduke's assassination was the pretext they needed to put Serbia in its place. The assassin may have been a Bosnian Serb, a citizen of their empire, but his inspiration had clearly come from the independent kingdom of Serbia, which had been agitating for years for its southern Slav neighbors to throw off the imperial yoke. On July 23, 1914, the Austrians delivered an ultimatum to Serbia so unreasonable in its demands that it was tantamount to a declaration of war.

Suddenly a local Balkan problem threatened to become a much wider conflict. Imperial Russia was the traditional protector of the Serbs, and Nicholas had personally promised to defend Serbia's independence. If Austria attacked Serbia, then Russia would be obliged to declare war on Austria. And, despite some desperate last-minute maneuvering, this is exactly what happened. On July 28, Austro-Hungarian artillery began bombarding Belgrade, the Serbian capital. The next day Tsar Nicholas ordered his armies along the Austrian frontier to mobilize.

Perhaps even then a wider European war might have been avoided were it not for the intemperate actions of Kaiser Wilhelm. The kaiser had dismissed Russia's allies, the French, as militarily inconsequential. He didn't even consider the possibility that England might side with France and Russia against Austria and Germany, and he doubted that cousin Nicky, whom he had been able to manipulate in the past, would really follow through and fight Germany. (The Russian armies were far from ready for war.) But when it became clear that the kaiser would throw his forces unreservedly on the side of Austria rather than mediating the growing crisis, Nicholas bowed to necessity and ordered a general mobilization. After that the First World War was virtually inevitable.

The opening of the war was greeted in Russia, as everywhere else in Europe, with overwhelming enthusiasm in an orgy of nationalist feeling that took even the participants by surprise. Nothing like it had attended any of the numerous patriotic celebrations of Nicholas II's reign — not the coronation or the tercentenary or the commemorations of the Napoleonic Battles of Poltava and Borodino in 1909 and 1912 respectively. Angry workers joined bitter revolutionaries in an explosion of loyalty to Russia and the tsar; peasants other than Rasputin were seen kissing countesses, while tens of thousands of people fell to their knees outside the Winter Palace and sang the imperial hymn when Nicholas and Alexandra appeared to greet them on the balcony on the day that war was declared.

"Never before, never after, did I feel so certain of Russia's future glory," said fourteen-year-old Gleb Botkin, "never so boundlessly devoted to the Emperor, who suddenly appeared in my imagination as some great deity, moving solely by his will heaven and earth, shaping the destinies of the whole human race. That our hopes proved vain and foolish ... is a matter of indifference to me. Those were heroic moments when all of us were rendered oblivious of the petty considerations of everyday existence and were willing, nay, eager, to sacrifice everything, including our very lives, to an abstract ideal of universal happiness and glory."

Only the imperial family wept — the tsar because of his failure to avert hostilities he knew would cost his country dearly, his children out of fright, and the empress owing to the letter from Rasputin that she held in her hand. (In the crucial days that led to war, Rasputin was at Pokrovskoe recovering from the recent assassination attempt.) "Again I say a terrible storm cloud hangs over Russia," the *starets* had written. "Disaster, grief, murky darkness and no light. A whole ocean of tears, there is no counting them,

"At that moment the tsar was really the autocrat, the military, political and religious director of his people, the absolute master of their bodies and souls."

— Maurice Paléologue,
French ambassador
to Russia, in 1914

A present-day view of the balcony of the Winter Palace (opposite), on which Nicholas and Alexandra appeared (inset) on the day that war was declared on Austria and Germany in August 1914.

Crowds in Palace
Square (opposite) cheer the declaration
of war and the imperial family.
A war poster (above) shows the Russian
bear chasing Kaiser Wilhelm and
Austrian emperor Franz Josef up a
tree. (Below) The tsar with
Grand Duke Nicholas ("Nikolasha"),
commander in chief of the
Russian armies.

and so much blood.... Russia is drowning in blood. The disaster is great," Rasputin concluded, "the misery infinite." His letter, which still exists, was signed "Grigory" and marked with the sign of the cross.

The war brought out the best and the worst in Alexandra and Nicholas both — the best in their sincere and absolute dedication to the cause of Russia's victory and the relief of her suffering soldiers, the worst in their failure to see that war could not be an answer to Russia's problems at home. It was the Japanese conflict of 1904 magnified ten or twenty times. The First World War was never an ideological conflict, despite all the bluster about Democracy and the Hun: the universal rejoicing that greeted the fall of the Romanovs in 1917 is sufficient testimony to the embarrassment Russia's allies had felt to be fighting alongside an autocrat, the "bloodthirsty tyrant" of popular imagination, whose wife — it was no longer a secret anywhere in the world — was a religious fanatic and ostensibly the mistress of a Siberian peasant. But without the aid of the Russian armies, with their enormous manpower and seemingly endless capacity for sacrifice, the war against Germany could never have been brought to a successful conclusion. Russia bled for the western powers, a fact no Russian ever forgot.

In those early optimistic days, however, when the Allied powers talked of the war being over by Christmas, morale was high and illusion persistent. Within a month of the formal declaration, the tsar left for the first of many tours of his army's headquarters. "I am so happy for you that you can at last manage to go," the empress wrote him that September, "as I know how deeply you have been suffering all this time.... Egoistically I suffer horribly to be separated — we are not accustomed to it & I do so endlessly love my very own precious Boysy dear." And truly, the tsar was never happier than when

he was with military men. The generals, among them his uncle, Grand Duke Nicholas Nicholaievitch, the commander in chief, were men whom he might not have liked but whom he could trust and respect — especially Uncle "Nikolasha," who towered nearly seven feet tall and was already a hero to the Russian people.

As for the empress, "she became overnight a changed being," Anna Viroubova remembered. Alexandra threw herself into nursing work, taking her daughters and Ania with her. "Every bodily ill and weakness forgotten," Ania continued, "she began at once an extensive plan for a system of hospitals and sanitary trains for the dreadful roll of wounded which she knew must begin with the first battle." By the end of 1914 eighty-five hospitals and ten "medical trains" had been established in Russia under Alexandra's direct patronage. The Winter Palace in St. Petersburg, the Catherine Palace at Tsarskoe Selo, the Petrovsky and Poteshny palaces in Moscow were all transformed into emergency medical centers, with rooms set aside for the wives and mothers of the wounded.

After two months of intensive training, Alexandra, Ania, Olga and Tatiana were certified as qualified nurses, while the two younger grand duchesses, Marie and Anastasia, were established as "patronesses" at a smaller hospital — a *lazaret* — in the Feodorovsky Gorodok at Tsarskoe Selo. They were the only creatures in the imperial complex who still went about in civilian dress. Everyone else was in uniform, including Alexandra and the elder girls, who rarely, if ever, doffed their habits as Russian sisters of mercy. According to Ania, "The Empress was spared nothing, nor did she wish to be."

"Arriving at the hospital shortly after nine in the morning," Ania went on, "we went directly to the receiving wards where the men were brought in after having first aid treatment in the trenches and field hospitals. They had

*T*he Armorial Hall of the Winter Palace today (left) and as it looked when converted to a hospital ward in 1914 (opposite left inset). The empress and her two eldest daughters (right) trained as nurses to help with "war relief." One of the grand duchesses' uniforms (below) has been preserved.

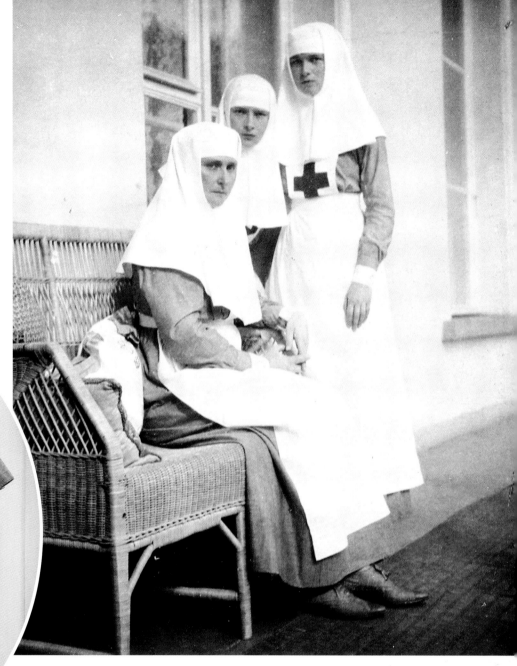

Grand Duchess Tatiana (opposite right inset) assists in an operation at the empress's hospital at Tsarskoe Selo, and with the rest of her family (minus the tsar), poses for a photograph (right) with the wounded. The empress is seated at center, with Olga directly behind her. Anastasia and Alexei are to the right, Marie and Tatiana to the left.

traveled far and were usually dirty as well as bloodstained and suffering. Our hands scrubbed in antiseptic solutions, we began the work of washing, cleaning and bandaging maimed bodies, mangled faces, blinded eyes, all the indescribable mutilations of what is called civilized warfare.... I have seen the Empress of Russia in the operating room of a hospital holding ether cones, handling sterilized instruments, assisting in the most difficult operations, taking from the hands of the busy surgeons amputated legs and arms, removing bloody and even vermin-infested dressings, enduring all the sights and smells and agonies of that most dreadful of all places, a military hospital in the midst of war."

But as usual the empress's commitment to principle took its toll on her popularity. She was criticized from the start for her hands-on approach to the crisis, her belief that active work in nursing was a sufficient example to lead the nation. It was not. She was needed as a public figure, but she and her daughters almost never left Tsarskoe Selo after 1914 except to tour hospitals, always in their nursing habits. Nor would Alexandra have understood the complaint of the Russian aristocracy that it was beneath the dignity of an empress to assist in medical operations, to bandage wounds or turn her gaze on a wounded soldier who (as she wrote the tsar) was "scarcely a 'man' any more, so shot to pieces, perhaps it must be cut off as so black but hope to save it."

Many of the soldiers themselves were mortified to discover that their empress was also their nurse. For every "suffering lad" who called out "Tsaritsa! Stand near me! Hold my hand that I may have courage!" there were ten who were "deeply embarrassed" by her ministrations. The fact that she was German compounded the unease.

At the entrance to the smaller of the two hospitals at Tsarskoe Selo (above), Anastasia (left) and Marie (center) pose with soldiers. The hospital was in the Feodorovsky Gorodok (right), a "modern" village built by Nicholas in the so-called New Russian Style of architecture.

124

Had she sung and danced her way through the war or ordered a hundred dresses à la Mary Lincoln, she could not have been less loved.

Anti-German hysteria swept through all Allied countries. In London in 1917, Alexandra's sister Victoria of Battenberg saw her husband dismissed as First Lord of the Admiralty and their surname changed to Mountbatten, while the British royal family, German to the core, ceased to be Saxe-Coburg and suddenly emerged as the House of Windsor. But in the Russian capital anti-German sentiment was the fiercest of all and inevitably heightened resentment of the German-born empress. At the outbreak of hostilities, St. Petersburg was renamed Petrograd, the German embassy was burned and a huge number of the Baltic-Russian nobility with names like Taube and von der Osten-Saacken-Tettenborn were reduced to digging out documents that proved their ancient descent from the servants of

Catherine the Great. The empress's German origins became a convenient peg on which to hang the general discontent; soon the rumor was that the kaiser had a private telephone line into his cousin Alexandra's Mauve Boudoir. She was "despised," Gleb Botkin recalled, while Russians were merely "disappointed" with the tsar as the war dragged on and no one came any nearer to victory.

While there is no real doubt that Alexandra had discarded her German loyalties and become a fierce Russian patriot, the popular rage against her had some technical justification. During the war the empress found herself with a brother and a sister on the opposing side in Germany, another sister in Russia and a third in England, all of them blithely corresponding for the duration of hostilities through their neutral cousins in Sweden. The evidence is convincing that Alexandra's brother Ernie, the grand duke of Hesse, made a clandestine visit to Tsarskoe Selo in 1916 to discuss the matter of a separate peace between Russia and Germany — an act

This imperial Easter egg of 1915 honors the women of the Romanov family who became Red Cross war nurses. Shown left to right are the tsar's sister Grand Duchess Olga, his daughter Olga, the empress, Tatiana, and his first cousin Grand Duchess Marie Pavlovna.

of treason on both sides. Already the previous year, in April 1915, Alexandra wrote the tsar:

I had a long, dear letter fr. Erni — I will show it you upon your return. He says that 'if there is someone who understands him (you) & knows what he is going through, it is me.' He kisses you tenderly. He longs for a way out of this dilemma, that someone ought to begin to make a bridge for discussions.

"So he had an idea of quite privately sending a man of confidence to Stockholm, who should meet a gentleman sent by you (privately) that they could help disperse many momentary difficulties. He had this idea, as in
Germany there is no real hatred for Russia. So he sent a gentleman to be there on the 28 — (that is 2 days ago & I only heard to-day) & can only spare him a week. So I at once wrote an answer (all through Daisy) [Louise, Crown Princess of Sweden] & sent it to the gentleman, telling him you are not yet back, so he better not wait — & that tho' one longs for peace, the time has not yet come....

"W. [Kaiser Wilhelm] knows of course absolutely nothing about all this.

The first year of the war had not gone well for Russia. Although its timely advance into East

"In the Great War ledger, the page on which the Russian losses were written has been torn out. No one knows the figure.... Sometimes in our battles... we had to remove the mounds of enemy corpses in order to get a clear field of fire."

— German field marshal
Paul von Hindenburg

Russian casualties in the war with Germany were staggering — more than three million by 1917. (Opposite) Troops enter a captured town on the southwestern front, but even victories incurred great losses (above).

Prussia in August 1914 had saved Paris by diverting German divisions from the western front, the losses had been terrible. By the beginning of 1915 Russia had lost a million men and one-quarter of its army had been killed, wounded or captured. And despite the heady advances on the southern front that brought Russian armies within striking distance of Vienna in the spring of 1915, the tsar's forces were no match for their real adversary, Germany. When the German juggernaut finally materialized late that spring, there was no stopping it. And when it was over, most of Russian Poland lay in German hands.

It was at this point that the tsar, at the urging of his wife (and Rasputin) but against the advice of every thinking person in the government, took command of Russia's military forces, replacing his highly competent relative, Nicholas Nicholaievitch, as commander in chief of the army and navy. (Alexandra hated Uncle Nikolasha, who had emerged as one of Rasputin's most stubborn critics, and she argued vehemently for his dismissal.) In September 1915 Nicholas left Tsarskoe Selo more or less permanently for the *Stavka*, or general headquarters, at Mogilev on the banks of the Dnieper

River in Belorussia. Nicholas was no military tactician, nor did he pretend to be. His decision was emotional, symbolic and led to a temporary boost in morale but no immediate change in Russia's military fortune.

The temporary gain was more than offset by the rapid disintegration of the government Nicholas had left behind, for all practical purposes, in the hands of the empress, who leaned ever more heavily on the political advice of Rasputin. Although they met only rarely during the war years, they kept up a regular correspondence during which Rasputin urged on her the appointment or dismissal of government ministers and even went so far as to offer advice on the military conduct of the war. From September

The tsar (above) entering the gate of the Stavka, the Russian army headquarters at Mogilev. In propaganda posters (opposite) he was depicted as an ancient knight of Muscovy and (inset) as a modern commander leading his troops into battle.

1915, with the tsar away at the front, Alexandra was unofficial regent, a position in no way illegal or even irregular under Russian law or tradition. Her defenders have gone a long way in recent years toward demonstrating that Alexandra did not singlehandedly bring down the monarchy as is often alleged, that the series of mediocrities and fools whom Nicholas appointed to his cabinet in the last days of the dynasty were not all chosen by her or, for that matter, necessarily under the guidance of Rasputin.

The tsar, however, cannot have remained unaffected by the advice and criticism Alexandra dispatched from Tsarskoe Selo in a head-bursting barrage of angry and rambling letters, many of which survive. This one was "no good," she complained, that one was "against Our Friend," a third — the tsar's foreign minister, Serge Sazonov — was "such a pancake." "No, hearken to our Friend," she wrote the tsar at one point, "believe Him. He has yr. interest and Russia's at heart — it is not for nothing that God sent Him to us — only we must pay more attention to what He says. His words are not lightly spoken and the gravity of having not only His prayers but His advice is great." The *appearance* of the empress's power and of Rasputin's influence over her was as important as its reality.

"Oh, Lovy," Alexandra wrote Nicholas at Mogilev, "you can trust me. I may not be clever enough — but I have a strong feeling and that helps more than the brain often. Don't change anybody until we meet, I entreat you, let's speak it over quietly together."

She traveled to see her husband only infrequently, but despite their separation the tsar was enjoying probably the last unbroken stretch of contentment he ever had. He was not merely playing at soldiers at the *Stavka*, though little was required of him beyond appearances, consultations and nods of the head. Toward the end of 1915, after several successful (and, for Alexei, wildly exciting) visits to the front, Nicholas persuaded Alexandra to let the tsarevitch live with him at headquarters. She consented on the condition that "his studies not be interrupted," and the unusual intimacy that two of the boy's tutors, Pierre Gilliard and Sydney Gibbes,

enjoyed with the members of the imperial family dates essentially from this decision.

"The teaching staff [at Mogilev] was a very small one," Gibbes recalled, "consisting of two or three persons only, but it was all very friendly and gay and, according to the Tsarevitch, infinitely preferable to Tsarskoe Selo. The Emperor seemed greatly pleased by the new arrangement, and sometimes would have us sit in his Cabinet while he was working. Once he overheard the Tsarevitch telling me that when he went home for good he was going to take the big cut glass ball that hung on the electric chandelier. 'Alexei,' the Emperor shouted out, 'that isn't ours.'" The

Alexandra perches on the tsar's desk (above left) during a visit to the Stavka in May 1916. The year before, Alexandra had permitted Alexei to live with his father at headquarters. Nicholas and Alexei are pictured resting by a trench while on a walk (top), at lunch with officers and aides (above) and (opposite top) reviewing departing troops. (Opposite bottom) Earlier in the war, father and son examine a captured German machine gun at Tsarskoe Selo.

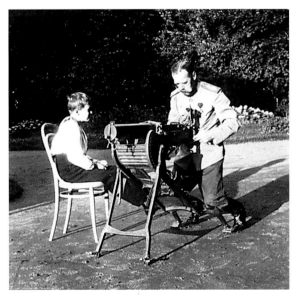

boy's unmitigated pride and delight at the chance to share his father's life — in an exercise that Nicholas hoped would spare him the crippling shyness he himself had suffered as a result of his upbringing — is particularly touching in view of its short duration. His letters home were filled with news about the "soldiering" life, about regiments, trains and "Papa's" every word. Even so the empress and her "girlies" sometimes descended on the *Stavka*, and a day never passed without at least one letter from Alexandra: "Good morning, my precious ones, how did you sleep, I wonder!... Oh, how I miss you both!" The experiment in bachelor living lasted only as long as

Alexei's health, however, which began to deteriorate drastically as 1916 drew to a close. A massive nosebleed had already taken him home to Tsarskoe and the last of Rasputin's "miracles."

The court physicians did what they could, but Alexei's condition continued to deteriorate. Finally the empress sent for Rasputin. It was probably the last time he ever set foot in the Alexander Palace. Anna Viroubova, who witnessed the visit, recorded it for posterity: "He came into the room, made the sign of the cross over the bed and, looking intently at the almost moribund child, said quietly to the kneeling parents: 'Don't be alarmed. Nothing will happen.'

That was all. The child fell asleep and the next day was so well that the Emperor left for the *Stavka*. Dr. Deverenko and Professor Federov told me afterwards that they did not even attempt to explain the cure."

By late 1916 Russia was reaching the point of no return. On the stalemated eastern front thousands upon thousands of young Russian men continued to die in a war that now seemed pointless. Away from the fighting, the country was falling into economic chaos, and the tsar's government began to disintegrate as the empress, by this time, "saturated with veronal" and "dead from fatigue," listened to none but her beloved *starets*. At the beginning of December, Vladimir Purishkevitch, a right-wing member of the Duma well known as one of the staunchest defenders of the monarchy, denounced Rasputin before his colleagues. Purishkevitch urged the elected representatives of the people to "have the courage to tell [the tsar] that the multitude is threatening in its wrath. Revolution threatens and an obscure *moujik* shall govern Russia no longer." Soon it became an open secret that Purishkevitch belonged to a group of conspirators plotting to rid Russia of the evil holy man.

Rasputin had heard rumors that his life was in danger. Sometime in December 1916 it is claimed that he sat down to write a remarkable letter in which he contemplated his own murder and prophesied its dire consequences for Russia. Authentic or not, the letter provides a chilling portent of what was to come:

I write and leave behind me this letter at St. Petersburg. I feel that I shall leave life before January 1. I wish to make known to the Russian people, to Papa, to the Russian Mother and to the Children, to the land of Russia, what they must understand. If I am killed by common assassins, and especially by my brothers the Russian peasants, you, Tsar of Russia, have nothing

to fear, remain on your throne and govern, and you, Russian Tsar, will have nothing to fear for your children, they will reign for hundreds of years in Russia. But if I am murdered by boyars, nobles, and if they shed my blood, their hands will remain soiled with my blood, for twenty-five years they will not wash their hands from my blood. They will leave Russia. Brothers will kill brothers, and they will kill each other and hate each other, and for twenty-five years there will be no nobles in the country. Tsar of the land of Russia, if you hear the sound of the bell which will tell you that Grigory has been killed, you must know this: if it was your relations who have wrought my death then no one of your family, that is to say, none of your children or relations will remain alive for more than two years. They will be killed by the Russian people.... I shall be killed. I am no longer among the living. Pray, pray, be strong, think of your blessed family.

Grigory

The story of Rasputin's death has been told so often and in so many dramatic forms as to properly belong in the realm of legend, but it has lost none of its power and fascination. The leader of the conspiracy was Prince Felix Yussupov, the twenty-nine-year-old heir to the greatest fortune in Russia and the husband of the tsar's niece Irina. Described in his own time as "delicate," effeminate and even "Bohemian," Yussupov had earlier fallen under Rasputin's spell. In fact, he was a flagrant homosexual whose fixation with Rasputin owed more to erotic fascination than the patriotism he later claimed as the motivation for the murder. And the murder itself was a vicious killing committed in drunkenness by a group of men who were probably no less depraved than Rasputin himself.

Yussupov's co-conspirators included the tsar's cousin Dmitri — Grand Duke Dmitri Pavlovitch — one of the very few Romanovs whom Alexandra had sincerely loved. All of her

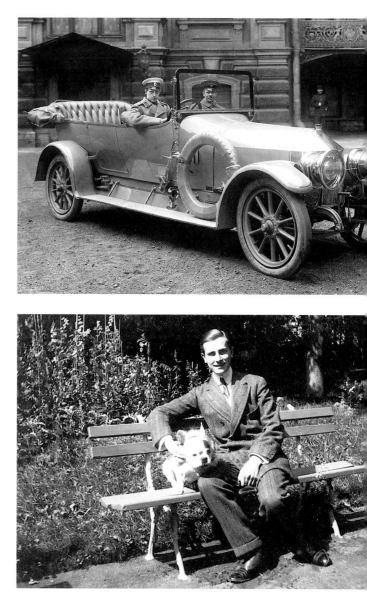

Grand Duke Dmitri Pavlovitch (below, at the wheel) was the tsar's first cousin and an intimate family friend. His involvement with Prince Felix Yussupov (bottom) in the murder of Rasputin was devastating for the empress. (Opposite) The Yussupov Palace on the Moika Canal, where Rasputin was killed on December 30, 1916. Mortally wounded, he staggered outside the door seen at the left end of the building.

daughters had a crush on him. He was beautiful, dashing, wide-eyed and dense. He seems to have been drawn into Yussupov's plot to kill Rasputin as much in the spirit of high jinks as for any political consideration, and he was the only member of the group who refused to discuss it later on. Joining Yussupov, Dmitri and Duma member Purishkevitch were an army doctor and an army officer.

It seems impossible that other members of the Romanov family were ignorant of the plot.

At no time in his life was Yussupov able to keep quiet about anything connected with himself or his image. "His desire to be talked about at all costs made no distinction as to method or manner," recalled Pavlovitch's sister, Marie Pavlovna. And Purishkevitch couldn't help revealing the plans to other members of the Duma.

Finally the appointed day, December 29, arrived. Despite the rumors of a plot to kill him, Rasputin did not suspect Yussupov, who had recently been more ingratiating than ever. He

readily agreed to a late-evening rendezvous at Yussupov's Petrograd residence on the Moika Canal.

At first, according to Yussupov, everything went as planned. Yussupov ushered his "friend" into the palace cellar and plied him with poison cakes and poisoned Madeira wine while the four other conspirators waited anxiously on the floor above. But though Rasputin ate heartily — more than enough to kill an ordinary man — he showed barely a sign of distress. Finally, after

more than two hours had passed, Yussupov could stand it no longer. He rushed upstairs, borrowed Dmitri's Browning revolver, returned to the cellar and shot the *starets* in the back.

At this point the line between fact and legend grows even murkier. No sooner had the doctor pronounced Rasputin dead than the corpse came back to life and lunged at the man who had shot him, tearing an epaulet off his jacket. In terror Felix fled upstairs and hid while Rasputin, roaring in rage, followed him on all fours. The wounded man somehow made it into the palace courtyard, then managed to regain his feet and began to run for the gate, shouting "Felix! Felix! I will tell everything to the empress." Purishkevitch, the only one who had followed him this far, fired several times before he finally brought Rasputin down. The five plotters then wrapped the body in a curtain and shoved it into the back of Purishkevitch's car. Below the Petrovsky Bridge they pushed the corpse through a hole in the ice that covered the Neva River.

How much of this story is true is impossible to tell. Rasputin's body was disinterred and burned after the Revolution, and no public investigation had been ordered at the time of the slaying on account of its political sensitivity. The story that the empress ordered Rasputin's burial in a private chapel near Tsarskoe Selo is certainly false. She wanted his body sent home to Siberia, but was persuaded by the prime minister of the moment, Alexander Protopopov, to bury him locally "until the mood of the city had quieted" sufficiently to transfer the corpse. She appeared with her husband, daughters and Anna Viroubova at the private early-morning inter-

ment. The girls placed an icon on the *starets'* chest before the coffin was closed, and the empress left a pathetic note: "My dear martyr, give me thy blessing that it may follow me always on the sad and dreary path I have yet to follow here below. And remember us from on high in your holy prayers. Alexandra."

The empress had reached what may have been her darkest hour. Fearing that Ania would be the next target for assassins, Alexandra insisted that she move into the palace. "Besides everything," she wrote to a lady-in-waiting, "try for a moment to realize what it is to know a friend in daily, hourly danger of also being foully murdered. But God is all mercy." No pretense of optimism or any but a desultory political conviction was maintained after this at Tsarskoe Selo. It was "all up," as the empress said in one of those quirky Britishisms that distinguished her speech in a crisis.

Her closest companion in the last weeks before the Revolution was Lili Dehn, the wife of an officer of the dowager empress's yacht, *Polar Star*, and one of the few of Alexandra's intimates to emerge from Russia with her integrity still intact. Her book, *The Real Tsaritsa*, while undoubtedly naive, is free of the usual self-exculpation.

"Oh, Madame," said Lili one evening as she sat with the empress and her daughters at a "musical evening" at the palace, "why are you so sad tonight?"

The empress turned and looked at her. "Why am I sad, Lili?" she replied. "I can't really say, but the music depresses me.... I think my heart has been broken."

Rasputin's body, bound with ropes, was pushed beneath the ice under this bridge (left) on the "Little Neva." The battered corpse (inset) was pulled from the water the next day.

A Last Respite: Mogilev, 1916

During the summer and fall of 1916, Alexandra and her four daughters made several trips to the Russian army's headquarters at Mogilev. Since May, Alexei had been back with the tsar at the *Stavka*, sleeping on a cot in his father's room. During each visit, which lasted about a week, the empress and the grand duchesses stayed on the imperial train and participated in all the hikes, picnics and excursions arranged for them. According to Count Grabbe, commander of the tsar's elite guard, "The grand duchesses loved coming to Mogilev. The trips enabled them not only to escape briefly from their cloistered life and be with their father but provided opportunities for meeting attractive officers; and for Olga and Tatiana the visits came as a welcome respite from the many tiring hours spent at Tsarskoe Selo taking care of the wounded...." These outings were also the last reprieve the family would have from the war and the worsening political climate. The following months would bring the death of Rasputin, revolution and the tsar's abdication.

A page from one of the imperial photo albums (below) documents a day trip on the Dnieper River near Mogilev. Even the empress was along for this excursion, although she had to be carried from the boat. The boys in white with Alexei were military school cadets invited to keep him company. (Opposite) The tsar relaxes on deck with Tatiana and, on shore (right), stands triumphant over Alexei. Olga, the most studious and somber of the girls (bottom right), sits with her notebook during a quiet moment at Mogilev.

CHAPTER SEVEN

Abdication

The Revolution came like the death of a friend who had been "lying sick for years and years," according to Sydney Gibbes, the English tutor at Tsarskoe Selo. It was neither avoidable nor unexpected, yet it took everyone by surprise. It was "a quite unbelievable event," recalled Gibbes, and "a sad, sad time for all concerned." Gibbes was, as yet, a constitutionalist, very nearly a republican, but the horrors he witnessed in Russia over the next several years swung him firmly into the Romanov camp. When it was all over he took vows, became a bishop of the Orthodox Church and kept his memories of the imperial family on their road to "Calvary" as the "most cherished possession" of his life. "So sweet," he wrote in 1929 to the exiled Anna Viroubova, "so sad."

Like everyone in Petrograd, Lili Dehn had heard the talk about the coming Revolution; heard, too, about plots, perfectly genuine, to assassinate the empress. "Life in general was excessively difficult and painful," she remembered, "so much so that, when my husband arrived from Murmansk and asked Count Kapnist how things were going, the Count replied, 'You'll soon see for yourself and you'll be horrified. We have gone back to the days of Paul I.'" (Tsar Paul I had been strangled at the Michael Palace in St. Petersburg in 1801, in a conspiracy involving all three of his sons.)

At the start of 1917 Alexandra had good reason to fear for her own and her children's safety. By this time even the most loyal members of the tsar's extended family were estranged from him and the empress. Long before Rasputin's murder, Nicholas's mother had told her son that if the *starets* were not removed from Petrograd she would leave the capital herself. In 1915 she did, taking up residence at Kiev for the duration of the war. Not even Grand Duchess Elizabeth was able to talk sense into her younger sister. At their last meeting, just before Rasputin was killed, Alexandra had refused to listen to Ella and sent her away in anger.

But none who took on the empress in the waning days of the tsar's reign did so more loudly than "Sandro," Grand Duke Alexander Mikhailovitch, the tsar's once-beloved cousin and brother-in-law, and the father-in-law of Felix Yussupov. Shortly after Rasputin's death, Sandro went to Tsarskoe Selo and attempted to bring the empress to her senses. (By this stage she was overstimulated by drugs and drinking pots of coffee for "medicinal" reasons.) They met in the imperial bedroom, the empress reclining on

*T*he ruins of the train station at
Tsarskoe Selo (above). From here in March 1917, Nicholas made his last trip to army headquarters.
(Opposite) The crumbling imperial crest of Nicholas and Alexandra marks the station walls.

*"Be Peter the
Great,
be Ivan the
Terrible ... crush
them all under
you....
It is war and at
such a time
interior war is
high treason."*

— Alexandra, in a letter
to Nicholas, 1916

*T*he empress
*alone at Tsarskoe Selo during the war,
her face prematurely aged but her
will unyielding.*

the large double bed she shared with her hus-band, and the tsar himself quietly sitting in the shadows smoking a cigarette. For the last time Sandro begged Alexandra to stop resisting the notion, the very concept, of reform.

"All this talk of yours is ridiculous," the empress replied, and the interview degenerated to the point where Sandro's voice could be heard throughout the halls of the Alexander Palace. "Remember, Alix," he shouted, "I remained silent for thirty months. For thirty months I never said ... a word to you about the disgrace-ful goings on in our government, better to say in *your* government. I realize that you are willing to perish and that your husband feels the same way, but what about us?... You have no right to drag your relatives with you down a precipice." At this point the tsar quietly intervened and led his old friend out of the room.

After Rasputin's murder, an open letter to the tsar, signed by Grand Duke Alexander and most of the senior members of the Romanov family, asked Nicholas to refrain from punish-ing either Prince Yussupov or Grand Duke Dmitri for their participation in the crime.

"No one has the right to commit murder," the tsar replied with no prompting from his wife. "In any case, I know that the conscience of many of you gives you no rest." In the words of A. A. Mossolov, the court chancellor, "The disintegration of the family could not have been more complete." Nicholas settled on banishing Felix and Dmitri from St. Petersburg.

⁂

In the period immediately following Rasputin's death, that is, the first two months of 1917, Nicholas did not return to the front and spent most of his time at Tsarskoe Selo. He knew about the mounting disorders in the capital, the strikes and riots and insistent demand for bread, but believed that wartime Russian patriotism would prevail over revolutionary sentiment.

The war, however, had disrupted every aspect of Russian life, and as its progress stalled, it became difficult to convince anyone that the bloodshed was worth another million lives. (By the time of the Revolution three million Russian soldiers had died.) Prices rose while food and fuel disappeared. In the cities, where conditions were the most miserable, the economy had vir-tually collapsed. To make matters worse, in early February Russia was plunged into the harshest winter in years. The cold caused locomotive boil-ers to burst, and the huge snowdrifts made many railway tracks impassable. The transportation breakdown not only exacerbated the already des-perate situation in urban areas; it meant that cru-cial supplies — both food and arms — were not reaching the front where roughly six million Russian soldiers in uniform also faced starva-tion. With hindsight, some sort of massive social upheaval was inevitable. And when the Revol-ution in Petrograd finally broke out, it was a manifestation of aimless discontent nebulous in its goals. But the ultimate catastrophe might have been averted with a little more sense and a lot less conspiracy.

Tsar Nicholas was not the only one who failed to see the cataclysm coming. In January, Lenin, still exiled in Switzerland, told a group of workers, "We older men may not live to see the decisive battles of the approaching revolution." And when, on February 27, the hugely popular left-wing Social Democrat Alexander Kerensky rose in the Duma and called openly for the over-throw of the tsar, his words were virtually lost in the rebellious cacophony that typified debate in that less-than-sophisticated legislative assembly. A few days before the Revolution broke out, Sir George Buchanan, the British ambassador, felt secure enough to go on vacation in Finland. And the sovereign was sufficiently sanguine that on March 7, after receiving a telegram from the staff at army headquarters requesting his presence, he decided to return to the *Stavka*.

"I am going to the G.H.Q. tomorrow," Nicholas told his wife.

"Cannot you possibly stay with us?" she asked, surprised.

"No, I must go. I cannot really imagine what can have made my presence at Headquarters so urgently necessary now," he continued. "I shall have to go and see myself."

All that winter there had been talk about a palace coup d'état, about the need to remove or even annihilate the empress. Threats on her life were an everyday occurrence, so it is hard to imagine what might have persuaded Nicholas to part from her at this time, especially as he could offer no explanation for why he was going.

Later, many believed that the tsar had been lured from the palace by his ministers and generals who, suddenly sensing revolution in the air, hoped to make him more malleable by separating him from his wife. Most assuredly that was Alexandra's own view. And without her beside him, Nicholas proved incapable of resisting the men who shortly forced his abdication.

On March 8, 1917, events in Petrograd began to spiral out of control. It started with a minor riot over bread, accompanying a much larger strike among textile workers in the capital. By the next day, huge crowds had filled the streets of Petrograd, but the police, on orders from the Duma, took no action against them, and the Cossacks, for once, did not carry whips (the usual Russian implement of crowd control). The authorities stood peacefully by as the throng spread through town, and even went so far as to assure them, "Don't worry. We won't shoot."

By Saturday, March 10, the crowds had been bolstered by tens of thousands of strikers, whose absence from their jobs brought the city to a virtual standstill. All day and late into the night the tsar's cabinet met in emergency session. Realizing the need for decisive action, the ministers finally cabled Nicholas at the front, urgently begging him to appoint a new government that might be more acceptable to the people. Unwilling to believe that things could have fallen apart so fast, Nicholas cabled back, "I order that the disorders in the capital, intolerable during these difficult times of war with Germany and Austria, be ended tomorrow. Nicholas."

It was one of the most pathetically ineffective commands in recorded history. Sunday brought the Petrograd garrisons onto the streets to face still vaster crowds than the day before. But many of the soldiers refused to fire and most who obeyed their commanders and shot at the demonstrators did so reluctantly. Again an urgent message went to the tsar, this time from the president of the Duma, Michael Rodzianko, whom Nicholas had once dismissed as "the biggest and fattest man in Russia." He did not even bother to answer Rodzianko's urgent telegram. The tsar's response to this last cry for his personal intervention was to order four regiments from the Galician front to the capital and to suspend the Duma.

By Monday, March 12, these measures had proved to be pitifully inadequate. First one, then another of the Petrograd regiments had joined the swelling mutiny. By the end of the day almost every military unit in the capital had expelled or murdered its officers and gone over to "the people." Meanwhile the multitudes surged through the streets setting fire to government buildings, including the law courts. The leaders of the Duma, realizing that it was now their government or no government at all, ignored the tsar's order to suspend their sitting and effectively placed themselves at the head of the Revolution. Before the day was done, the Mensheviks and other moderate labor and factory groups had called for union with the Soviet of Soldiers' and Workers' Deputies, which met

The Fourth Duma meets at the Tauride Palace (opposite) in 1916. (Below) After the Revolution, the chamber has a different appearance as the site of a congress of the Soviet of Soldiers' and Workers' Deputies. (Bottom) A street protest in Petrograd in 1917 passes the British embassy.

like the Duma, in the Tauride Palace. A blood-bath was thus averted, but at the same time the seeds were sown for the far bloodier revolution that was about to come.

By March 14 the transfer of power was complete. The Duma and the Soviet were solidly in charge.

While Petrograd fell into the lap of the revolutionaries, a few miles away at Tsarskoe Selo the empress was preoccupied with an epidemic of measles that had brought down her children (and Ania) and left them in critical condition. (Complications developed for all four of the girls as well as Alexei — abscesses, fevers and ruptured eardrums.) Remarkably, Alexandra seems to have been completely unaware of just how quickly the situation in the capital was deteriorating. The tsar's last prime minister, the ancient and ineffectual Prince Nicholas Golitsyn, continually downplayed the disturbances and assured her there was nothing to worry about. It wasn't until March 12, when Lili Dehn came down from town for a visit, that Alexandra began to realize the danger she and her family were in.

A few days earlier, Dr. Botkin had left his house at Tsarskoe Selo and moved into the palace to nurse the imperial children as their condition worsened. By the day after Lili's visit, the insurrection had spread to Tsarskoe itself, where Botkin's daughter Tatiana heard the shouts for " 'Bread! Bread!' ... 'Down with Alice!' and still coarser epithets attached to the Empress's name."

"This may turn out worse than 1905," Dr. Botkin remarked on one of his quick visits home. All manner of rumors were already flying through town: that the tsarevitch had died, that his father had fled the country, that "a crowd of revolutionaries, 8,000 strong, was marching on Tsarskoe Selo from Petrograd with machine guns and armored automobiles intending to destroy the Palace.... And really something

indescribable was going on in the streets," Tatiana Botkin remembered. "Drunken soldiers without belts and all unbuttoned were running back and forth carrying off all they could lay hands on in the shops. Some carried bales of dry goods, others boots, still others, though already quite drunk, were making off with bottles of wine and vodka, while some had entwined themselves all over in red silk ribbons.... The rank and file of His Majesty's Convoy pranced through the streets all perfumed and pomaded, with red bows; they had all forgotten the exceptional position they had occupied at Court, the favor and attention that had been lavished on them by their Sovereigns."

The empress now realized that the situation was serious, but despite urgings from Rodzianko and others, she was not prepared to flee. Her children, falling sick one by one, were too ill to move and she would do nothing until the tsar arrived (too late, he had finally begun the journey home, although Alexandra did not not yet know it). "When the house is on fire," Rodzianko protested, "the invalids are the first to be taken out," but the empress had made up her mind. She would wait. By the next day, with the railroads surrounding Tsarskoe Selo already in rebel hands, all escape routes were effectively sealed. The empress, her family and her servants were, for all practical purposes, prisoners in their own palace, even if troops still loyal to the tsar had arrived to protect them.

That morning a force of 1,500 men, including members of the *Garde Equipage* (the marine guard the family knew so well from their cruises on the *Standart*), took up defensive positions around the Alexander Palace. A feared attack by an unruly mob of mutinous soldiers failed to materialize, and by nightfall an uneasy calm had descended.

Late that night Grand Duchess Marie, who, with Anastasia, was only beginning to get

The empress (center) photographed during the war with Anna Viroubova (left) and Lili Dehn, two of the faithful who were with her at the Alexander Palace in March of 1917. (Opposite) Alexandra and her daughter Marie went to these gates to plead for the loyalty of the palace guard during the Revolution.

sick, accompanied her mother on a review of the palace guard to plead for their loyalty. It was bitterly cold, but Alexandra simply "threw a black fur cloak over her white nurse's dress," as one of her trusted maids of honor, Baroness Sophie Buxhoeveden, recalled, and "went out herself to speak to the soldiers."

"She went through the courtyard and all through the Palace basement," the baroness remembered, "where the men came in turns to warm themselves, telling the soldiers how fully she trusted in their fidelity to the Emperor, and how well she knew that if the need arose they would defend the heir.... The scene was unforgettable. It was dark, except for a faint light thrown up from the snow and reflected on the polished barrels of the rifles. The troops were lined up in battle order in the courtyard, the first line kneeling in the snow, the others standing behind, their rifles in readiness for a sudden attack. The figures of the Empress and her daughter passed like dark shadows from line to line, the white Palace looming a ghostly mass in the background."

Inside, Anastasia was also dealing with circumstances for which nothing could have prepared her. She spent most of her time with Lili Dehn and kept her sense of humor even as the world she knew was falling to pieces. "Don't worry," she remarked when Lili accidentally broke a vase in the empress's drawing room. "It isn't ours. It belongs to the government."

"During the night," Lili wrote, "we got up and looked out of the windows. A huge gun had been placed in the courtyard. 'How astonished Papa will be!' whispered Anastasia. We stood for a few minutes watching the weird scene. It was so bitterly cold that the sentinels were dancing round the gun in order to keep warm. Their figures were sharply defined against the arc-lights — it seemed like some new Carmagnole; in the distance we heard shouts of drunken voices and occasional shots — and so the night passed.

"At 5 A.M. ... we went downstairs to the Empress's bedroom. She was awake, and as she opened the door she whispered: 'Hush ... Marie is asleep: the train is late.... Most probably the Emperor won't come until ten.' The Empress was fully dressed, and she looked so sad that I could not help saying impulsively: 'Oh, Madame, *why* is the train late?'

"She smiled wanly but did not reply. As we went back to our bedroom, Anastasia said in agitated tones: 'Lili, the train is *never* late. Oh, if Papa would only come quickly.... I'm beginning to feel ill. What shall I do if I get ill? I can't be useful to Mama.... Oh, Lili, say I'm not going to be ill.'

"I tried to calm her, and I persuaded her to lie down on her bed and sleep; but the poor child was actually sickening for the measles. [She] could not reconcile herself to the idea of being ill: she cried and cried and kept on repeating: 'Please, don't keep me in bed.'"

The empress, too, was at her wit's end. "Lili," she said, "I must not give way. I keep on saying, '*I must not*' — it helps me." She was now barely able to walk, and her frantic telegrams to the tsar at Mogilev had all been returned with a mark from the military postal authorities: "Address of person mentioned unknown." Meals, said Lili, "were silent and horrible affairs: I felt as though each morsel would choke me."

Early on the morning of March 15, the last of the troops guarding the imperial family, the *Garde Equipage*, deserted the Alexander Palace and returned to the capital, apparently on the order of their commander, Grand Duke Kyril Vladimirovitch. The previous day Kyril, a cousin of the tsar, had donned a red armband and led his soldiers through the streets of Petrograd to swear fealty to the Duma. He was the first of the Romanovs to betray the emperor.

In vain the empress waited for her husband to appear. When she finally learned that the train bringing him home had been detained at Pskov,

less than a day's train ride away, she wrote both to express her outrage and to shore up the tsar's courage. Because power, telegraph and telephone communications had been cut off, her letter had to be smuggled to Pskov in the trousers of two Cossack soldiers.

"My heart breaks from the thought of you living through all these tortures and upsets totally alone," Alexandra wrote, "& we know nothing of you, & you know nothing of us.... I wanted to send an aeroplane, but all have vanished. The young men will tell you all so I have nothing to tell about the state of affairs. It is all hateful, & events are progressing with colossal speed. I firmly believe, though — & no one shall shake this belief — that all will be all right.... Clearly they don't want to let you see me so above all you must not sign any paper, constitution or other such horror — but you are alone, without your army, caught like a mouse in a trap, what can you do? This is supremely base and mean, unprecedented in history, to detain one's sovereign.... What if you show yourself to the troops in other places and gather them around? If you must make concessions, under no circumstances are you obliged to honor them since they were obtained in ignoble fashion."

❧

After breakfast on March 15, 1917, aboard the imperial train at Pskov, Tsar Nicholas II received a small delegation led by General Nicholas Ruzsky, commander of the Northern Group of Armies. Ruzsky told the tsar he was in regular communication with the president of the Duma, then solemnly handed him a fistful of telegrams from his top generals. They all bore the same bleak message: for the good of the country he must resign the throne. Grand Duke Nicholas, the general the tsar respected most, "begged on my knees" for his relative's abdication. The grand duke had seen what Nicholas could not — that the balance had now shifted too far, that even

*A*board the imperial train (left),
the tsar was urged by his generals to abdicate on March 15, 1917.
Later that day, in the train's dining car (inset), Nicholas confided to
Count Grabbe that he hoped now to fulfill his life's desire and keep a farm,
perhaps somewhere in England.

*"With
the stroke of
a pen,
the tsar had
transformed
himself
from the ruler
of all Russia
to a
person with
no rights
whatsoever...."*

— Count Alexander
Grabbe, commander of
the tsar's elite guard

*F*lanked by imperial
*eagles, the tsar poses for a photograph
on the train that would later be the
scene of his abdication.*

their loyal troops were barely under control, that the country was on the verge of chaos, and that only something as drastic as this had any hope of saving the Romanov dynasty.

Nicholas turned pale and walked to a window. For what seemed an interminable few minutes he said nothing. Then, abruptly, he turned and spoke: "I have decided that I will give up the throne in favor of my son, Alexei."

Whole books have been filled with varying accounts as to why he relinquished the throne so easily. In *Nicholas and Alexandra*, Robert K. Massie argues that it was a supreme act of patriotism by a man who "cared far more about winning the war than he did for his crown." Others have used this incident as proof of the tsar's weakness of character, his fatalism. But the Russian historian Edvard Radzinsky probably comes closest to the truth when he writes simply that Nicholas was tired, that he had no idea which way to turn, that he knew on some level that his wife's advice had been a disaster and that he only wanted to be left in peace. It must have been an enormous relief. "All around me," the tsar confided to his diary after resigning his crown, "I see treachery, cowardice, and deceit."

A few hours after his abdication — and after a frank talk with Dr. Federov, one of the family's physicians — Nicholas realized the impossibility of his twelve-year-old hemophiliac son's ruling in his place, and he amended the form of abdication in favor of his brother Michael. Perhaps he dreamed at that moment of the quiet life his family might lead away from the cares of state that had finally brought him down.

❧

Word of Nicholas's abdication reached the palace at Tsarskoe Selo only a day after it happened, but was dismissed as a rumor until one of his uncles, Grand Duke Paul Alexandrovitch, arrived to confirm it to the empress.

"It's all lies!" she shrieked. "The newspapers

invented it! I believe in God and the Army!"

"God and the Army are on the side of the Revolution now," replied the grand duke. Alexandra's face "was distorted with agony," Lili Dehn remembered. "Her eyes were full of tears" as she "tottered rather than walked" out of her study, took Lili by the hand and sobbed, "*Abdiqué.*" (Why she spoke in French at such a moment can only be surmised. A portrait of Marie Antoinette had hung in her drawing room since 1896, when the French government gave it to her during an official visit to Paris.)

"The people are to assume the Regency," she remarked to Lili later, completely bewildered at the thought. More than anything, Alexandra worried that her son might be taken from her, and she was actually relieved to learn that the tsar had abdicated for Alexei as well as himself. She asked Pierre Gilliard, the French tutor, to break the news to the boy.

"You know your father does not want to be tsar anymore, Alexei Nicholaievitch," said Gilliard gently.

"What!" cried Alexei. "Why?"

"He is very tired and has had a lot of trouble lately."

"Oh, yes. Mama told me.... But who's going to be tsar, then?"

"I don't know," said Gilliard. "Perhaps nobody now."

Across the hall the grand duchesses burst into tears when their mother told them what had happened at Pskov. She had to write it down for Tatiana and Anastasia, now lying sick with the others, whose eardrums had burst and who were temporarily deaf.

Alexandra rushed to reassure her husband when she finally learned he had abdicated, immediately dispatching another smuggled letter to buoy his spirits: "My beloved, Soul of my soul.... I wholly understand your action, oh my hero. I know that you could not have signed anything that contradicted what you swore at your coronation. We know each other to perfection, we have no need of words, we shall see you again on your throne, restored by your people and troops to the glory of your realm." For Alexandra herself, however, words of comfort were few and far between. Of all the Romanov relatives in Russia, only one wrote to console her — Nicholas's sister Xenia, whose husband, Grand Duke Alexander, ironically, was the empress's chief opponent in the family.

By the time Alexandra learned of her husband's abdication, preparations were already well under way for the family's departure from Tsarskoe. Boxes were being packed; servants had been advised discreetly that a sudden exit might be necessary. Later, among monarchist exiles, it became an item of faith to recall that the tsar and his family had refused to leave Russia at the moment of crisis, but in fact they were not in control of events, and only the illness of the children had earlier prevented Alexandra from fleeing toward Mogilev and her husband.

Now it was too late. Their adored uncle, Grand Duke Michael, had renounced the throne less than one day after learning it was his, and the Romanov dynasty came to an end. "Misha, it turns out, has abdicated," Nicholas wrote in his diary. "His manifesto ends with a four-line addendum about elections for a Constituent Assembly in 6 months. God knows what gave him the idea of signing such rot!" Nicholas still did not understand that the Revolution had been necessary.

His children, nevertheless, when they awoke on March 17, were prisoners of the new regime — the "Red Dawn" that ultimately plunged Russia into a deeper misery than anything known under the tsars.

❧

At Pskov it did not occur to Nicholas that his services to Russia would no longer be required.

Incredibly enough, he imagined he could still serve out the war in some military capacity, and on March 16 he returned to the *Stavka*. "It may have been too much for him to see [the empress] and the children right after his downfall," Edvard Radzinsky has hypothesized. "He may have wanted to give them time to get used to the situation. Also, he had to say good-bye to the army. There was a war in progress, and he discharged his duties as commander-in-chief to the end."

His mother arrived at army headquarters from Kiev, no word of recrimination on her lips — no word about anything, apparently — as she dined, took tea and played bezique for several days with Nicholas in his train. Neither could know, of course, that this was their final meeting, and that when the tsar said good-bye to a number of his uncles and cousins at the front it would be forever.

No evidence indicates that Nicholas ever again thought about or discussed his own abdication except to regret it. He had believed it would bring peace, he said; he had thought it was what the people wanted. As time went on and he watched his former empire slide into chaos, he had only one thought, the words he used at the end of his farewell speech to his soldiers: "May God save Russia!"

"Nicholas II was not stupid," says Dominic Lieven in his excellent political biography of the last tsar. "A Russian monarch could not save himself or his dynasty simply by putting on a top hat and becoming a citizen king.... Under the Russian system of government, the Emperor bore ultimate responsibility for everything. The burden was crushing, not least because a corollary of autocracy was that the Russian people tended to accept responsibility for nothing, blaming their own sins and their country's failings on the empire's rulers. Nicholas II loved his country and served

Grand Duke Michael (above) gave up the throne one day after Nicholas ceded it to him. He was the first Romanov to be murdered the following year by the Bolsheviks. (Opposite) Revolutionary guards at the Alexander Palace. The former tsar and tsarina were shocked by their "indolence" and laxity.

it loyally to the best of his ability."

The ex-tsar did not get home to Tsarskoe Selo until March 22, being announced at the gates of the Alexander Palace as "Nicholas Romanov" and watching sadly as the vast majority of his aides and servants — trusted members of the imperial entourage with names like Sablin, Mordvinov, Drenteln, Grabbe and Leuchtenberg — slunk from the train and disappeared from sight.

Inside, Alexandra was burning her diaries. It was already known that anyone who chose to remain at Tsarskoe would be "isolated from the outside world" by resolution of the new government, and that a special commission of inquiry would be established to investigate charges of treason against the tsar and the empress. The captivity had begun.

CHAPTER EIGHT

Captivity

It was Lili Dehn who had suggested to the empress that she burn her correspondence "at once," immediately on hearing about the tsar's abdication and several days in advance of Alexandra's formal arrest by the provisional government.

"It may be argued that I was guilty of the worst Vandalism ... in an historical and artistic sense," Lili wrote later, "but I was right on the score of friendship.... I dreaded the possibility of either letters or diaries falling into the hands of the Revolutionaries. I knew that the worst construction would be placed by the 'Sons of Freedom' on anything unusual which these papers might contain." With a fierce fire burning day and night in her drawing-room grate, it took Alexandra the better part of a week to destroy the private records of her life: her diaries first of all, along with her correspondence with her father, her brother, Queen Victoria and untold numbers of royal relations and friends. She kept the bulk of her letters from the tsar, curiously enough, documents that might have been the most sensitive of all had Nicholas been capable of writing an intriguing sentence. It may even be that Alexandra preserved these intimate papers intentionally as written proof of her own and her husband's "innocence."

In April, when she was interrogated by Alexander Kerensky, Russia's new minister of justice who soon became head of the provisional government, the empress admitted freely, even boldly, "that the Emperor and herself were the most united of couples ... and that they had no secrets from each other; that they discussed everything, and that it was not astonishing that in the last years which had been so troubled, they had often discussed politics.... It was true that they had discussed the different appointments of ministers, but this could not be otherwise in a marriage such as theirs." What the rest of Alexandra's papers might have revealed about her influence on the government (and specifically about her wartime dealings with her brother, the Grand Duke of Hesse) remains a tantalizingly open question. As it was, Kerensky emerged from his interview with the empress with a single remark to the tsar: "Your wife does not lie."

"I have always known it," Nicholas replied.

He had shocked everyone in the palace with the great change in his appearance. (Not only was he exhausted, physically and mentally, but for months he had been taking cocaine, a common remedy in those days for fatigue.) He was "deathly pale," said Lili Dehn, "his face was covered with innumerable wrinkles, his hair was

The central hall of the Alexander Palace, seen from across the snowy park.

quite gray at the temples, and blue shadows encircled his eyes. He looked like an old man."

For a period of eighteen days, on Kerensky's order, Nicholas and Alexandra were kept apart, allowed to see each other only at meals and only in the presence of soldiers, but Kerensky found no evidence of "treason" against them and, to his credit, refused to concoct any, despite the mounting clamor in Petrograd against "the Former Tyrant" and "the German Bitch." The belief that Alexandra had been conspiring with the Germans for the duration of the war extended well beyond Russia's borders and is probably the real reason she and her family were denied political asylum by their allies in 1917.

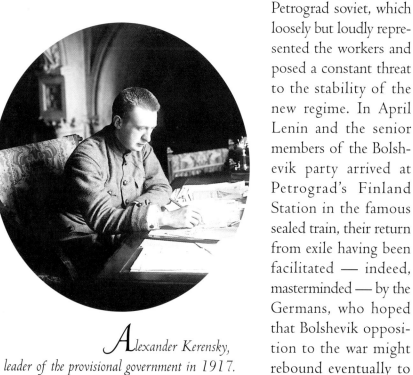

*A*lexander Kerensky, *leader of the provisional government in 1917.*

"The Empress is not only a Boche by birth but in sentiment," said the British ambassador to France, Lord Francis Bertie, when the question arose of sending the Romanovs into exile there. "She did all she could to bring about an understanding with Germany. She is regarded as a criminal or a criminal lunatic, and the Emperor as a criminal from his weakness and submission to her promptings." England, in any case, not France, was the imperial family's preferred destination if exile became necessary. Just four days after his abdication, Nicholas asked the provisional government for safe passage to England for himself and his family, and on March 22 the British government, under Prime Minister David Lloyd George, made a formal offer of asylum,

anxious only that the world understand that it did so "on the initiative of the Russian government."

"It's the last chance of securing these poor unfortunates' freedom and perhaps of saving their lives," said Paul Miliukov, the new Russian foreign minister, without a trace of exaggeration. In Petrograd, at every turn, the provisional government was obliged to answer to the demands and charges of the recently established Petrograd soviet, which loosely but loudly represented the workers and posed a constant threat to the stability of the new regime. In April Lenin and the senior members of the Bolshevik party arrived at Petrograd's Finland Station in the famous sealed train, their return from exile having been facilitated — indeed, masterminded — by the Germans, who hoped that Bolshevik opposition to the war might rebound eventually to Germany's advantage.

The Bolshevik membership was still small at the time — estimated at no more than thirty thousand — but the party was better organized than any other revolutionary body in Russia, and within six months its ranks had swelled dramatically. Calls for Nicholas and Alexandra's incarceration at the Fortress of Peter and Paul, their "trial" for treason and even their summary execution were no idle threats. At Tsarskoe Selo cries of "To the palace! To the palace!" were heard on the streets for many weeks (while a number of fancy shops and at least one department store

*A Soviet depiction of the arrival of
Vladimir Lenin at Petrograd's Finland Station on the night of April 16, 1917,
where he was greeted by a cheering crowd waving red banners.*

were looted by drunken crowds at Tsarskoe in the mistaken belief that *they* were the palace).

It was King George V, in the end, Nicholas and Alexandra's "devoted cousin Georgie," who shut the door on their hoped-for exile in England. The king had "received letters from people in all classes of life," according to his private secretary, Lord Stamfordham, "expressing [their] adverse opinions" to the plan. The presence of the Romanovs in England, Stamfordham feared, "especially of the Empress," would "raise all sorts of difficulties" for their British relations in wartime.

"You have probably heard rumors of the Emperor and Empress of Russia, together with many Grand Dukes, coming to England to find asylum here," said an assistant secretary to King George. "Of course the King has been accused of trying to work this for his royal friends. As a matter of fact His Majesty has been opposed to this proposal from the start, and has begged his ministers to knock it on the head. I do not expect that these Russian royalties will come, but if they do their presence here will be due to the War Cabinet and not to His Majesty." For years the role of the British royal family was minimized, even concealed, in accounts of the Romanovs' demise, and blame for the ultimate withdrawal of Britain's offer of asylum was put squarely on the shoulders of the "radical" Lloyd George and his leftist Liberal government. At Tsarskoe Selo, however, where the only sound from England was a polite inquiry from Queen Mary, through Kerensky, about the state of Alexandra's health, no one remained long in doubt about the nature of loyalty among princes.

The tsar had broken down and wept in the empress's arms on his first day back from the front — this according to Anna Viroubova, whose continued presence at the palace was regarded by most of its other inhabitants as a serious threat to their safety because of her long and close association with Rasputin. If Alexandra, in her own mind, was the Marie Antoinette of the Russian Revolution, Ania was its Princesse de Lamballe, the intimate friend of the queen of France who was dragged from her apartments during the French disturbances and slaughtered by the angry mob. Ania's near-fatal bout with measles made her more difficult than ever, and she monopolized the empress's attention in these critical days. She was a demanding woman at the best of times — jealous, petulant and "childish," in Alexandra's description. Now she wept, moaned, whimpered, complained, begged for company and shrieked every time she heard the sound of gunfire.

"We've all gone mad," said one of the soldiers to Gleb Botkin when Gleb asked why he and his comrades kept firing their rifles into the air. (The revolutionary soldiers had also been shooting the deer and even the swans in the park at Tsarskoe Selo.) Apparently not all of the Sons of Freedom were convinced that the Revolution would succeed: "They'll hang every one of us, so we may as well do some shooting in the meantime." When Ania, along with Lili Dehn, was finally taken to St. Petersburg for questioning on April 3, there was something like a sigh of relief from everyone but Alexandra, who blamed Dr. Botkin for answering in the affirmative when Kerensky asked if Ania was well enough to be moved.

"How can you?" the empress exclaimed when she heard that Botkin had "betrayed" her friend. "How can you? You — who have children of your own!" Ania herself later charged Botkin with "craven fear," but in fact his decision saved her life. She was away from the palace when the rest of the retinue were later sent with the imperial family to Siberia. Lili Dehn had just enough time to say good-bye to Anastasia before the soldiers took her away.

"She was in bed," said Lili. "I kissed her many times and told her I would never forsake them." The empress pointed to the sky as Lili and Ania left and declared, "We shall meet in another world." It was "bitterly cold" in the one they were in, Lili remembered, "and a bleak wind howled around the Palace and drove the snow in stinging dust around my face.... In this manner we saw the last of Tsarskoe Selo." Ania was close to fainting from terror.

"Poor unfortunate woman," the tsar remarked. "What will become of *her?*" He, too, had been burning his papers and jotting the usual pallid entries in his diary:

9 [22] March, Thursday. Arrived quickly and safely at Tsarskoe Selo at 10:30. But Lord, what a change! There are guards outside and around the palace, and ensigns of some kind inside the entry. Went upstairs and there saw my sweetheart Alix and my dear children.... Had lunch and dinner in the playroom with Alexei. Took a walk with Valya [Prince Vassili] Dolgoruky [one of the suite who had not deserted] and worked with him a bit in the garden, since we are not allowed to walk any further....

10 [23] March. Slept well, despite the conditions we now find ourselves in. The thought that we are together gladdens and consoles me.... Looked through papers, put them in order, and burnt them....

11 [24] March. In the morning received [Count Paul] Benckendorff [the grand marshal of the court], learned from him that we shall be staying here quite a while. A pleasant thought. Continued burning letters and papers.

The entries went on in this vein. On March 27, Nicholas was pleased to report that he "had plenty of time to read for [his] own pleasure" and also, happily, "time to sit upstairs

The deposed tsar shovels snow while under house arrest in March of 1917.

with the children." The Swiss tutor, Pierre Gilliard, whose "voluntary imprisonment" began with the arrest of the empress, noted in his own diary that Nicholas seemed "very gay" when he visited his daughters in their sickroom, where they were slowly recovering from measles. He "gave the impression of a schoolboy on vacation," Gilliard thought, despite the humiliations that were being heaped upon him thick and fast. The tsar had been granted permission for a short daily walk in a restricted area of the palace grounds, which the soldiers took as an opportunity to harass their former commander in chief.

"You can't go there, *Gospodin Polkovnik*," they barked, calling Nicholas by the only formal title he still enjoyed — colonel. "We don't permit you to walk in that direction, Mr. Colonel.... Stand back when you are commanded." Only once was Nicholas observed to lose his temper, when one of the officers who was following him in the park intentionally stepped on his heel.

"The Emperor," said Tatiana Botkin, "without turning around, swung his cane backward at the same moment with such force that neither this officer nor any other ever attempted such tricks again." Apart from boredom and the deprivation of his accustomed physical exercise (it was "shooting" he missed the most, he said), Nicholas's main preoccupation was still the successful prosecution of the war. The "degeneration" of the soldiers around him filled him with disgust, and he was able to bear reports of the Russian army's retreat at the front only by putting them down to his country's well-known love of "exaggeration." The tsar seems honestly not to have minded the blatant hostility of his jailers.

"Not for anything in the world," said one of them bluntly when Nicholas offered his hand.

"But, my dear fellow, why?" the tsar replied. "What have you got against me?"

Nicholas was more concerned about the safety and peace of mind of his daughters who, when they recovered from the measles, wearing bright spring outfits and wigs to disguise their shaved heads, normally accompanied him on his daily walks. In May permission was granted for the imperial family to dig a kitchen garden outside the palace, something to occupy the endless stretches of time. The tsar's methodical planning and supervision of his rows of carrots and cabbage led one of the soldiers to remark that had he not been born a Romanov "he'd have owned the country anyway," so tireless was his weeding and tilling of the ground. But even these innocent outdoor excursions were sometimes canceled as crowds assembled at the palace gate, "pressed around it on all sides," as Tatiana Botkin said, "and accompanied each gesture of the Grand Duchesses and His Majesty by taunts and coarse remarks. Of course there were

Nicholas can be seen (above at right) sharing a furrow in the vegetable garden with Pierre Gilliard (left, facing camera). Snapshots from the family's album (opposite) show (clockwise from top): Tatiana and Countess Hendrikova carrying turf; Tatiana and Anastasia wheeling a water barrel; the empress observing the activity while embroidering in her wheelchair.

Showing off their shaved heads (top left), the tsar's four daughters pose in the garden. Their hair had begun to fall out after a bout of measles, and Alexandra (top right, in the garden with Nicholas) had ordered their heads to be shaved to facilitate its regrowth. Usually the girls wore wigs — as in the photograph at right, which shows Olga, Alexei, Anastasia (holding the King Charles spaniel Jimmy) and Tatiana resting between chores in the garden.

a few of them who came with aching hearts to take one more look at the adored family, but they were not more than one or two."

It was the primary question on the family's mind: where had everybody gone? What had become of their loyal subjects, and how could Russians suddenly have become so hateful and rude? To appreciate the shock the family must have experienced, it is necessary only to reflect that up till now, by etiquette of the court, no one had been allowed to converse with them unless invited to do so, or even to address them without having been greeted by name. The new commandant of the palace guard, Colonel Korovichenko, was himself "exceedingly tactless and rude," Tatiana Botkin remembered. He had

159

charge of censoring the imperial family's correspondence, among other things, and seemed to take particular pleasure in mocking their endearments and mode of expression.

"What an 'appetizing' book you have in your hand," he remarked to one of the grand duchesses after she and her sisters had gently complained about the quality of the food they were getting. "One is tempted to eat it." These taunts were nothing, of course, compared to the lewd remarks hurled later at the girls, and for the time being it was the empress who suffered most from the gibes of the soldiers and the mob. She was no longer allowed the use of her private balcony at the palace, her trips to church were sharply curtailed, and in the newspapers, where every pretense of restraint had suddenly been lifted, she saw the lampoons and bitter political sketches that portrayed her without compunction as a modern Messalina. One, in particular, showed the empress scrubbing her back in a tub of her subjects' blood.

"If Nicky killed a few more of these revolutionaries," the caption read, "I could have a bath like this more often." The staff endeavored to keep Alexandra from seeing the worst of these attacks, but she could not — would not — be tricked. She had an almost uncanny way of walking into a room whenever bad news was being discussed. It was as though she sought it out for some purpose of her own.

"It generally happened that when the soldiers talked to the Emperor or the children their hostility disappeared," said Sophie Buxhoeveden. "They saw they were not the cruel monsters they had been taught to believe. But they were always more hostile to the Empress and showed by their

conduct the sort of propaganda that had been at work among them." Anti-German epithets were the least of it. In March Alexandra endured the news of the disinterment and desecration of Rasputin's corpse — it was doused in gasoline and burned on a pile of logs in the Pargolovo Forest — and when she went outdoors (which was not often) "the soldiers always kept close to her, listening to her talk.... They often smoked their vile tobacco straight into her face, or exchanged gross jokes to see their effect." Witnesses speak alternatively of the empress's serenity and agitation in the face of these insults, there being a fine line, undoubtedly, between religious hysteria and inner peace in a character such as hers. "She is great, great," said Paul Benckendorff in one of the most honest tributes ever paid to the empress, "but I have always said she is one of those characters who rise to the sublime only in misfortune."

"I am remembering the past," Alexandra wrote Lili Dehn three months after her husband's abdication. (Lili had been questioned and released after leaving Tsarskoe Selo in April.) "It is necessary to look more calmly on everything. What is to be done? Once He has sent us such trials, evidently He thinks we are prepared for it. It is a sort of examination — it is necessary to prove that we did not go through it in vain." She was giving religious instruction to her children, the division of their regular lessons falling otherwise on Gilliard, Baroness Buxhoeveden, Catherine Schneider (who had gone to England so many years before to teach Russian to the empress), Dr. Botkin and the tsar himself, who greeted Gilliard one morning with the friendly salute, *"Mon cher collègue."* That Alexei's education, in particular, should not be interrupted

*T*his bridge (left) in the Alexander Park
once marked the boundary of the captive tsar's domain. In April 1917, he and Tatiana (inset) broke up ice
floes in the canal under the watchful eye of a revolutionary guard.

was thought to be essential by everyone at the palace. The twelve-year-old tsarevitch, naturally, had only a partial understanding of the reality of events, and remarked in a note to a friend that when — if — he ever became tsar, "no one [would] be allowed to lie" to him. At Tsarskoe, he said, "everyone" had lied, including his beloved Derevenko, one of two sailor-attendants who had been his constant companions almost from the moment of his birth. At the time of the Revolution, Derevenko went over to the radicals; he lounged in a chair in the tsarevitch's bedroom and ordered him around until Gilliard put a stop to it.

"Insolently he bawled at the boy ... to bring him this or that, to perform any menial service," Gilliard recalled. "Dazed and apparently only half conscious of what he was being forced to do, the child moved about trying to obey." A huge to-do ensued later on in the spring, when the soldiers guarding the Alexander Palace found Alexei playing with a toy rifle and sounded the alarm: "They are armed!" The cry went up before the rifle itself was confiscated (only to be smuggled back to the tsarevitch, piece by piece, by the commandant of the palace).

"There were spies everywhere," said Baroness Buxhoeveden, "and some of the underservants spied upon us, repeating what we said in the guard-room. We once found a footman kneeling

In captivity at Tsarskoe Selo, Alexei (above) plays with his spaniel, Joy, and (inset) emerges from a swim. (Opposite) Colonel Kobylinsky oversaw the confinement of the family at Tsarskoe Selo and in Tobolsk.

at a door, listening to the conversation inside, so even in our rooms we had to be careful not to say anything that might be misinterpreted." Outside the intimacy of their private chambers, the imperial family and all of the staff were forbidden to speak any language but Russian.

"A word in French to M. Gilliard, whose Russian was very bad at that time, would be followed by great unpleasantness," the baroness wrote. "Towards the end of the time at Tsarskoe, an assistant commander, Damadianz, was always hiding in the bushes when the Empress was in the garden, listening to everything she said. Neither parents nor children complained of all this. 'Funny, isn't it?' was all the Grand Duchesses said." Easter, nevertheless, was a sorry holiday that year. "The pulse of life had stopped," said Sydney Gibbes, the English tutor; the imperial family had suddenly become "very human." Gilliard noted the extreme sadness of everyone present in the palace chapel during the Easter service. At the traditional late-night breakfast celebrated everywhere in Russia at the hour that "Christ Is Risen!" — even though Anastasia had recovered from measles and was joking with the soldiers — the gloom was inescapable. Count Benckendorff took a fresh look at Alexei and praised the tsarevitch's "excellent heart."

"If his disease should be mastered," Benckendorff wrote, "and should God grant him life, he should one day play a part in the restoration of our poor country. He is the representative of the legitimate principle; his character has been formed by the misfortunes of his parents and his own childhood. May God protect him and

save him and all his family from the claws of the fanatics in which they are at present."

❧

In May, on Kerensky's order, a new commandant was appointed at the Alexander Palace: Eugene Stepanovitch Kobylinsky, a colonel of the Petrograd Life Guards who would oversee the life of the imperial family for the next eleven months until the Bolshevik party seized power in Russia and relieved him of his command. Kerensky's periodic arrival at Tsarskoe Selo was "no joy to anybody," in Tatiana Botkin's words — almost invariably it meant bad news. To the Romanovs the hero of the Revolution was little more than a strutting and ill-mannered martinet, roaming

through their rooms, leafing through their papers and torturing the empress with threats of separation from her family. (As time went by, it's true, the tsar came to admire Kerensky, and declared with maddening hindsight that he wished he had "known about the man" before this so that he might have given him a position in the government.) In choosing Kobylinsky to accompany the Romanovs into Siberian exile, however, to watch over the revolutionary guard and manage what remained of the emperor's estate, Kerensky displayed an undeniable sensitivity to the Romanovs' plight. When it came to the Revolution, Colonel Kobylinsky was neither for nor against the monarchy or the imperial family. He was able to serve them as an honest soldier, clear in purpose and devoted to Russia. He served, indeed, as an "ordinary Russian," the kind of soldier the family said they liked.

"People on the Right were incensed to know that a colonel of the old-time guards could take upon himself the position of Their Majesties' jailer," said Tatiana Botkin, who blamed the failure of Russian monarchists to "cultivate" Kobylinsky for the eventual murder of the tsar, his family and her father at Ekaterinburg. Kobylinsky "did all he could for the Tsar's family," Tatiana insisted, "and it was not his fault if the short-sighted monarchists could not make out that much and never even turned to the one man who had it in his power to organize their rescue. He was only waiting for some help from outside, which he could scarcely call for, since his every action, every word, almost his every thought was constantly watched by three hundred adversely disposed suspicious soldiers."

In July 1917, after the first unsuccessful Bolshevik uprising in the capital, Tatiana's father was called with Kobylinsky to Petrograd, where Kerensky told them that the imperial family was about to be moved to Siberia, to the town of Tobolsk. "I chose Tobolsk," said Kerensky later, "because it was an out-and-out backwater ... had a very small garrison, no industrial proletariat, and a population which was prosperous and contented, not to say old-fashioned. In addition ... the climate was excellent and the town could boast a very passable Governor's residence where the Imperial family could live with some measure of comfort." The decision to move them had come on the heels of the famous "July Days" when, responding to massive defeats for the Russian armies on the eastern front and a general retreat of the nation's forces, a new rebellion broke out in Petrograd, routing the Bolsheviks temporarily and ensconcing Kerensky at the head of the provisional government, but giving further notice that the "bloodless" revolution of the previous March would probably be the last of its kind. Russia was sliding into violent chaos, and the safety of the imperial family could no longer be guaranteed so near the stirred-up capital.

Since the failure of England to grant them asylum, the imperial family had been hoping against hope that Kerensky might send them to Livadia, their adored Crimean retreat. This would enable them, technically, to remain in Russia while enjoying the spectacular benefits of a seaside resort. That Siberia had been chosen instead was no secret to any of them by the time they boarded a special train on the early morning of August 14. They had been told to pack furs and warm clothing, and the staff, such as remained, were given a final chance to "save their skins" — the revolutionaries' phrase — before the family's departure. Only the so-called under-servants chose to do so, however, and the

Romanovs were followed into Siberian exile by the familiar band of loyalists: Gilliard, Gibbes, the Botkins, Catherine Schneider, Sophie Buxhoeveden and another lady-in-waiting, Countess Anastasia Hendrikova.

There were, in addition, adjutants for the tsar: Prince Vassili Dolgoruky and General Iiya Tatishchev, two men who hated each other personally but were united now by their loyalty to the former emperor. There were cooks, stewards, valets and maids, among them Clementy Nagorny, the second (and still intensely loyal) of the tsarevitch's sailor-attendants, Alexandra Tegleva ("Shura"), who was Grand Duchess Anastasia's nurse, and Anna Stepanovna Demidova, "a tall, well-built woman rather inclined to be stout," in Sydney Gibbes' recollection, "who in direct contrast to her physical appearance was of a singularly timid and shrinking disposition."

For the moment the imperial family and their remaining retainers were safe, or so they thought. "We trust you," the tsar told Kerensky. "If you say we must move, it must be. We trust you." The last night at Tsarskoe was an endless, somber affair filled with anxiety and floods of tears. "The hour appointed for their departure was 1 A.M.," said Tatiana Botkin, "but they did not leave till nearly 6 A.M. The Grand Duchesses wept copiously, the Empress, too, was much perturbed, and my father went from one to the other with a bottle of soothing drops, comforting them all." The family spent the long night sitting on their trunks and suitcases in the famous semicircular hall of the Alexander Palace, waiting for the signal to leave, occasionally retiring to their rooms for a rest they never got. Soldiers appeared from moment to moment with the sharp command, "Get ready!" Before departure Kerensky allowed the emperor to see his brother, Grand Duke Michael, in whose favor Nicholas had abdicated the throne in March. They were not left alone together, however, and could discuss nothing of

Today a lecture room for the navy, the once-elegant semicircular hall of the Alexander Palace (above) was where the family and their retinue gathered before their departure for Siberia. The empress was carried in her wheelchair through a window (right) as the party left at dawn for the Alexandrovsky train station (far right).

consequence in Kerensky's presence.

"The brothers ... were most deeply moved," Kerensky recalled. "For a long time they were silent ... then they plunged into that fragmentary, irrelevant small-talk which is so characteristic of short meetings: How is Alix? How is Mother? Where are you living now? and so on." Outside in the hall the tsarevitch made an effort to see "Uncle Misha," but permission was declined. The day before had been Alexei's thirteenth birthday. At the empress's request the holy icon of Our Lady of Znamenie had been brought to the palace as a blessing on her son.

"The ceremony was poignant," Count Benckendorff recalled. "All were in tears." Alexandra herself was nearly frantic with grief as the precious belongings of a lifetime were packed and labeled. She tried to bring everything she could: rugs, portraits, pictures, screens, knick-knacks, mementos, icons and, not least, a fortune in family jewelry — the diamonds, emeralds, pendants and pearls that belonged to her and her daughters. When the time came to go, the weeping empress was lifted by servants from a window of the palace and carried to the car that took her to the Alexander Station at Alexandrovsky, fifteen miles away. There the soldiers saw her walk weakly but with dignity, holding fast to her husband's arm, down the rails to the waiting train, which had been disguised for security purposes as a vehicle of the Red Cross. It flew a Japanese flag, and it may be that Kerensky, as he later insisted, hoped the train might speed his captives straight out of Russia to safety.

"What shall the future bring to my poor children?" the empress wrote in a note to Baroness Buxhoeveden, who was detained at Tsarskoe by illness and only later arrived at Tobolsk. "My heart breaks thinking of them." Her face was ashy white as she left the Alexander Palace for the last time, and no one doubted that she felt the full force of her family's desolation.

"The sunrise that saw us off was beautiful.... We left Tsarskoe Selo at 6:10 in the morning. Thank God we are all saved and together."

— From Nicholas II's diary

Sunrise over the Alexander Palace. The imperial family left here at dawn on August 14, 1917, and were taken by train to Siberia. None of them would ever return.

Ironically, the summertime journey to Siberia provided the imperial family with the most exhilarating few days they had enjoyed in months. They were allowed to walk whenever the train stopped and to roam in the woods in search of flowers and berries, though the curtains of their private carriage were always drawn at stations and large towns. Inside, according to the tsar's diary, it was "stifling and dusty," nearly eighty degrees Fahrenheit in the daytime. Altogether the trip proved incredibly slow. On August 17 the Romanovs passed through the city of Ekaterinburg, a mining town already known to them as the center of revolutionary activity in the Ural Mountains.

Months later, in her own comical English, Grand Duchess Anastasia described the trip into exile in a letter to a friend:

My dear Friend. I will describe to you who [how] we travelled. We started in the morning and when we got into the train I went to sleap, so did all of us. We were very tierd because we did not sleap the whole night. The first day was hot and very dusty. At the stations we had to shut our window curtanse than nobody should see us. Once in the evening I was looking out we stoped near a little house, but there was no staition so we could look out. A little boy came to my window and asked: 'Uncle, please give me, if you have got, a newspaper.' I said: 'I am not an uncle but an anty and have no newspaper.' At the first moment I could not understand why did he call me 'Uncle' but then I remembered that my hear is cut and I and the soldiers (which where standing next to me) laught very much. On the way many funy things had hapend, and if I shall have time I shall write to you our travell father on. Good by. Don't forget me. Many kisses from us all to you my darling. Your A.

Revolutionary soldiers and deputies packing up the contents of the palaces at Tsarskoe Selo after the Romanovs left for Siberia. The steamer that took the family to Tobolsk passed by Rasputin's hometown of Pokrovskoe, seen today (opposite top) and in a photo taken in 1917 (inset) by the children's English tutor, Sydney Gibbes. Rasputin's parents' home still stands in the town (opposite bottom).

On August 18, at the port town of Tyumen, the imperial captives were transferred from their train to the steamer *Russia*, which took them up the rivers Tur, Tobol and Irtysh in the direction of Tobolsk, where the railroad did not run. Later that day they passed the village of Pokrovskoe, where Rasputin had lived and which he had once predicted they would see for themselves. The empress turned to her servant, Alexei Volkov, with the words, "Here lived Grigory Efimovitch. In this river he caught the fish he brought to us in Tsarskoe Selo." It was an omen, Alexandra felt sure, and somewhat assuaged her disappointment at not being sent to the Crimea.

The revolutionary spirit had not yet "infected" this part of Siberia, and no one seemed to object when the imperial family, on their arrival at Tobolsk, were given the finest house in town for their prison: the white two-storied governor's mansion, so called because it had once been the official residence of the governors of Tobolsk province. The house as yet was unfit for habitation, and the Romanovs lived on board the *Russia* for more than a week while their rooms were cleaned and painted, their furniture installed and special favors obtained, among them a piano for the grand duchesses and spring mattresses for their parents, who could not be expected to sleep on camp beds like the others.

"We had supper," the tsar remarked on their first night at the dock, "joked about people's astonishing inability to arrange even for lodgings, and went to bed early." The street on

The tsar saws wood with Pierre Gilliard (opposite) behind the governor's mansion in Tobolsk. (Inset) The mansion today. Outside the fenced compound (below), revolutionary soldiers from Petrograd stand guard. The Kornilov house across the street (bottom) was where Dr. Botkin, his children, and other members of the imperial suite lived.

which the governor's mansion stood had recently been renamed Freedom Street (Ulitza Svobody), but that was as far as radicalism seemed to go in Tobolsk. Practically the entire town came down to the shore to greet their boat on arrival.

"We were all amazed at the girls," said one local resident many years later. "Their hair was shorn like little boys'. We thought that was the fashion in Petrograd." Many of Tobolsk's inhabitants were the descendants of political prisoners, exiled years before to Siberia by Nicholas II's ancestors, but none appeared to be holding a grudge, and the imperial prisoners were treated with honor, even deference, by most of the residents in town.

It was a different matter with the several detachments of soldiers, three hundred of whom had been brought from Tsarskoe Selo for the purpose of guarding the imperial family. By common agreement of the prisoners, one of the detachments was "friendly," one was "neutral," and one was "revolutionary," continually insisting on the rights of "the People" and generally making a nuisance of themselves. A case of wine, for example, sent to the tsar in Tobolsk with the express permission of Kerensky, was dumped into the river on the grounds that the soldiers themselves were forbidden to drink while on duty.

In September a "civilian" commissar, Vassili Pankratov, looking like "an old black raven," was appointed by the provisional government to oversee the Romanovs' captivity, his authority superseding, though not replacing, that of Colonel Kobylinsky. One of his first acts was to order that the Romanovs be photographed front and profile in the manner of convicts.

Pankratov himself had spent fifteen years as a political prisoner at the Schlusselberg Fortress in St. Petersburg. Along with his assistant, Alexander Nikolsky, he gave "revolutionary lectures" to the guards, many of whom, in

point of fact, did not know how to sign their names. Money is what had brought all the soldiers to Tobolsk, the certainty of pay and a chance to escape the turmoil in the capital. As a result of Pankratov's "political conversations," however, according to Tatiana Botkin, the entire company soon "split into parties and quarreled," while Colonel Kobylinsky, striving to maintain a semblance of order, "went gray and looked ten years older by the end of that winter." It is a tribute to the charm of the tsar's four daughters (if not the gentle nature of Russian soldiers) that as time went by the girls managed to win over most of their jailers in games and private chats and the kind of innocent flirtation in which they must have been dying to indulge. Even Pankratov eventually became friendly, and after a few months at Tobolsk, Grand Duchess Marie told Sydney Gibbes that she wouldn't mind living there forever if she could only go for a walk.

None of them could. In the first several days of their imprisonment the imperial family was allowed free access to the building across from their own, the somewhat larger, pink and elaborate Kornilov house, which had been requisitioned from a local merchant to house the imperial staff. The enthusiasm with which the crowds saluted the former monarch and his family whenever they sat out on the balcony or appeared at a window put an end to these excursions, however. A wooden fence was erected around their prison, simultaneously enclosing a side street that would serve as the only area for physical recreation.

In October a young friend of Grand Duchess Olga, Rita Hitrovo, arrived unannounced at Tobolsk, carrying letters, gifts and encouragement from Petrograd. The soldiers concluded she was part of a monarchist plot (which she might well have been) and sent her back to the capital. After that no one who had not already received permission to enter the governor's mansion was allowed to do so, so that Dr. Botkin's children, for instance, and Sophie Buxhoeveden, who arrived in Tobolsk somewhat later than the rest, never saw the imperial family again except from a distance as they walked in the courtyard, appeared at a window or sat on the balcony of the house.

Inside, the tsar and his children tried everything they could think of to keep busy. They sawed or chopped wood, "swinging their hatchets with unusual dexterity," recalled Tatiana Botkin. They walked in circles, jumped up and down, stood on their heads and waved at passersby. When winter came they built a snow mountain in the courtyard, as they had frequently done at Tsarskoe Selo, and "fought like Trojans" while they still could, "hurling themselves and each other in the snow and laughing at the top of their voices." When Nicholas and Alexandra both appeared on top of the ice hill one morning, however, to say good-bye to a detachment of departing soldiers, the mountain was razed to the ground. After that, for most of the time, the children just sat on the balcony, taking what sun there was and dreaming, undoubtedly, of freedom.

Inside the house, lessons continued and the girls were never idle. They sewed, embroidered, drew, read and finally (it was a great highlight of their captivity) acted in plays under the direction of their tutors. But there was no disguising the tedium of their exile. Alexei was allowed to play with a couple of local boys — inside the house — and with "Kolia" Derevenko, the son not of the thankless sailor who had deserted him in the Revolution but of Dr. Botkin's colleague, Vladimir Derevenko, who had followed the family to Tobolsk and, as a medical specialist, went in and out of the governor's mansion more or less as he pleased. But for much of the time the tsarevitch was in bed, laid up with a cold, or a cough, or a pain in the joints that Alexandra feared might be a hemorrhage, and most of the entries in his diary-in-exile open with the same five words: "Today passed just as yesterday." Only now and then did anything like emotion creep into the pathetic record of Alexei's days: "It is boring!... God help us! God have mercy on us!"

"Yes, the past is over," his mother remarked in a letter to Anna Viroubova, who after five harrowing months in the Fortress of Peter and Paul found herself at liberty in Petrograd. "I thank God for all I had & was given — and will live in my memories, which no one can take away.... I left all the [photograph] albums in a trunk [at Tsarskoe Selo].... I drive things away, they destroy me, all too fresh in my memory." The empress spent most of her time at Tobolsk in her room, where she escaped the worst of the revolutionary scene and aged incredibly over the winter months.

"What did Grigory see in that old woman?" said a man who had known Rasputin. The empress and all her daughters except Anastasia had grown razor-thin in exile. According to the empress, Anastasia was "now very fat, as Marie *was*, round and fat to the waist, with short legs." "You could hardly find anyone so thin" as Tatiana, said Sydney Gibbes in a thumbnail sketch of the tsar's daughters at the end of their lives. Olga suffered the most from boredom, he remembered; Tatiana was "haughtier" than she used to be, and "it was impossible to guess her thoughts." Marie, skinny as she had become, could still "easily" lift Gibbes off the ground, while Anastasia's "mental development seemed to have been suddenly arrested." It seems not to have entered their parents' minds that the lives of the children were actually in danger. Almost contentedly, Nicholas and Alexandra expected nothing for themselves but martyrdom, and the experience of exile, the empress said, would be "easier" for them.

*T*he tsar's eldest daughter, Olga (above), chopping wood at Tobolsk. (Below) Nicholas and his children enjoy the sun on the roof of the greenhouse and (opposite top left) take exercise with members of their retinue. (Opposite top right) The room shared by the four girls. (Opposite bottom left) A sketch of the governor's house and (right) watercolors done by the girls in Tobolsk. In the center is Anastasia's English workbook, showing corrections by Sydney Gibbes.

"When will it all finish?" she wondered in a letter to Ania. "How I love my country, with all its faults!... Believe in the people, darling. The nation is strong and young and soft as wax."

In November 1917, in a stunning coup d'état, the Bolshevik party seized power from the Kerensky government in Petrograd and in a matter of months, under Vladimir Ilyich Lenin, transformed Russia officially into the world's first communist state. Only after the conclusion of the four-year Russian civil war was Lenin's government able to consolidate the new regime. But from the beginning Lenin, along with Jacob Sverdlov, Leon Trotsky, and other leading Bolsheviks, ran the country in a manner that owed much to the style of the tsars — brutally, without mercy and with the eventual formal declaration of a "Red Terror" in Russia that was meant to bring the population into line and very shortly did.

In the winter months, with the rivers frozen, the town of Tobolsk was accessible only by horse and cart (or sleigh), and it took several weeks for news of the Bolshevik coup to reach

the captives in the governor's mansion. Sydney Gibbes "had never seen the Emperor so shaken" as the day he heard about Lenin's triumph: "For the moment he was completely incapable of saying or doing anything, and nobody dared to say a word. Then gradually our normal life began again, but with a certain difference: The rising danger was apparent to everybody.... It was clear that [the family's] position had become extremely precarious and might very well end in tragedy." Commissar Pankratov later reported that the tsar was depressed by the turn of events — "but depressed most of all by the looting of the wine cellars in the Winter Palace!"

"Couldn't Mr. Kerensky have put a stop to that license?" Nicholas asked.

"Obviously not," said Pankratov. "A mob, Nicholas Alexandrovitch, is always a mob."

"How can that be?" the tsar inquired. "Alexander Feodorovitch [Kerensky] was put in by the people. A real favorite of the soldiers.... Regardless of what happened — why tear apart a palace, why allow the plunder and destruction of riches?"

At first, in what proved to be the lull before

A painting of the looting of the
Winter Palace (opposite) in November 1917, and (above) imperial crests lying in
Palace Square after being removed from the palace facade.

the storm, there were no obvious changes in the routine or the command at Tobolsk. Lessons continued, prayers were sung, and boredom ruled.

Christmas came, and with it the last semblance of "useful" activity in the governor's mansion. According to custom, the imperial family gave presents to all of their servants, down to the last footman, and this year a number of the soldiers also received gifts of knitted scarves, gloves and caps.

"The day before Christmas Her Majesty asked my father if we had a Christmas tree," Tatiana Botkin recalled, "and, hearing that we had not, immediately sent one of the servants into town to get us one, adding to it a few candlesticks, gold-rain, snow, and candles clipped by His Majesty's own hands. On the evening of the same day we each received a piece of embroidery — the work of Their Highnesses — a book-mark water-colored by Her Majesty, and a present: my father a vase, my brother a book, and I a charm for my watch — a gold nugget with a diamond."

Alexandra had been taking a great interest in the Botkin children, especially the youngest, Gleb, who told his father in Tobolsk that he intended to study for the priesthood. "My father had complained to [the empress] of my hatred of the revolutionaries and my general state of depression," Gleb remembered, "which he regarded as a wrong attitude to maintain. But Her Majesty thought, to the contrary, that it was my father who had adapted himself too easily to the new regime, and sent me many kind messages." Repeatedly she asked the commandant if the Botkins might come over to play cards or study or simply sit with her own children, so bored by now that whenever they left the house for their daily exercise they began looking at their watches to see when they might go in again. But permission was refused, and the two households had to be content with daily waves and occasional correspondence.

Gleb Botkin was a budding poet (something that endeared him especially to moody Grand Duchess Olga) and a talented

"To my sweet darling Mama... May God's blessing be upon you and guard you for ever. Your ever loving girl, Tatiana."

Tatiana's last Christmas present to her mother (left) was a notebook bound in mauve cloth bearing the empress's "lucky" symbol, the swastika. Years later, the Nazis would corrupt this ancient Hindu sign.

176

artist who amused the grand duchesses and their brother with satiric cartoons, a series of brilliant watercolors depicting the various personalities of the Russian Revolution as animals in uniform. His father brought the drawings to the tsar's children as fast as Gleb could produce them — one of the few opportunities they had for honest laughter.

The early winter of 1918 was mild for Siberia, but in February the blizzards began and the tsar's children again fell sick, this time with German measles. The illness did not last long, and it was everyone's turn to break out laughing just before Lent, when Anastasia revealed more than she intended during a performance of the play *Packing Up*, a "vulgar" Edwardian comedy directed by Sydney Gibbes, in which the youngest grand duchess took the male lead. "At the end of the farce," Gibbes recalled, "the husband has to turn his back, open his dressing gown as if to take it off — Anastasia wore an

old one of mine — and then exclaim: 'But I've packed my trousers; I can't go.' The night's applause had excited the Grand Duchess. The piece had gone with a swing and they were getting through the 'business' so fast that a draught got under the gown and whisked its tail up to the middle of her back, showing her sturdy legs and bottom encased in the Emperor's Jaeger underwear. We all gasped; Emperor and Empress, suite and servants, collapsed in uncontrolled laughter. Poor Anastasia could not make it out." She was a trouper, nevertheless, and when *Packing Up*, by popular demand, was repeated a second time, she made sure the audience got its money's worth. It was the only play to be presented at Tobolsk twice that winter, and it was the last time anyone saw the empress — the Princess Sunshine of years before — laughing hard and long.

By March, Tobolsk was "infested with Bolshevism," Tatiana Botkin remembered, and new

recruits from Petrograd and Tsarskoe Selo arrived to replace the existing guard. Pankratov was dismissed, and on Moscow's order the imperial family was placed on soldiers' rations. Money for their upkeep had long ago evaporated. The tsar was supporting not just his family but the entire staff of suite and servants out of his own pocket — that is, from the remainder of the funds that had been brought with the family from the state bank in Petrograd. Now Moscow decreed that the retinue would be cut in half and all the retainers, with the exception of the doctors, sent to live with the imperial family in the governor's mansion itself. This presented "a great inconvenience," as the Botkins recalled, and ended in some comical doubling- and even tripling-up of the staff. Catherine Schneider, the empress's *lectrice*, took a single room in company with her own two maids, while General Tatishchev and Prince Dolgoruky, the emperor's mutually antagonistic aides-de-camp, were forced to bunk together and regularly

*F*aithful members of the retinue at Tobolsk. At lunch (above left) are, from left: Olga; adjutant General Tatishchev; tutor Pierre Gilliard; Countess Hendrikova, a lady-in-waiting; Tatiana and tutor Catherine Schneider. Schneider and Hendrikova are shown outdoors (above, second and third from right), as is the tsar's aide, Prince Dolgoruky (right).

entertained the whole household with their violent discussions.

"We must not become petty, we must not be small," said Tatishchev in his better moments, but it wasn't easy to keep a cool head. Sydney Gibbes, whom the Botkins thought a "pig-headed Englishman," flatly refused to move in with his Swiss colleague, Gilliard, and went off to live in "a warm and roomy little barn" with his maid, Anfisa (much to the amusement of the four grand duchesses, who had already predicted that Gibbes would "never live anywhere without Fisa"). The empress did her best to provide compensation for the discharged servants, but most of them didn't bother to wait for their money. They robbed the larder, presented Alexandra with bills for their services and before leaving the house got so drunk that many passed out in the hall outside the children's rooms. At meals, butter, sugar, coffee and eggs all disappeared from the table — any kind of "luxury" was regarded by the Bolsheviks as suspiciously (and by now criminally) "aristocratic." The imperial family's visits to church had already been suspended in December when the local priest, Father Alexeiev, made the mistake of praying for the family's health with a mention of their titles, a holdover from tsardom expressly forbidden by the new regime. (Subsequently a makeshift chapel was constructed inside the governor's mansion and services were held there with the assistance of nuns and priests from the shrine of St. John of Tobolsk.)

Further indignities were not long in coming. In March the tsar was ordered to remove his officer's epaulets from his uniforms and jackets. They bore the monogram of his father, Alexander III, and their forced removal was an outrage, almost a sacrilege, to the whole family. That same month the Bolshevik government signed a peace treaty with the Germans at Brest-Litovsk, putting an end to Russia's involvement in the First World War and simultaneously surrendering something like a third of Russia's eastern territory to the Germans. Nothing since the moment of his abdication had so upset the tsar and the empress. Nicholas called it "a nightmare ... much worse and more shameful than events in the Time of Troubles," while Alexandra declared that she couldn't even think about Brest-Litovsk "without a terrible pain in [her] heart." There were many in Russia, she realized, who would regard the Germans as a relief from the Bolsheviks, but for her they were "far worse — such an unbearable pain — but everything generally hurts now — all one's feelings have been trampled underfoot."

"Great God," Alexandra exclaimed in a letter to Lili Dehn, "what have they come to, to wait for the enemy to come and rid them from the internal foe. And who is sent as the leader? Aunt Baby's brother. Do you understand?"

She was writing in code. Aunt Baby was the nickname given to the empress by Lili's son, Alexander, and her brother was Ernie, the grand duke of Hesse, whose attempts to rescue Alexandra and her family were as sincere as his meddling in Russian politics was murky and inscrutable. The grand duke's role in subsequent events remains obscure. For years rumors swirled about a secret codicil in the Treaty of Brest-Litovsk, in which the German kaiser ostensibly demanded a guarantee that no harm would come to his cousin the empress and her daughters — "German" princesses, in the kaiser's view, and, in any case, potentially valuable pawns. That spring Count Benckendorff advised Count William Mirbach, the German ambassador in Petrograd, that "if the Tsar and his wife and children died, Kaiser Wilhelm would be personally responsible" — something of a switch among monarchists who were otherwise trying to play down the imperial family's connections with Germany.

In December 1917 the family was forbidden to attend church services in Tobolsk, so a makeshift altar was erected in the house (bottom) and nuns (below) came from the town to sing mass. (Opposite) Below the windows of the governor's mansion, a revolutionary procession passes the Kornilov house.

"Be calm," came Mirbach's reply. "I know all about the situation in Tobolsk, and when the time comes, the German Empire will act." There was talk of the grand duke of Hesse as a potential regent of Russia under a restored monarchy, and the efforts of a number of addlepated loyalists to rescue the Romanovs from Tobolsk were clearly funded by him. "I would rather die in Russia than be saved by the Germans," Alexandra declared, as if she had a choice in the matter. Furthermore she quite plainly believed that the Brest treaty would never be legal until her husband signed it. Her fear that Nicholas might "cooperate" with the Bolsheviks, willingly

or otherwise, was the reason for her profound agitation at the beginning of April when a new commissar arrived in Tobolsk from Moscow, where Lenin had moved the Russian capital at the start of 1918.

The envoy's name was Vassili Yakovlev — such, at least, was his alias. There are as many questions about Yakovlev and the true nature of his mission as there are theorists on the subject. Even at Tobolsk in 1918 he seemed shrouded in mystery — a distinguished, elegant, respectful Bolshevik, bowing to the empress and gently inquiring about the tsarevitch's health. Rumors spread in the governor's mansion that

Yakovlev was really Trotsky in disguise or that he had come to take the whole imperial family to England, Norway, Germany or Japan. The tsar, at least, and most certainly the empress, believed that Yakovlev had been sent to bring Nicholas to Moscow for trial.

Unfortunately, however, he arrived at the very moment that the Bolsheviks in Siberia and the Ural Mountains began to show their muscle. At Omsk in western Siberia, the local soviet regarded Tobolsk as its personal fiefdom and made it its goal to "spread Bolshevism" in the town. Across the Urals toward Moscow, the Bolshevik leaders at Ekaterinburg had their own

fascination with the tsar. There "the People" were dreaming of vengeance, and the Ural soviet was determined that Nicholas not escape retribution. Elsewhere civil war was breaking out, as armed resistance to the Bolsheviks mounted all over Russia and the so-called Czech legions — more than 40,000 Austro-Hungarian prisoners of war — took matters into their own hands and began a march across Siberia in an effort to leave the country. Whatever Yakovlev's actual mission, it seems clear that conflicting ambitions, combined with the imperial family's own preternatural bad luck, prevented him from fulfilling it.

Why they had not been rescued before now was a matter of some perplexity to everyone on the scene. In Petrograd Anna Viroubova was leading the drive for funds and "loyal servants" to save the imperial family, while different efforts on the part of their friends in the Crimea seemed, for a time, almost certain of success. In the end there was a failure of organization that even many of the monarchists in exile did not hesitate to put down to Russian incompetence. "I must say that our monarchists, in planning to organize the escape of Their Majesties, did not even trouble to inform themselves definitely of the conditions at Tobolsk, or even to study the geographical layout of the town," said a rueful Tatiana Botkin. Pierre Gilliard wondered why the whole of Siberia had not been flooded with attempted rescuers. "For pity's sake," he exclaimed, "if [the Swiss] were running this thing, every loader, every ship's captain, every *yamschik* on the way would be our own men."

"And really," Dr. Botkin's daughter continued, "nothing would have been easier than to scatter our own men among the employees of the steamships and post drivers. There remained another very simple method — that of bribing the whole guard, many of whom had already

said to Their Highnesses, 'Just as soon as the Bolsheviks pay us, we will go.' Surely they would have offered no resistance if the money had come from monarchists." Incredibly, there seems to have been persistent confusion about exactly *who* was supposed to be rescued: the tsar, the heir, the empress and her daughters, or all of the family together. The considerable sum of money collected vanished in the hands of Boris Soloviev, a Petrograd parvenu and the son of a treasurer of the Holy Synod, who had married Rasputin's daughter Maria in 1917 and thereby earned credentials as the Romanovs' rescuer that he plainly did not have. At the moment of the tsar's removal from Tobolsk, Soloviev contrived to make himself scarce, and finally disappeared altogether with a great deal of money in his pocket.

Yakovlev appears to have been charged initially with the task of removing the whole of the imperial family to Moscow at the same time as the tsar. But Alexei had again fallen ill — desperately ill, as it happened, following a tumble from riding a sled down the stairs that caused intense internal bleeding. As he grew older the boy appears to have more and more often tempted fate and even to have deliberately brought on attacks. It was "as if he did it on purpose," said the tsar.

Now he was "frightfully thin," the empress reported, "with enormous eyes." It was "as bad as at Spala."

"Mama, I would like to die," Alexei groaned from his bed. "I am not afraid of death, but I am so afraid of what they will do to us here." When Yakovlev took stock of the boy's condition, he apparently changed his plan and declared that the tsar alone would accompany him from Tobolsk. Nicholas refused, whereupon Yakovlev answered that if he didn't come along, Moscow would only send another envoy who might prove less amenable than himself.

"Be calm," said Yakovlev. "I am responsible with my life for your safety. If you do not want to go alone, you can take with you any people you wish. Be ready. We are leaving tomorrow [morning] at four o'clock."

Thus was Alexandra confronted with the most difficult decision of her life. She could not let her husband leave without her, nor could she desert her ailing son. Up till then she had "always known what to do." Now, suddenly, she didn't. She wept. She prayed. She beseeched the Lord to flood the rivers so that no one could travel at all. It was Grand Duchess Tatiana, finally, who told her mother, "You cannot go on tormenting yourself like this," and forced her to a decision. "Yes," said the empress. "I will go with the Tsar."

"You know what my son is to me," she remarked to her staff as they hastily packed for her journey, "and I must choose between him and my husband. But I have made up my mind. I must be firm. I must leave my child and share my husband's life or death." Their love remained in many ways as intense as when they were first engaged in 1894.

She looked around her and decided that Marie should come with them — "darling Mashka," "an angel and the best of us." The choice made sense. Olga's spirits were too low, said the empress, Tatiana's level head was needed to look after Alexei and manage the house and Anastasia was "too young to be taken into account." But Marie was solid, absolutely reliable; according to Sophie Buxhoeveden, the experience of the Revolution had turned her overnight "from a child into a woman." Her sisters' tears on hearing this news were not from jealousy or frustration, but genuine sorrow. The family had never been separated this way before. Tea that evening was taken in almost total silence, the girls gathered in a group at their mother's shoulders, Alexei moaning softly in the other room. He had just

*In April 1918, Alexei (inset) was recovering
from a bout of bleeding brought on from sliding down the stairs (above) on a sled. The empress was forced to
make the agonizing choice of leaving her son to accompany her husband to Ekaterinburg. (Below) This photo of the
carts that took Nicholas, Alexandra and Marie from Tobolsk was hastily shot by Gibbes on April 26, 1918.*

been told that his parents were leaving.

"It was the most mournful and depressing party I ever attended," said Sydney Gibbes, matter-of-fact to the last. "There was not much talking and no pretense at gaiety. It was solemn and tragic, a fit prelude to an inescapable tragedy." Leaving with the tsar and the empress were Prince Dolgoruky; the cook, Kharitonov; two valets, Trupp and Chemodurov; and Anna Demidova, the empress's maid, quivering with fear and murmuring, "Oh, Mr. Gibbes, I am so frightened of the Bolsheviks. I don't know what they will do to us!" Dr. Botkin, too, left with them that night, though Alexandra had not expected him to.

"What about your children?" she asked him pointedly, perhaps recalling Botkin's "betrayal" of Anna Viroubova at Tsarskoe Selo.

"My duty has always been with Your Majesties," Botkin replied, and the empress squeezed his hand in gratitude. Across the street, from their window at the Kornilov house, Botkin's children looked down and saw their father for the last time as the party was bundled into filthy peasant carts and drove off. Nicholas sat in the first with Yakovlev; Marie and the empress followed in the next, where a mattress and some straw had been placed on the ground for their "comfort." The rest of the prisoners took up the rear.

"My father saw me," said Tatiana Botkin, "and turning around signed me repeatedly with the cross.... Then again soldiers. Demidova with soldiers, Chemodurov with soldiers, more soldiers and mounted soldiers on every side. All this dashed past me with incredible rapidity." She looked away toward the governor's mansion where she saw Olga, Tatiana and Anastasia — "three figures in gray suits" — standing on the steps. "They gazed for a long time into the distance, then turned and slowly, one after the other, entered the house."

*"Though we know that
the storm is coming nearer and nearer,
our souls are at peace. Whatever happens
will be through God's will."*
— From Alexandra's last letter to Anna Viroubova from Tobolsk

CHAPTER NINE

The House of Special Purpose

The worst of it, they all agreed, was the uncertainty: the tsar, the empress and Marie not knowing where they were being taken, and the rest of the family not knowing where they had gone. The children had filled their father's pockets with loving notes and words of encouragement before his convoy left Tobolsk. From Olga: "God protect you, bless you and have pity on you, my dear darling Papa. Don't worry about Alexei.... God knows the reasons and will bring us out of this." From Alexei: "I hope you get there soon. I'm going to try to eat a lot and get well quickly. I am so glad our sharpshooters are traveling with you." From Anastasia: "May God and all the saints protect you, my dearest Papa. In thoughts and prayers we are always with you. I can't begin to imagine how we're going to stay here without you." Tatiana, evidently, was too upset to write anything at all, and a note from Marie, hastily scribbled on the first day of their journey and

smuggled back to the governor's mansion by a member of the escort, could scarcely have cheered her up. "A dreadful journey," Marie said. "We are jolted terribly on these awful roads."

It was worse even than Marie let on. At no time of the year were the roads of Siberia a pleasure to travel. In the early spring, before the snows had fully melted, they were a nightmare, rutted and muddied to such an extent that the

empress could only declare afterward that her "soul was shaken out" by the ordeal. "Road perfectly atrocious," she wrote in her diary (which, since the Revolution, she had kept exclusively as a neutral record of events), "frozen ground, mud, water up to the horses' stomachs, fearfully shaken, pains all over." Alexandra and Marie traveled the nearly 200 miles from Tobolsk to Tyumen literally on the floor of their cart, with nothing but a few cushions and a rotted mattress for support. They were wearing thin Persian lamb coats and twice crossed the frozen rivers by foot on wooden planks, the ice being too thin to support the horses and carts. At night the family and Yakovlev stayed in peasants' houses while their horses were replaced.

On the day before they reached Tyumen (and, mercifully, the railroad), the team was changed at Pokrovskoe, directly in front of the house where Rasputin had lived. The empress's letter describing what must have been an affecting experience either never reached her children or was lost. We

Tobolsk (opposite) in 1918, photographed by Sydney Gibbes.
(Inset) After the departure of their parents, Anastasia, Tatiana and Olga take tea in the governor's mansion with a convalescing Alexei.
(Above) A view of Tobolsk today, from the river.

know only that the *starets'* widow, Praskovia Dubrovina, looked down at the prisoners from her balcony and blessed them in the usual fashion by signing the cross in the air. At Tyumen, despite her bumps and bruises, Alexandra begged Commissar Yakovlev to telegraph her daughters with the message that they had "arrived, all well."

But they were not going to proceed to Moscow, as they discovered soon enough. At Tyumen, Yakovlev installed the Romanovs in the first-class carriage of a waiting train while he headed for the telegraph office. What he did there and to whom he spoke remain a matter of conjecture and dispute. In Moscow responsibility for the fate of the imperial family had fallen into the hands of Jacob Sverdlov, "President of the Central Executive Committee of the All-Russian Congress of Soviets," better remembered as Lenin's right-hand man and de facto minister for internal affairs. It was Sverdlov who originally signed the order to bring the tsar to Moscow and who now played a game behind Yakovlev's back, encouraging the Bolshevik leaders at Ekaterinburg in their determination to take charge of the imperial prisoners while simultaneously ordering Yakovlev to proceed as planned by bringing the Romanovs to the Kremlin. For security purposes the family was referred to in telegrams as "the Baggage."

"Everything Yakovlev does is a direct execution of my order," Sverdlov proclaimed, but since no one in Siberia had any but a transient power, the statement was meaningless, and Sverdlov knew it. Yakovlev had heard news of a party of Ekaterinburg Bolsheviks waiting to ambush his train and murder the tsar on the way to the Urals. In order to avoid it, whether on his own initiative or at Sverdlov's command, he headed east toward Omsk. The plan was to move south from there and finally west to the capital.

This was all the excuse Ekaterinburg needed to intervene with force of arms. Isaac Goloshchekin, the military commissar of the Ural soviet headquartered in Ekaterinburg, was an intimate friend of Jacob Sverdlov (if indeed the Bolsheviks had "friends"). Goloshchekin knew, or guessed, that Moscow had no definite plan for the future of the tsar and that the Ural soviet would be doing the Kremlin leadership a favor by taking charge of the Romanovs. How much of this Yakovlev also knew will never be determined. From this point on, until its own collapse more than seventy years later, the Soviet government publicly disavowed all responsibility for the murder of the imperial family, insisting that the matter had been decided entirely on the initiative of the Ural soviet.

At Ekaterinburg the Bolshevik leaders now accused Yakovlev of attempting to "flee" with the imperial prisoners. "To all, to all, to all!" their telegrams shrieked. Yakovlev was branded a traitor to the Revolution, and Ekaterinburg, hitherto Omsk's bitterest rival in the region, suddenly got friendly with the Omsk soviet, whose soldiers now halted Yakovlev's train. The tsar and his family were trapped.

"Omsk Soviet would not let us pass Omsk," Alexandra remarked in her diary, "and feared one wished to take us to Japan." Even in the unlikely event that Japan was Yakovlev's real destination, it no longer mattered. The train and its "Baggage" were promptly escorted to Ekaterinburg where, on April 30, 1918, the Romanovs were delivered to the chairman of the Ural soviet, Alexander Beloborodov. In one of Russian history's more frightful gestures, the local soviet issued a receipt for the captives:

1) The former tsar, Nicholas Alexandrovitch Romanov.

2) The former tsarina, Alexandra Feodorovna Romanova.

3) The former Grand Duchess Marie Nicholaievna Romanova.

In Moscow, Jacob Sverdlov was the man who — with his friend Lenin — decided the fate of the imperial family. Ekaterinburg was later renamed Sverdlovsk in his honor. (Opposite) The central station at Ekaterinburg in 1918. Fearing an angry mob, the Bolshevik leaders brought the Romanovs to a secondary depot a few miles away.

All to be kept under guard
in the city of Ekaterinburg.

They were taken in open cars accompanied by the sound of spitting, jeers and shouts of "Show us the Romanovs!" to a building the Bolsheviks were already calling the "House of Special Purpose." It was a cream-colored town-house belonging to a prosperous "bourgeois" engineer by the name of Ipatiev, who only two days earlier had been ordered to take his things and vacate the premises. Ironically, the owner's name was the same as that of the monastery at Kostroma where Michael Romanov had been hailed as tsar 305 years before.

Ipatiev's house was a mansion by Ekaterinburg's standards, built of stone on the side of a hill in the most fashionable part of the city, not far from Ascension Cathedral. It stood on Ascension Square, which the men who shortly murdered the tsar's family would rechristen "The Square of National Vengeance," just as Ekaterinburg itself, in honor of the crime and the man who allowed it, was subsequently renamed Sverdlovsk.

Even before the tragedy, no one went to Ekaterinburg and reported that they liked it. "I shall never forget my first impression of this fatal town," Lili Dehn wrote after she, Anna Viroubova and Rasputin passed through the place in 1916. They were returning to Petrograd from Tobolsk, where the empress had sent them to inspect the relics at the shrine of St. John. "Directly we got out of the train I felt a sense of calamity — we were all affected."

Founded in the eighteenth century for the purpose of mining diamonds and named in honor of Catherine I, Ekaterinburg was and is a workers' town, a radical town with a history of violence and organized crime that long predated the murder of the tsar. Nicholas knew the nature of the place before he got there. "I would have gone anywhere but to the Urals," he confessed. "Judging by the newspapers, people there are bitterly hostile to me."

Nicholas described his family's final prison as "clean," but objected, on the day of his arrival, to the Bolsheviks' insistence on searching — rifling — every piece of their luggage, "right up to the last vial in Alix's pharmacy."

"This is an insult!" Alexandra declared, while Nicholas leaped to her defense: "Up till now we have dealt with decent people!"

"You are not at Tsarskoe anymore," the emperor was told; if he "opened [his] mouth again," the Bolsheviks said, he would be sentenced to hard labor. By the time he wrote in his diary that night, he had calmed down considerably.

"We have been assigned 4 rooms," Nicholas reported, "a corner bedroom, a lavatory, next door a dining-room with windows onto a little garden and a view of a low-lying part of town, and finally a spacious hall with arches in place of doors." The whole house was a mass of arches, curves and curls that decorated the rooms, doorways, roof and windows of the lower floor — a semi-basement. This "cellar" was actually a part of the ground floor, which had been built into the hillside and was accessible from the Romanovs' quarters only by descending a staircase, walking out through the courtyard and re-entering the house where it burrowed underground.

"A very high wooden fence has been built around the house," Nicholas went on. "A chain of sentries has been posted there and in the little garden too." In fact there were ten guardposts in and around the house. It was a fortress, impenetrable and impossible to escape. Marie described the reality of the place to her sisters in two or three letters that the Bolsheviks allowed her to send.

The Ipatiev house (opposite) was regarded as one of the finest in Ekaterinburg and had been completed only a few years before it was commandeered by the Ural soviet. (Below) The drawing room of the house, and its exterior (bottom) after a palisade had been erected around it. (Right) Alexandra scratched a swastika and the date of her arrival on a window frame of her bedroom in Ekaterinburg.

"We were brought here in automobiles after getting off the train," she wrote. "For lunch, at four-thirty, we were invited to share the communal soup. We weren't able to unpack our things till evening, because all of our suitcases were being rifled, including the medicines and the candy."

"Medicines" and "candy" were the Romanovs' code for the family jewels, a great number of which had been left in Tobolsk where Olga, Tatiana and Anastasia, helped by the remaining servants and staff, were frantically concealing them in the hems of their skirts, the buttons of their jackets, the rims of their hats, in pillows, cushions, underwear and corsets. On arrival at Ekaterinburg, the tsar's adjutant, Prince Dolgoruky, had been arrested at the station when it was found he was carrying more than eighty thousand rubles in cash. He was shot within days (though the family never knew it). The jewelry was all they had left to see them through — or out, "should God permit that to happen." Marie continued, "Everything was in a terrible state ... even the inside of the suitcases: dust and filth, everything disturbed and destroyed.... I really have nothing to write to you about.... The dining room is dark.... There is dust everywhere, we can't figure it out, since there aren't any carpets.... Even this paper is dirty: all our stationery was soiled on route.... Everyone who comes into the house inspects our rooms. Every time Mama has to get out of bed and greet them in her dressing gown.... It's difficult to write about anything cheerful, because there's all too little cheerfulness here. On the other hand, God doesn't abandon us. The sun shines, the birds sing, and this morning we heard the bells sounding matins.... Oh, my darlings, how I long to see you!"

For the next five weeks, until the family was reunited, most of the letters on both sides spoke of nothing but God and pain, the gloom being relieved only occasionally by incongruous chipper remarks: Marie and Anna Demidova had washed the empress's hair, "Baby" had gone for a walk, such-and-such a friend had written from Tsarskoe or Petrograd or the Crimea, where a number of the family's relatives had found a tenuous safety within feet of the sea and the chance of escape. The dowager empress was there with the tsar's sisters, Xenia and Olga, and their families. Olga had recently divorced her husband, Prince Peter of Oldenburg, and married a colonel of her mother's guard. She had had a baby, Tikhon, and was nursing him herself. Hard as it was for the imperial couple to believe, she "seem[ed] to be happy."

Others in the family were not so fortunate. Nicholas's brother Michael, and Ella, the empress's sister, were both imprisoned at Perm, west of Ekaterinburg, along with Grand Duke Serge Mikhailovitch and several young princes of the imperial house. In Petrograd the tsar's uncle, Grand Duke Paul, and three of his cousins were held in the Fortress of Peter and Paul. By now none of those in prison could have held out much hope of survival.

In Ekaterinburg a measure of hope returned at Easter, which Nicholas, Alexandra and Marie celebrated on a makeshift altar in the Ipatiev house. In Tobolsk the children enjoyed something like a proper service with the help of the nuns of St. John. Almost all of the letters from the period of separation are marked with crosses and the pious greeting, *"Khristoss Voskressiye!"* — "Christ is Risen!" And on a window of her bedroom in the House of Special Purpose, Alexandra drew a swastika: it was her "lucky" symbol.

On May 15 the windows of the house were nailed shut and whitewashed so the prisoners could not look out. After that the curtains were rarely opened because, as Marie said, darkness and the comfort of a lamp were preferable to the head-numbing glare of sunlight through paint.

Nicholas turned fifty on May 19 (the day of Job, as he liked to remind himself) and was frankly amazed that he had made it that far. The commandant of the Ipatiev house, Alexander Avadeyev, was a drunken, bullying lout whose normal response to any request from the tsar and his family was to curse, spit and shout, "Oh, to hell with them!" The "rudeness" the family had known from their previous jailers was small preparation for the indignities they encountered in their final prison. The doors were removed from most of the rooms, and a sentry was posted outside the single lavatory. When the empress, Marie or, later, the other girls were obliged to relieve themselves, they were not allowed to do it alone.

On the wall above the toilet were pornographic sketches of the empress with Rasputin, filthy jokes, insults and, frequently, smeared excrement. "Don't forget to look at the drawings," the soldiers would say to the grand duchesses before they entered. "Please be so kind as to leave the seat as clean as you found it," said a pathetic note to the guards placed beside this filth. The guards forced the girls to play revolutionary songs on the battered piano in the parlor: "Let's Forget the Old Regime" and "You Fell a Victim to the Struggle." It is said that the Bolsheviks sometimes spat in the family's soup before serving it to them — *if* they served it to them, which they sometimes didn't. The family ate without benefit of linen or silverware, often dining on nothing but black bread and tea; no matter what, their food was simply warmed over from whatever the guards had left uneaten. "Darling," said Grand Duchess Olga in one of her last letters to Ania, "you must know how dreadful it all is."

At Tobolsk the grand duchesses and Alexei had already had a taste of what was in store for them at Ekaterinburg — so plainly and so frighteningly that Gilliard, Gibbes and others in the retinue began to wonder seriously about the advisability of allowing the children to join their parents. Yet another commissar, "Rodionov" (it was an alias, as many Bolshevik surnames were) had taken command from the exhausted Colonel Kobylinsky and seemed bent on humiliating the girls. He was "a right snake," said Anastasia's nurse, Shura Tegleva. In the governor's mansion the doors remained on their hinges but were not allowed to be locked.

But the grand duchesses would not hear about not joining their parents — it was all they longed for and talked about. In the third week of May when the snows had melted and the rivers were open — even though Alexei was not fully recovered — the tsar's children once again boarded the steamer *Russia*, this time to sail back to Tyumen. A number of the faithful, among them Gleb and Tatiana Botkin, had been warned privately that no one who went with the grand duchesses and Alexei to Ekaterinburg would remain at liberty; worse, that they would not even be imprisoned with the Romanovs themselves but tossed in the local jail. Tatiana Botkin, told that under no circumstances would she be allowed to rejoin her father, wisely decided to stay in Tobolsk. She could surely be of more use "on the outside," she said. Most of the others stampeded for the boat and, sure enough, were imprisoned and later murdered in Bolshevik hands. As foreign nationals, Pierre Gilliard and Sydney Gibbes were both set free. So were a number of others, with no explanation and amid mounting rumors that they had "betrayed" the family, sold a few secrets and begged for their lives. Baroness Buxhoeveden attributed her unexpected release by the Bolsheviks to her "foreign" surname — it was Danish by origin — but, as

The port of Tyumen (below), showing the gangway where the tsar's children disembarked from the steamer Russia on the way to Ekaterinburg. Photos taken by Sydney Gibbes on board the steamer show Alexei and Olga (right), and Tatiana in the foreground and Anastasia in profile at the window (far right).

one Romanov scholar has correctly pointed out, "the even more obviously foreign name of 'Catherine Schneider' did not prevent the poor woman from being shot."

At Tyumen, Alexei, Olga, Tatiana and Anastasia boarded the train that would take them to their parents. During the journey the girls were forcibly separated from the remainder of their suite and rode out the trip by themselves. It was during this separation that some of the Bolshevik guards attempted to rape them. "The Grand Duchesses had to spend the night in open cabins and at night the sharpshooters got the idea of going in to them," according to a friend of one of the soldiers in question. "He always told the end of the story differently: either someone forbade them, or they passed out drunk first.... Whether he wasn't telling everything or was simply bragging, I don't know." To this day no one does. Stories later spread in monarchist circles of the girls being tied naked to chairs and gang-raped by crazed revolutionaries. The tale was doubtless exaggerated, but the threat of sexual assault was never far away. Alexei and his tutors, obviously, could provide no real protection against the swaggering lewdness of Red Army soldiers nursing a grudge. Colonel Kobylinsky, who might have succeeded, had stayed in Tobolsk when the children were transferred, felled by an attack of colitis and completely worn out, in any case.

When the train reached Tyumen the tutors watched as Olga, Tatiana and Anastasia were forced to drag their own luggage through the mud. It was pouring rain that day, and Alexei, at least, had the advantage of being carried to a waiting car by his attendant, Nagorny. In the miserable circumstances, with all or most of their illusions gone, it is touching to know that all was "great joy" in the Ipatiev house when the children finally arrived. "No end to the mutual questions and answers," the tsar remarked. "The poor things endured much moral suffering in Tobolsk and during their three-day journey." Now that the children had arrived from Tobolsk, a second, taller palisade was erected around the one that already existed outside the house, shutting out the world completely. But they were together now, that was all — that was all that had ever mattered.

❧

They lived for less than two more months, through Marie's nineteenth birthday and Anastasia's seventeenth, in a darkening atmosphere of terror and uncertainty that owed nothing to the exaggeration of monarchists. The last days of the Romanovs properly have been called a living hell, and the horror of their eventual murder — it can't be called an execution — still has the power to cut through history, politics, wars, revolutions and every consideration of expediency and "the times." A litany of the family's suffering in the weeks before they died can be pieced together mainly from secondhand accounts, inasmuch as the Bolsheviks were liars and the Soviet records concerning the death of the tsar are only now slowly emerging from the morass of the Bolshevik archives in Moscow. We know that the grand duchesses, when they arrived at Ekaterinburg, were subjected to a lengthy inspection and that the empress, after that, forbade them ever to remove their corsets. We know that the family was given a half hour each day to walk in the enclosed garden, that Alexei was in wretched shape and only occasionally left his bed, and that one of the grand duchesses was shot at one day when she tried to open a window to peer at the sky. "In my opinion," said the tsar in his diary, "[the sentry] was just fooling around with his rifle the way guards always do."

Scaring the children out of their wits appears to have been a particular pleasure for the Bolsheviks, however. At one point Anastasia submitted a request for a new pair of shoes, or even an old pair from her luggage in the loft, and was

On the train to Ekaterinburg, Pierre Gilliard sits next to Anastasia's nurse, Alexandra Tegleva ("Shura"), whom he would later marry.

*T*his rear view of the Ipatiev house
(above) shows the small garden where the family was allowed a brief afternoon
exercise period. (Left) The room shared by the grand duchesses (seen here in a
photograph taken after the Bolshevik evacuation of the city) had an ornate glass
chandelier (inset), which was later taken to England by Sydney Gibbes.
Also found in the house after the murders was Grand Duchess
Olga's diary (below).

191

told brutally "that those she had would last for the rest of her life." From the window of their room, if they stood on a chair and peered out a crack at the top, the grand duchesses could just make out the dome of Ascension Cathedral. The Bolsheviks occasionally toyed with the family's nerves by pretending they were about to be moved, and in June a series of mysterious letters arrived at the house with the pledge to rescue the family. The notes were either smuggled in by nuns from a local convent or deliberately planted by the Bolshevik authorities to trap the imperial family in a "counter-revolutionary" attempt to escape — historians are still divided on the subject. The notes, which were written in French, appeared to have come from friends on the outside. "The friends sleep no longer and hope the hour so long awaited has arrived. The revolt of the Czechoslovaks menaces the Bolsheviks more and more seriously.... Be watchful of every movement from without, wait and hope.... Be ready all the time, day and night. Make a sketch of your two rooms, the places of the furniture, of the beds.... One of you should not sleep between two and three o'clock all the following nights." The empress, at least, believed in the authenticity of the plot, for she replied in detail as to the layout of the house: "The second window from the corner, facing the square, has been open for two days — day and night — the seventh and eighth windows facing the square at the side of the main entrance are always open."

It was the tsar, however, who apparently put an end to the family's cooperation with the real or imaginary plan: "We do not want to and cannot flee," he wrote in a letter discovered many years later in Soviet archives. "We may be rescued only by force as it was by force that we were taken from Tobolsk. Therefore do not count on any active aid on our part.... Above all, in the name of God, avoid bloodshed....Give up the idea of carrying us off. If you are guarding us, you may

*D*r. *Botkin (above),
the family's faithful physician,
was imprisoned with them in the
Ipatiev house. (Opposite) Those in
the house could hear the bells of
Ascension Cathedral and catch a
glimpse of it through the top of the
whitewashed windows.*

always come and save us in the case of imminent danger. We are fully ignorant of what is going on outside, receiving neither papers nor letters. Since it has been permitted to open the windows, the guard has been increased, and one is forbidden to put one's head out of the window, at the risk of receiving a bullet in the face."

In the first days of July, when the advancing Czech Legions in Siberia were joined by a loose conglomeration of anti-Bolshevik forces to form the "White" Army in the civil war, the interior guard at the Ipatiev house was changed, and so was the commandant, Avadeyev. The Romanov's new chief jailer was "a dark gentleman" — it may have been the family's euphemism for a Jew — whom they at first mistook for a doctor. He was Jacob Yurovsky, a former jeweler and photographer's assistant, now a senior member of the Ural soviet. "This specimen we like least of all," Nicholas observed.

The decision to murder the entire family and, simultaneously, all of the Romanovs in the Ural region, was probably reached in Moscow at the beginning of July, and conceivably sooner than that. That the nod came from Lenin personally is not much doubted by historians, despite the absence of written proof and the lingering suspicion in Russia that he could not have authorized such an appalling crime.

Even before the murder, rumors flew that the Romanovs had been spirited from Ekaterinburg, whisked off to England, "spared" by Papa Lenin. On June 8, a bomb went off in the courtyard of the Ipatiev house (there was no explanation for it), and later an airplane was seen flying over the roof. In this plane people said, one, some, or all of the imperial family had escaped. On July 14, 1918, when mass was sung for the last time in the house, the officiating priest, Father Storozhev, noticed that the whole family seemed changed. They were not cheerful, he said; they did not converse in the manner he was used to.

"Something has happened to them in there," the priest concluded. He didn't know what it was, and neither does anyone else. Rudolf Lacher, an Austrian prisoner of war who found himself attached as an orderly to Commandant Yurovsky, later claimed to have seen the imperial family the night they vanished from the face of the earth. As they filed down the stairs, Lacher reported, the girls were "clutching each other" and sobbing. Later he heard the sound of gunfire and saw "bloody bundles" — bodies wrapped in sheets — being loaded onto a truck in the courtyard. The sight seems to have left him unmoved. "They weren't my relatives," Lacher explained. Another Austrian in the town, Heinrich Kleibenzetl, who had the job of cleaning and repairing the uniforms of the Ipatiev house guard, confirmed Lacher's account in all but one detail. He, too, had heard the sound of gunfire, along with a single female cry, "Mama!" But when he got home that night — he lived in a house across the street as an assistant to a local tailor — he found "one of the Grand Duchesses," wounded but alive, being tended in his bed. She was unconscious, her face had been beaten and she was covered with blood. Later, under oath, Kleibenzetl declared that the girl was Anastasia.

So many stories have been put forward, so many claims and counterclaims. In the late 1950s and through the 1960s during the famous Anastasia trials in Germany, a lawyer for Anna Anderson, the woman who claimed she was the emperor's youngest daughter, joked that if you added up everyone who pretended to have witnessed the massacre in the Ipatiev house, to have heard the shots and screams, to have rescued a living body or disposed of a dead one, "you'd have a World's Fair, not a top-secret murder in the middle of the night." The truth about the Ekaterinburg tragedy has been rendered indecipherable by different Bolshevik factions and the scores of people, drunk and sober, icily determined or inflamed with rage, who hoped to play a part (and, naturally, the *main* part) in the so-called National Vengeance.

The empress's diary (though not the tsar's) was dutifully maintained almost to the hour of the murder:

July 3 (16). Tuesday. Irina's [Princess Irina Alexandrovna, daughter of the Tsar's sister Xenia and Grand Duke Alexander] 23rd BD [birthday]. 11.[A.M.] Gray morning, later lovely sunshine. Baby has a slight cold. All went out ½ hour in the morning. Olga and I arranged our medicines [i.e., the jewels, a constant preoccupation of the family in the last days]. T. [Tatiana] read. 3. [P.M.] rel [religious] readings. They went out. T. stayed with me and we read the b [books] by pr. [prophets] Amos and pr. Avdiy. Talked. Every morning the superint. [Commandant Yurovsky] comes to our rooms, at last after a week brought eggs again for Baby. 8. Supper/ Suddenly Lika Sedniev [the kitchen boy] was fetched to go and see his uncle and flew off. Wonder whether it's true and we shall see the boy back again. Played bezique with N. 10½ to bed. 15 degrees.

The removal of young Sedniev was sudden and unexpected enough to arouse the suspicions of everyone in the house. A few days earlier the tsar's valet Chemodurov had been released on the grounds of "ill health," while the tsarevitch's attendant Nagorny was also removed (and shot, though the family did not know it) when he dared to defend Alexei against the brutal treatment and insults of the guard.

On the final night in the Ipatiev house, July 16–17, 1918, Dr. Botkin had begun a letter to a friend in Moscow. Although the doctor had been warned that his life was in danger, he had refused to desert the imperial family.

I am making a last attempt at writing a real letter — at least from here — although that qualification, I believe, is utterly superfluous. I do not think that I was

fated at any time to write to anyone from anywhere. My voluntary confinement here is restricted less by time than by my earthly existence. In essence I am dead — dead for my children — dead for my work.... I am dead but not yet buried, or buried alive — whichever, the consequences are nearly identical.... The day before yesterday, as I was calmly reading ... I suddenly saw a reduced vision of my son Yuri's face [Dr. Botkin had two elder children besides Gleb and Tatiana, Yuri (George) and Dmitri, who had died in battle in 1914], but dead, in a horizontal position, his eyes closed. Yesterday, at the same reading, I suddenly heard a word that sounded like Papulya [dear Papa]. I nearly burst into sobs. Again — this is not a hallucination because the word was pronounced, the voice was similar, and I did not doubt for an instant that my daughter [Tatiana], who was supposed to be in Tobolsk, was talking to me.... I will probably never hear that voice so dear or feel that touch so dear with which my little children so spoiled me.... If faith without works is dead, then deeds can live without faith.... This vindicates my last decision ... when I unhesitatingly orphaned my own children in order to carry out my physician's duty to the end, as Abraham did not hesitate at God's demand to sacrifice his only son.

Here Botkin's letter breaks off, presumably interrupted around midnight by the sudden appearance of Commander Yurovsky. There was "firing in the town," Yurovsky told him, and the family would be obliged to "evacuate" the house.

Dr. Botkin now went to rouse the imperial family for their purported evacuation from Ekaterinburg. For days they had heard artillery fire in the distance — the sound of the advancing White Army, which they probably guessed would never reach them in time.

Earlier in the day, in fact, a telegram had gone from Ekaterinburg to Moscow in which the local soviet declared that it "could not wait to do what has been agreed upon." Whether an answer came back from Moscow or not is still unknown. It was payday in Ekaterinburg, and the guards,

"The Romanovs did not suspect anything. The superintendent went for them personally and led them down the stairs to the lower rooms...."

— From an account of the execution written by Commandant Jacob Yurovsky in 1920

The final page of Alexandra's diary (opposite) records her last day and concludes just hours before her death.

almost without exception, were drunk by late evening. As it was, Yurovsky experienced some difficulty finding enough soldiers, even among the Ipatiev house guard, who were willing to shoot the girls. About half of the death squad, according to most reports, were Letts — Latvian mercenaries — who presumably had no nationalist or leftover religious compunction about slaughtering either women or children.

After being wakened by Dr. Botkin, the family washed, dressed and were ready to leave in about half an hour, the women having carefully put on the clothing in which their "medicines" were sewn. With them were Botkin and the three servants who still remained: the cook, Kharitonov, the valet Trupp and Anna Demidova, who carried a cushion that was also found, later, to be filled with jewels. Anastasia is alleged to have carried the children's pet spaniel Jimmy in her arms.

The Romanovs walked down the stairs and out of the house, then doubled back through the courtyard and entered the long hall that led to a small basement room. It had been emptied of furniture, and the empress, imposing to the last, exclaimed, "What, may we not sit?" Two chairs, accordingly, were brought in — one for Alexandra and the other for the tsar, who had carried Alexei and held him now in his lap.

After a tense wait the double doors of the cellar opened and Yurovsky, with ten or twelve soldiers behind him, entered. Accounts vary widely as to what the commandant actually said, but the central point was the "necessity" of the Romanovs' deaths.

"Your relatives have tried to save you," Yurovsky declared, according to the most widely known version of his speech. "They have failed, and we are now obliged to shoot you all."

"What?" cried the tsar, in a nearly exact duplication of his words many years earlier in Japan, when the Otsu fanatic attacked him with

*T*he dining room of the Ipatiev house *(above)* where the imperial family ate their last meal. *(Left)* The stairs descending from the upstairs bedrooms to the courtyard and the lower part of the house. *(Right)* The entry at the back of the house to the cellar where the family was shot. *(Opposite)* The massacre as rendered by a magazine artist in 1922.

his sword. *"What?!"* Apparently the order had to repeated, and according to Yurovsky, when the reality sank in, "a wail rose up among" the victims. There were a few "incoherent exclamations" and a hurried attempt on everyone's part to make the sign of the cross. Then the firing began.

The emperor was shot first and fell backward with staggering force, either because his position at the front of the group had trapped him in the first rain of bullets or, as Edvard Radzinsky suggests in *The Last Tsar,* because "everyone crowding in the doorway of that terrible room, all twelve revolutionaries, had come to kill the Tsar." It was the same with Alexandra who was blown from her chair during the first volley of gunfire and died from a bullet in the head.

Her children were not so lucky. The amount of time it took to silence them came near to unhinging the murderers themselves. Commandant Yurovsky had ordered the squad "to aim straight for the heart," but he seems to have been concerned mainly about containing the flow of blood to make it easier to clean up afterward. He never guessed that the diamonds and jewels the grand duchesses had sewn into their corsets would turn the garments into bulletproof vests. The bullets bounced off their chests and ricocheted, Yurovsky reported, "jumping around the room like hail." What Russia's finest revolutionary soldiers must have thought about the ability of the emperor's daughters to repel their attack can only be imagined. Only fifteen months had passed since the tsar had ceased to be legally divine. Desperately the drunken assassins began stabbing and club-

bing the four girls amid the billowing gunsmoke.

When the firing had ended, almost everyone was still alive on the floor — the children, the servants and Dr. Botkin — and had to be finished off in one way or another. Alexei was "still moaning" and apparently clutching his father's khaki jacket. There are reports that one of the soldiers kicked him in the head before Yurovsky took his own pistol and "shot him two or three times at point-blank range."

It was even worse for the women, stated one guard: "The Tsar's two youngest daughters [Marie and Anastasia], pressed up against the wall, were squatting, covering their heads with their arms, and then two men fired at their heads.... The lady-in-waiting [Anna Demidova was meant] was lying on the floor still alive.... One of the comrades began plunging the bayo-

net of his American Winchester into her chest. The bayonet was like a dagger, but it was dull and would not penetrate. She grabbed the bayonet with both hands and began screaming. Later they got her with their rifle butts."

A guard ran in from the courtyard to say that the shots, moans and screams could be heard from the streets and that the murderers had better desist, but still the victims refused to die.

Finally, after twenty or thirty minutes, everyone in the room "lay still," in the words of one of the killers. The bodies of the family and their servants were lifted onto makeshift stretchers and carried through the courtyard and the hall of the house to the front door, where a truck was waiting to take them out of the city for burial. Nicholas was brought first, his body wrapped in the sheet from his own and Alexandra's bed. Then came the grand duchesses — all of them, apparently, still "rustling" and alive. "One of the daughters" actually sat up on the stretcher and "cried out" before she was again attacked with bayonets and clubbed on the head; "the others," says one report, "also turned out to be still alive."

The murderers appear to have had no idea which of the daughters was which; the girls are mentioned interchangeably by name in the different accounts of the massacre. Alive or dead, the bodies had to be taken out of Ekaterinburg before dawn. The murderers now tossed the children onto the truck and drove into the night, leaving behind a tragedy that stirs us to this day.

CHAPTER TEN

Aftermath

The most common misconception about the massacre at Ekaterinburg, one that still stubbornly finds its way into encyclopedias and history books, is that the tsar's assassins formed part of a "firing squad." The image suggests a row of soldiers taking careful aim at their victims as they stand against a wall and swiftly, efficiently, shooting them down. There could be no less accurate description of the barbarous slaughter in the cellar of the Ipatiev house. In the first place, the room was far too small for a mass execution — barely seventeen feet by fourteen. To have even a chance of hitting their victims squarely, most of the murderers had to cram into the doorway, backed up in rows of three and four, and to fire over each other's shoulders.

"There were eleven or even twelve murderers for eleven victims, who were not even tied," says Ian Lilburn, a British historian who assisted Anna Anderson's lawyers during the Anastasia trials in Germany. "*One* assassin would have performed the task more easily, and indeed this would have more been consistent with the usual Bolshevik practice of shooting their victims individually in the back of the neck." Why this brisk and virtually foolproof mode of execution was not employed at Ekaterinburg on the most important political prisoners in Russia is only the first of many questions historians need to ask in confronting the unimaginable sloppiness of the crime. Equally puzzling is the fact that the murder of the imperial family was left in the hands of a drunken, sadistic band of thugs, so totally disorganized and incompetent that they afterward needed three whole days to bury the bodies. It is constantly claimed, in Soviet and western sources alike, that the Bolsheviks hoped "to hide all traces of the crime." If that is so, they chose a peculiar way to do it, involving as many people as possible in the murder, in the subsequent cleaning of the blood-stained cellar and especially in the disposal of the bodies. No murder in history could have been less secret than this, and it may be that the Bolsheviks' purported attempts to conceal it became the primary goal only when the full horror of the deed began to sink in — and when it became

This photograph of the murder room in the Ipatiev house plainly shows where the victims stood. It was taken after White Army investigators had dug out sections of the back wall and floor containing bullets and bayonet marks.

apparent, as it later on did, that two of the bodies were missing.

The original plan was to dispose of the imperial family's corpses speedily and permanently by tossing them down a mine shaft in the Koptyaki forest outside Ekaterinburg, an area of swamps and pits and disused mines. Commandant Yurovsky's famous "Note" describing the events (prepared two years after the fact and not published until 1989) is the nearest thing we have to a firsthand account of the burial. Despite its belated appearance and numerous internal contradictions, it confirms, if nothing else, the unrelieved distress and confusion of the next several days.

"Practically everything that could go wrong with the disposal of the bodies did go wrong," one commentator has said. "The burial squad repeatedly tried to pilfer the corpses — and was persuaded to desist only by the threat of summary execution. Nobody knew where the bodies were to be buried. Trucks either didn't show up or broke down at crucial moments. At one point Yurovsky fell off his horse, badly injuring himself." For a night and a day the bodies lay at the bottom of the Four Brothers mine at Koptyaki. But when it seemed that the whole of Ekaterinburg had discovered the whereabouts of the "secret" grave, Yurovsky ordered the corpses to be moved farther into the woods, where deeper mines could be found. Again the trucks broke down or got stuck in the mud, and finally the bodies of Russia's last imperial family were piled on top of one another and dumped in a hastily dug pit, only three feet deep, in a part of the forest by no means sequestered and in full view of the railway line. Some of the corpses were still bound with ropes, all had their faces smashed with rifle butts to prevent identification, and the grave itself was drenched with sulfuric acid to "prevent a stink" and to assist in the decomposition of the bodies. In his "Note" to the Kremlin,

Yurovsky described the effort of his burial squad to burn two of the corpses "apart from the others," ostensibly to make it more difficult for the Whites to identify the bodies by counting the deceased. "We wanted to burn A[lexei] and A[lexandra] F[eodorovna]," he reported, "but by mistake instead of her we burned the lady-in-waiting [Anna Demidova] and Alexei." No one has ever attempted a plausible explanation for this unlikely confusion of female corpses. For the time being, the Special Purpose had been fulfilled. "The world will never know what we did with them," a senior Bolshevik commissar is supposed to have remarked at the time. For seventy years the remaining bodies lay hidden in their shallow forest grave.

Three days after the murder, on July 20, 1918, with the White Army at the gates and the fall of the local Bolsheviks a foregone conclusion, the Ural soviet finally announced in Ekaterinburg that "the ex-Tsar, Nicholas Romanov, guilty before the people of innumerable crimes," had been shot on its own decision. "Romanov's family," said the Bolsheviks, had already been "transferred from Ekaterinburg to a place of greater safety." But in a coded telegram to Moscow (which many forensic experts regard as a forgery), the Ural soviet assured the Kremlin that "the entire family [had] met the same fate as the head," Nicholas. "Officially," the telegram read, the empress, Alexei and the savagely murdered girls would "perish in the evacuation."

*W*hen the Whites entered the Ipatiev house on July 25, 1918, they found it in disarray (above), with drawers open, their contents strewn about and, in the stoves, the remains of clothing that had been burned. (Opposite) The empress's wheelchair stands empty in a corner.

The refusal of the Bolsheviks to admit to the killing of the rest of the imperial family along with the tsar had the effect of keeping the monarchist faithful in suspense and led inevitably to tales of rescue and escape, some of them plausible, most of them bizarre, but none of them fully irrefutable in the absence of the corpses. When Ekaterinburg fell to the Whites on July 25, not to be recaptured by the Bolsheviks until the following year, a military investigation into the disappearance of the family was launched under the direction of General Michael K. Dieterichs, a rabidly anti-Bolshevik right-wing officer of Admiral Kolchak's Siberian forces. "Joan of Arc in riding breeches," his subordinates called him. His chief aspiration, much to the discredit of the Whites, was to blame the murder of the imperial family on "the Jews" and their imaginary overlords, "the Elders of Zion." It took General Dieterichs two unsuccessful tries before he found a magistrate who was prepared to bow to what he called a "political command" — that is, to make religious martyrs out of the Romanovs. The man finally chosen for the work was Nicholas Sokolov, a former assistant judge of the court of assizes at Omsk, whose deeply pious and otherwise painstaking forensic report was eventually published in Paris as the *Enquête judiciaire sur l'assassinat de la famille impériale russe* (Judicial Investigation into the Murder of the Russian Imperial Family). For many years Sokolov's report remained the standard account of the murder, until the Soviets fell in 1991 and the secrets of the Kremlin began to unravel.

So far, nothing has emerged from the archives of the late Soviet government that substantially contradicts the central conclusion of the Sokolov report: that the whole imperial family was shot, if not killed, in the Ipatiev house. Russian archives are a labyrinth, however, scattered among a number of official bureaus and ministries in Moscow and St. Petersburg and designed by the Soviets as much to confuse and obfuscate the truth as to enlighten anyone. The archives are like a smiling *matrioshka* doll, one layer hidden inside another, and so far as the murder of the imperial family is concerned, information is still trickling out. It will be years, if ever, before a thoroughly accurate picture of the murder can be formed. Sokolov's report, of course, was based on circumstantial evidence. He never found a single undisputed eyewitness to the murder of the family or a trace of their mortal remains — major drawbacks if the goal of the investigation, mandated by the White Army, was to prove the family's death in a legal, dynastic and religious sense.

Sokolov's explanation for the total disappearance of the bodies, while utterly preposterous, was accepted for years by most historians in the absence of anything better. The bodies had been hacked to pieces, Sokolov said, soaked in gasoline and burned on bonfires; what remained after burning was "dissolved in sulfuric acid" (a sheer impossibility in the absence of test tubes and proper laboratory conditions) and tossed down the shaft of the Four Brothers mine, where the corpses had in fact briefly lain. Apparently the Bolsheviks had burned the imperial family's clothes and other effects at the opening of the shaft, leaving a conspicuous display of hooks and eyes, belt buckles, rings and other jewelry scattered quite openly on the ground. No attempt had been made to conceal them or to clean up the debris, perhaps in an effort to divert the Whites' attention from the site of the final grave a few miles away. How Inspector Sokolov could have overlooked the grave itself remains incomprehensible: there is even a photograph of the site in his *Enquête judiciaire*, but the search for corpses was limited to the area in and around the Four Brothers.

All sorts of "evidence" began to appear at the mineshaft in huge profusion only *after* Sokolov

The muddy road in the Koptyaki forest where the corpses of the tsar's family were taken for burial.

got to work: bits of human "epidermis," a handful of charred "mammal bones," a denture that ostensibly had belonged to Dr. Botkin and somebody's missing index finger, which Sokolov, in an leap of pure monarchist fancy, declared to be that of the empress. In the meantime, all testimony suggesting that one or the other of the Romanovs had survived the carnage in the Ipatiev house — and there was plenty of it — was suppressed in Sokolov's concluding report, including the statements of eighteen witnesses from the city of Perm who declared that Empress Alexandra and all of her daughters had still been alive at Perm in September 1918, two months after their supposed deaths. Within weeks of the murder Anastasia had already been "sighted" many times — in prisons, hospitals, convents and peasants' huts — and was well on her way to mythical status. So many witnesses eventually came forward who remembered the Bolsheviks' frenzied search for the missing grand duchess that in less controversial circumstances it would undoubtedly have been accepted as a fact of history. One of the more credible and disinterested testimonies came from Count Carl Bonde, sent by the Swedish foreign ministry to inspect prisoner-of-war camps in Siberia during the civil war. Bonde declared, "In my capacity as the chief of the Swedish Red Cross mission in Siberia in 1918, I traveled in a private railway car. At some place, the name of which escapes my memory, the train was stopped and searched for the Grand Duchess Anastasia, daughter of Tsar Nicholas II. The Grand Duchess, however,

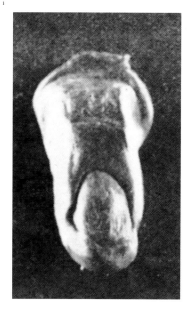

Investigators from the White Army look for traces of the family's remains at the Four Brothers Mine in the autumn of 1918. Among the evidence found was a finger (top), claimed to be one of the empress's, the burnt remains of six women's corsets (middle) and an ordinary belt buckle (below), thought to be identical to one worn by the tsar (bottom right).

was not aboard the train. Nobody knew where she had gone."

From the beginning, the rumors of escape focused on the two youngest children, Anastasia and Alexei. From the Whites' point of view, and remembering Russia's already well-established history of royal claimants and pretenders, the idea of a missing heir or heiress was a political nightmare. As if to squelch the legends once and for all, just in advance of the Bolsheviks' recapture of Ekaterinburg, more "evidence" turned up at the Four Brothers mine: wads of string, tinfoil, nails and the melted lead of a boy's toy soldiers, which Alexei had invariably carried around in his pockets; the burnt remains of six women's corsets, accounting all too obviously for the six women who supposedly perished in the Ipatiev house (as if the maid, Demidova, would have worn the same make of lingerie as the empress); and finally the children's spaniel, Jimmy, whose battered carcass, in a state of near-perfect preservation, suddenly appeared at the bottom of the mineshaft months after the imperial family's murder (the dog plainly had been dead only a few weeks when it was found). Swiftly, too, the Whites concocted the story of Anastasia carrying Jimmy in her arms on the night of the murder, though not one of the guards or soldiers mentioned anything about a dog in their records of the crime. Hereafter the luckless spaniel, whom Anna Viroubova had actually presented to Grand Duchess Tatiana at Tsarskoe Selo, became known as Anastasia's pet, the better to link the death of the grand duchess with the dog's.

As for Alexei, a claimant to his name and title appeared in Siberia as early as August 1918, only to be exposed by Pierre Gilliard, who went on to a long career as the Russian monarchist community's primary exposer of imperial fakes and as the world's preeminent (through strictly self-appointed) expert on the life and death of

The dowager empress on board HMS Marlborough *as she sailed into exile in April 1919.*

the last Romanovs. Gilliard certainly had his work cut out for him. From 1918 even until the present day an astonishing parade of pretenders, male and female, have claimed to be a child of Nicholas II.

In one case — and one alone — the claim may even have been authentic.

The Bolsheviks looked farther afield than Ekaterinburg in their effort to annihilate every living member of the Romanov family — "the former dynasty," as they inevitably called it. In June 1918 the tsar's brother Michael was shot in the woods at Perm; his body was never recovered. Alexandra's sister Ella was held for some time in and around the Urals, imprisoned in the company of Grand Duke Serge Mikhailovitch and four young Romanov princes. On July 18, just one day after the murder of "poor Alicky" at Ekaterinburg, Ella and the others were hurled alive down the shaft of an abandoned mine at Alapayevsk and left to die of their injuries, starvation and exposure. Ella died an Orthodox nun, the mother superior of a convent in Moscow and a martyr to the faith. At this writing she is the only member of the imperial family to have been canonized in Russia.

Altogether, seventeen of the Romanovs were murdered in the Revolution, while about twice that number managed to escape, some with ease and some with difficulty, some with money and some without. The tsar's decision to banish both Felix Yussupov and Grand Duke Dmitri for their role in the murder of Rasputin had the effect of saving their lives. They found themselves in the south of the former empire, where no member of the family fell permanently or tragically into Bolshevik hands. The tsar's sister Olga virtually walked out of the country through the Caucasus with her "commoner" husband, Colonel Nicholas Kulikovsky, and their infant sons. His mother, the dowager

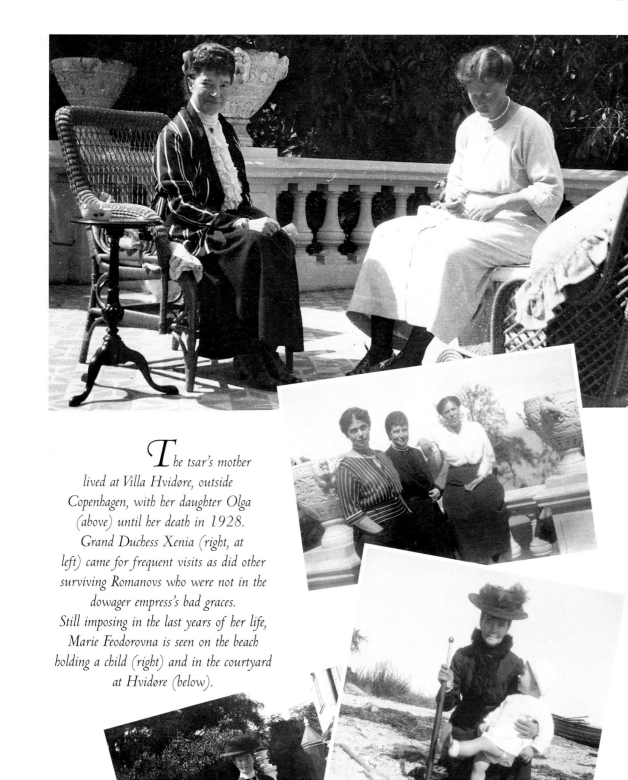

empress, with her daughter Xenia and Xenia's family, were rescued from the Crimea by Marie Feodorovna's nephew, George V; we may assume the King of England was suffering certain pangs of conscience over his failure to help "dear Nicky" at a moment when it might have made a difference. In April 1919, alarmed by reports of violence at Ekaterinburg, the king sent the HMS *Marlborough* to Yalta out of concern for "Aunt Minnie" and his Russian cousins. Even then, with the Bolsheviks about to recapture the Crimean peninsula, the dowager empress would not leave until everyone who wanted to go with her had got safely on board. Some six thousand Russian aristocrats thus sailed into permanent exile at British expense. It was the last time anyone heard "God Save the Tsar" played for the de facto head of the Romanov dynasty.

The dowager empress, after an extended stay in England with her sister, Queen Alexandra, eventually returned to her native Denmark. Following some "unsatisfactory" experiences as a guest in the Danish royal palace, she retired to Villa Hvidøre, a windswept mansion overlooking the Baltic on a hill above Copenhagen. Here she remained in effective seclusion until her death in 1928, at the age of eighty-one, looked after by her daughter Olga (whom she bullied mercilessly) and taking no part in the agonized, often ludicrous disagreements of the Romanov family in exile. She refused to endorse any potential claimant to the Russian throne, and never accepted the main conclusions of the Sokolov report, which determined the deaths of both her sons and her five imperial grandchildren. "It may have been pride," said her son-in-law, Grand Duke Alexander, who lived out most of his exile with his mistress in the south of France. "It may have been affection. It may have been superstition. But it was also statecraft. Until the titular head of the House of Romanov admitted that the throne was vacant, all claimants to *(continued on page 208)*

The tsar's mother lived at Villa Hvidøre, outside Copenhagen, with her daughter Olga (above) until her death in 1928. Grand Duchess Xenia (right, at left) came for frequent visits as did other surviving Romanovs who were not in the dowager empress's bad graces. Still imposing in the last years of her life, Marie Feodorovna is seen on the beach holding a child (right) and in the courtyard at Hvidøre (below).

(continued on page 208)

GRAND DUCHESS OLGA

Nicholas II's youngest sister, Grand Duchess Olga Alexandrovna, was the simplest, the most original and undoubtedly the most beloved member of the Romanov family in exile. In 1901, as a girl of nineteen (left), she had been pushed by her mother into marriage with a cousin fourteen years her elder. But the marriage was never consummated and in 1916, with the tsar's blessing, she married the man she had loved for some years, Colonel Nicholas Kulikovsky (oval inset). In February 1920 they escaped from Russia with their two sons Tikhon and Guri (above) and joined Dowager Empress Marie at Hvidøre. After her mother's death (and the sale of her jewels), Olga and the colonel purchased a dairy farm in Denmark. In 1945 the family immigrated to Canada, living on a farm outside Toronto. With advancing age, Olga and her husband moved to a bungalow near Cooksville, Ontario, where the colonel died in 1958. Two years later Olga herself was in failing health. On November 24, 1960, the woman born "in the purple" at the palace of Gatchina died in a small apartment above a Toronto barbershop.

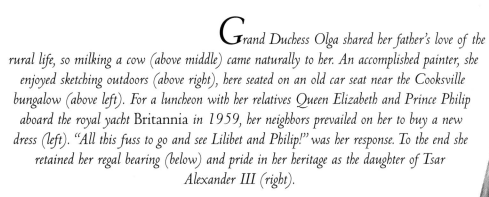

Grand Duchess Olga shared her father's love of the rural life, so milking a cow (above middle) came naturally to her. An accomplished painter, she enjoyed sketching outdoors (above right), here seated on an old car seat near the Cooksville bungalow (above left). For a luncheon with her relatives Queen Elizabeth and Prince Philip aboard the royal yacht Britannia in 1959, her neighbors prevailed on her to buy a new dress (left). "All this fuss to go and see Lilibet and Philip!" was her response. To the end she retained her regal bearing (below) and pride in her heritage as the daughter of Tsar Alexander III (right).

the throne were in the position of pretenders."

By 1921 there were something like two million Russian refugees in Europe, with a significant monarchist presence in London, Paris and Berlin. At the time, naturally enough, no one imagined that the Soviet regime would last, and everyone wanted to be ready when the moment came to pack their bags and go home. "We had been chased from the stage still wearing our brilliant costumes," said the thoughtful Grand Duchess Marie Pavlovna. "We had to make new ones now, and, above all, learn how to wear them."

Hardly anyone did. Marie Pavlovna herself worked for a time as a designer's assistant to Coco Chanel, and her brother, Grand Duke Dmitri, refusing till he died to talk about his role in the murder of Rasputin, sold champagne in Florida before marrying an American heiress, Audrey Emery of Cincinnati, Ohio. Most of the Romanovs who escaped from Russia were penniless in exile, not that pennies ever made much sense to them. A small book could be written about their financial misadventures after the Revolution. "They didn't know a ruble from a kopeck," said a niece of Nicholas II, a Romanov princess who had the good fortune to marry an American with money. The tsar's sister Xenia proved especially adept at falling victim to swindles (and bringing lawsuits to recover what she could). She lived out her life as a guest of the British royal family in Wilderness House, a cottage at Hampton Court lent to her by George V. Both of Nicholas's sisters kept themselves entirely aloof from monarchist politics — so much so that when one of Xenia's grandsons,

signing the guest book at a wedding in London, entered his name as "Prince Alexander Romanov," she crossed it out and wrote in its place, "A. Romanov, Esq."

But keeping the flame alive and adhering to the legitimate principle was the goal of almost every homesick Russian in exile. The politics of the emigration took an increasingly rightist turn through the 1920s and 1930s, when a number of Adolf Hitler's early supporters in Germany were Russian generals, barons, counts and grand dukes who hoped that the führer's noisy opposition to "Bolshevism" might provide them with the means to get home. By the end of the twenties, three grand dukes had been put forward as potential rulers of a reborn monarchist Russia: the tsar's second cousin, Grand Duke Nicholas Nicholaievitch, the most popular and sensible candidate, who wisely stayed above the fray; Grand Duke Dmitri, who was probably endorsed for his Hollywood looks; and Grand Duke Kyril, who would have been the rightful heir to the throne were it not for certain dynastic technicalities (his mother had not been Orthodox at the time of his birth) and the red armband he had worn during the March revolution. (Kyril had the added distinction of being married to the dead empress's ex-sister-in-law, the hated "Ducky," who had divorced Alexandra's brother Ernie in 1901 and married the grand duke in defiance of the tsar.) In 1922 Kyril gave himself the dubious title of "Protector of the Russian Throne." Two years later he outraged the majority of his compatriots in exile by declaring himself Emperor and Autocrat of All the Russias.

Most of the Romanovs who escaped the Revolution found themselves penniless in exile. The tsar's cousin Boris endorsed a brand of cigarettes (left). Prince George, son of Grand Duke Constantine (top), sold lamps. Grand Duke Dmitri Pavlovitch, a conspirator in the murder of Rasputin, married an American heiress, Audrey Emery (above), and lived in Palm Beach.

*G*rand Duke Kyril (top, with his wife, Victoria "Ducky," and son Vladimir) granted titles to those who supported his claim to be "emperor-in-exile." All three members of the family shown above have recently been interred in the Cathedral of Peter and Paul in St. Petersburg. Grand Duchess Xenia (above) was granted a grace-and-favor house at Hampton Court and died in 1960, a few months before her sister, Olga.

It was the one time the dowager empress broke her silence in Copenhagen and denounced a member of the family. "My heart was painfully depressed," she wrote in an open letter to Grand Duke Nicholas. "If it should please the Almighty to take unto Himself my beloved sons and grandson [Alexei], I believe that the future Emperor will be designated by our fundamental laws in unison with the Orthodox Church and altogether with the Russian people."

That they were all still thinking and talking about "the people" and "the laws" may be viewed as a given of political exile, even, in this case, as a symptom of shock. "All our conversation still turned around one subject — the past," wrote Grand Duchess Marie Pavlovna. "This past was like a dusty diamond which we held to the light in the hope of seeing the sun rays play through it. We spoke of the past, we looked back to it. And speaking of the past we sought for no lessons but tirelessly and aimlessly went over old ground seeking whom to blame for what had befallen us." Among the more honest monarchists, it was the empress who took the full force of her former subjects' considerable hostility. "That woman made a rag out of Nicky," the tsar's sister Xenia complained in exile. "She was never really one of us. She wouldn't even speak Russian unless she absolutely had to." Only Alexandra's murder at Ekaterinburg was able to transform her in the Russian mind into the sweet, pious, righteous tsarina she had all along desired to be. Only the perceived martyrdom of the entire family kept the bitterest resentments at bay. At a memorial service for the imperial family in Paris in the early twenties, looking around him at the huge crowd of weeping Russians in the church (not one of whom had lifted a finger to save the imperial family at the time of the Revolution), Gleb Botkin asked a neighbor what he thought

would happen if the tsar should suddenly walk into the room, alive and well and ready to assert his rights.

"They would do their best to murder him again," his friend replied.

Into this atmosphere of family resentment and political hallucination stepped "Anna Anderson," the woman who claimed until her death in 1984 to be Grand Duchess Anastasia. It was Anna Anderson who made Anastasia famous; her life was the subject of at least a dozen books, thousands of newspaper and magazine articles, five plays, three films (one of which won Ingrid Bergman an Oscar in 1956) and a dark ballet by Kenneth MacMillan that has become part of the permanent repertory at Covent Garden. No other claimant in the long and colorful history of royal pretenders has ever been taken so seriously by so many people, or come as close as Mrs. Anderson did to proving her case. Her suit for legal recognition as the daughter of the tsar occupied the German courts for nearly forty years and ended in a draw in February 1970, when the West German supreme court at Karlsruhe declared the case legally unresolved, "neither established nor refuted."

In the same ruling the judges affirmed that "the death of Grand Duchess Anastasia at Ekaterinburg cannot be accepted as a conclusively proven historical fact." Up to that point, before the opening of the Kremlin archives, the German courts had examined more evidence and heard more witnesses on the subject of the murder of the tsar and his family than any other body in the world, including Nicholas Sokolov and the White Army magistrates in Siberia. Though hardly a victory, it was a significant achievement for a woman whose opponents maintained with equal conviction that she was actually Franziska Schanzkowska, a former Polish factory worker who had lost her mind in a grenade explosion during the First World War. But it left Mrs. Anderson in a legal and historical limbo. Her only comment when the Karlsruhe verdict came down was characteristically taciturn: "We go on."

The judgment of the West German supreme court came fifty years to the day after the suicide attempt that is the first record of Anna Anderson's existence. On February 17, 1920, a young woman was rescued from the waters of the Landwehr Canal in Berlin, where she had evidently thrown herself in a moment of despair. Examined by the police, she refused to divulge any information about her identity and challenged them almost defiantly to discover who she was. "If people knew who I am," she declared, "I would not be here." The authorities noted at the time that she seemed "about twenty" years of age — Anastasia herself would have been eighteen and a half; that she spoke German badly, with a strong "eastern" accent; and that her body was covered with scars — "many lacerations," said the doctor's report. Her skull had been fractured (though the X rays proving this disappeared mysteriously in the wake of the scandal her claim provoked) and in at least four places — at the back of the head, in the arm, the chest and the foot — she had plainly been stabbed. Other experts later affirmed that the star-shaped scar that pierced Mrs. Anderson's right foot from top to bottom conformed exactly in shape and appearance to the mark that would have been left by the particular make of bayonet used in Russia during the First World War (and, of course, during the Revolution).

But the woman would not tell the Berlin police where the scars had come from. After weeks of stubborn silence she was taken to a public mental asylum where she remained for more than two years as a "depressed case" under the moniker "Miss Unknown." Only in March 1922, by which

time the Russian monarchist community in Berlin had been alerted to her existence, did the claim emerge that she was Anastasia, and it is not entirely clear that she herself was the first one who made it. Throughout her life, to a very real degree, Mrs. Anderson's claim was advanced on

$\mathcal{T}$*he first known photographs of Anna Anderson were mug shots taken by the Berlin police (opposite) after her appearance in Germany in 1920. She had tried to drown herself in the Landwehr Canal and refused to provide any information about her identity.*

Grand Duchess Anastasia (above) in the park at Tsarskoe Selo in 1916. (Above right) Anna Anderson in 1974 in Charlottesville, Virginia. (Above far right) A formal court photograph of Anastasia taken during the 1913 tercentenary.

her behalf by friends, lawyers and champions who thought it a high honor to be allowed to fight her battles. ("Anderson," of course, was an alias, picked out of a hat in 1928 in order to avoid reporters.) Mrs. Anderson seemed completely unconcerned about convincing the world of the truth of her story. She never once entered the courtroom, for instance, during her endless suits for recognition. She refused to provide a coherent account of her purported escape from Ekaterinburg, often declining to meet important witnesses who had come to see her, and refusing to speak Russian, unfortunately for her, except "spontaneously," under narcosis or when she was reasonably sure she was not being "tested." Plainly she knew the Russian language — no one in the early days of the controversy ever disputed this — and until her opponents had thoroughly muddied the waters with their talk of Polish peasants, the German authorities regarded Mrs. Anderson as a Russian national.

"Why will you not speak Russian?" asked Princess Xenia Georgievna — a daughter of Grand Duke George Mikhailovitch who had played with Anastasia as a child — in 1928. Mrs. Anderson answered with a remark that made the princess's blood run cold: "Because it was the last language we heard in that house." No one doubted that whoever she was, she had been traumatized, but the records of her life can be searched from top to bottom without finding a doctor or a psychiatrist who believed she was insane. She was not, though nervous breakdowns and a variety of despotic tantrums committed her to rest homes more than once in her life.

For many who remembered Anastasia as a child — the lively, merry, mischievous daughter of Russia's gloomiest rulers — it was difficult, and in most cases impossible, for them to recognize her in the emaciated, paranoid, ghostly figure whom they now saw before them. Her early supporters had enjoyed no substantial

connection with the Russian court and were thought to have endorsed her claim only with an eye toward obtaining a share of the legendary Romanov fortune, thought at that time to lie on deposit in the Bank of England. It was only in 1925, when Mrs. Anderson met the German crown princess, Cecile of Prussia (whose own mother was a Russian grand duchess, a sister of "Sandro," Alexander Mikhailovitch), that the case exploded into controversy and international attention.

"She looks like Xenia," the crown princess declared (meaning Nicholas II's sister). "I almost believe that it must be Anastasia." Others who had known the young Anastasia in Russia were frankly bowled over by the claimant's stunning resemblance to *all* the tsar's daughters, and the distinctly "royal" manner in which she comported herself from first day to last. No one who knew Mrs. Anderson with any degree of intimacy ever doubted that she was Somebody. Her astonishing inside knowledge about the private life of the Russian imperial family, moreover, was such that she was frequently able to identify photographs, mementos and events that no one else could. This left her in a peculiar double bind, of course, since without documentary support she was unable to prove her own assertions, while with it she could be — and was accused of — "studying" for her role.

It was Mrs. Anderson who first asserted, in 1925, that the empress's brother Ernie, the grand duke of Hesse, had made a secret trip to Tsarskoe Selo during the First World War in order to discuss a separate peace with the tsar. Over the years her story was confirmed by one important witness after another, including the family of the German kaiser and (in private, because in public they were cowards) most of the Romanovs. Her allegation earned her the permanent enmity of the grand duke and his descendants, not one of whom ever saw her but who became the prime

As a child Anastasia liked to take photographs of herself in the mirror (below). Anna Anderson also enjoyed doing this (bottom), although in 1928, when this picture was taken, she could not have seen the Romanov family photograph albums. (Opposite left) Anna Anderson in 1930 in New York City. (Opposite right) Anastasia at Tsarskoe Selo just after the revolution in 1917.

movers in an increasingly reckless effort to prove her a fraud. During the legal battles that marked the later stages of her life, the house of Hesse, represented after the death of the grand duke in 1937 by Empress Alexandra's nephew, Louis Mountbatten, spent "thousands of pounds" to fight her in court. Just before his own assassination by IRA terrorists in 1979, when a forensic study of the shape of Anna Anderson's ears concluded "with 100% certainty" that she was indeed Anastasia, an angry Russian cousin confronted Lord Mountbatten in London and asked him "how he had dared" to fight the woman so bitterly and so long when he had never set eyes on her in his life.

"We were told she was an impostor," Mountbatten replied — the usual answer among royalty whenever the issue was pressed.

Two of the main problems in resolving the case were the absence of witnesses who had known the tsar's daughters well, on the one hand, and who enjoyed authority within the Romanov family, on the other. The central witnesses were dead — Anastasia's parents, sisters and brother — and among the hordes of her relations all over Europe hardly one had known Anastasia well enough, or late enough in her life, to reach a definite conclusion. Contrary to popular belief, the dowager empress never met Mrs. Anderson and eventually refused even to hear her name mentioned in the room. Within the imperial family it was well known that the dowager's entourage in Denmark was worried about the effect Mrs. Anderson's claim might have on an old woman who still clung to the hope that all her grandchildren might be alive in Russia. "One was sacrificed to save the other," said one of the Romanovs — a remark made somewhat easier to bear by the fact that Mrs. Anderson was thought to be dying through most of the 1920s (she suffered from tuberculosis of the bones), and in any case was being supported financially by the dowager empress's brother, Prince Waldemar of Denmark. All of her life she was taken care of by one royal or noble personage or another. At Prince Waldemar's urging the tsar's sister Olga met Mrs. Anderson in 1925, but was so "agonized" by the responsibility of making a decision — and of confronting her mother with what might be a devastating truth — that she finally dropped out of the case altogether, signing affidavits in which she denounced Mrs. Anderson as a fraud while sometimes, strangely, referring to her in private as "my niece." Everyone in the Romanov family knows that Olga "hesitated for months" before committing herself to the denial of Mrs. Anderson's identity; that she was inclined to accept her as Anastasia — "My reason cannot grasp it," she said, "but my heart tells me that she is" — and that she reneged only under pressure from her mother and senior members of the dynasty.

"I am sending you all my love, am thinking of you all the time," Olga wrote Mrs. Anderson in Berlin. "It is so sad to go away knowing that you are ill and suffering and lonely. Don't be anxious. You are not alone and we shall not abandon you." Recently discovered documents at Columbia University relating to Olga's meetings with Mrs. Anderson confirm beyond reasonable doubt that her original attitude was "favorable," but the results of two separate investigations of the case commissioned on behalf of the exiled Romanovs in the 1920s have been "confiscated" — one by the Danish royal family (as relatives of the dowager empress) and the other by the heirs of the "tsar" Kyril, whose hostility toward Mrs. Anderson needs no explanation.

Those who had been closest to the imperial family remained divided. Both of the Botkin children, Tatiana and Gleb, met Mrs. Anderson and recognized her without reservation, and so did Lili Dehn years after the Revolution, when she visited Mrs. Anderson in Germany and experienced the surprise of her life.

"I had a shock," said Lili in her sworn affidavit, "a real shock when I first saw her — a poor, pale and wrinkled little face!"

Anna and Lili stayed together for six days talking about Tsarskoe Selo, about rugs in the palace and curtains on the walls. Looking at black-and-white pictures, Mrs. Anderson accurately named the color of a dress the empress was wearing, and by the time Lili left, she was a convert. "Do not bother to tell me that she has read these things in books," Lili said. "I have recognized her, physically and intuitively, through signs that do not deceive." Sydney Gibbes, on the other hand, who saw the claimant around the same time, was equally certain she was a fraud.

"If that's Grand Duchess Anastasia," Gibbes exclaimed, "I'm a Chinaman." Anna Viroubova kept away, much to the relief of both sides in the quarrel, and in the end, at least while Mrs. Anderson was alive, the matter degenerated into the realm of pure allegation, with one witness saying yes, the other saying no, and the claimant herself increasingly bitter and out of touch with reality. In 1968, after the loss of her last court case but one, she immigrated to America at the invitation of Gleb Botkin and shortly afterward married John E. Manahan of Charlottesville, Virginia, a local historian and genealogist almost as eccentric as she, who looked after her for the rest of her life.

Asked by a reporter if she would ever give up her claim, she pounded the table in front of her and exclaimed, "Never! To my last. No, no, no, no." She died in 1984 in Charlottesville and was cremated at her own request, leaving nothing behind but an outraged controversy and some tiny, faded locks of her hair.

❧

None of the main participants in the drama of Nicholas and Alexandra lived to see the fall of the Soviet Union, the advent of a tenuous democracy in Russia or the exhumation, in 1991, of the battered and broken skeletons of the tsar's family. The whereabouts of the secret grave had been known since at least 1976, when a team of "amateur sleuths" in Ekaterinburg, for reasons that are still unclear and with information that must have come from inside sources at the Kremlin, tracked it down. The discovery coincided almost exactly with the destruction of the Ipatiev house, which had stood as a museum of the "National Vengeance" during the 1920s and later as a simple reminder of the darkest days of the Revolution. In 1977 — again, for reasons impossible to divine — the house was bulldozed on the order of Boris Yeltsin, an Ekaterinburg native and at that time Communist Party chief in the city. Later Yeltsin referred to the demolition of the historic site as "an act of barbarism" and, as everyone sooner or later does in Russia, blamed it on Moscow.

Not until twelve years later, in 1989, was the discovery of the Romanovs' grave made public in an article by Geli Ryabov, a well-known crime writer in Russia and formerly an "official researcher" at the ministry of the interior in Moscow. "I felt that I was somehow responsible for all the cruelty in my country's history," Ryabov explained. "I decided it was my duty to discover the truth about the execution and burial of the Romanovs, and to tell people." In innumerable interviews and press conferences in Russia and abroad, Ryabov insisted that all eleven bodies were accounted for — the seven

The Ipatiev house was destroyed in 1977 (opposite) on orders from Boris Yeltsin, then Communist Party chief in Sverdlovsk (Ekaterinburg). (Below) Workers demolishing the house stand near the window of the basement room where the imperial family was killed.

members of the imperial family and their four servants — and that rumors, legends, court cases and claimants could all be put on the shelf. Western historians and journalists were jubilant at the news, since it seemed to vindicate their own intractable skepticism when it came to the murder of the Romanovs and offered the promise of peace at last on the Russian imperial front. When his story hit the newspapers Geli Ryabov was dramatically photographed like Hamlet, scowling and holding a skull in his hands, which he claimed was Alexei's. So far, however, no one but Ryabov and his team in Ekaterinburg had seen the skeletons, much less taken steps to determine their authenticity.

Two years went by before the grave was opened again, this time to reveal what Yurovsky's "Note" long ago had reported. Contrary to Ryabov's claim, two of the bodies were missing — Alexei's and "one of the grand duchesses'" (not the empress and not Anna Demidova, as Yurovsky had stupidly claimed). The result, in Russia, was a sudden explosion of Alexeis and Anastasias — aged men and women in all parts of the country clamoring to be considered claimants after decades of forced separation from their own history. No serious evidence of

any kind has emerged to shed light on the possible fate of the tsarevitch, though Radzinsky, in *The Last Tsar*, his best-selling narrative of Nicholas II's life and death, pinpoints a specific moment on the night of the murder, as the truck bearing the imperial family's corpses to the grave was stalled for some time in the darkness when one or another of the tsar's children might have been spirited away. It is farfetched, but no more so than Prince Felix Yussupov's account of the murder of Rasputin, which most historians continue to accept as an article of faith. The point about a miraculous escape is that it *is* miraculous, unexpected and logically inexplicable. It is hardly to be imagined that the Bolsheviks, in 1918 or at any time in the future, would have wanted the world to know how badly they had botched the "Special Purpose."

The missing bodies, in any case, have never been found, nor any trace of the "nearby" bonfire on which they were supposedly cremated. In 1992 the regional government in Ekaterinburg — the

successors to the old Ural soviet — called in a team of American forensic experts to see if the other skeletons might be formally identified. The invitation was issued without consulting Moscow, however, where a national investigation was already underway at Yeltsin's command and a state funeral was being planned should the bones turn out to be genuine. When the American team, headed by Dr. William Maples of the C. A. Pound Human Identification Laboratory at the University of Florida in Gainesville, unequivocally concluded that Anastasia's body was the one that was missing, Russian pride and the honor of Russian science were both deeply wounded.

"All the skeletons appear to be too tall to be Anastasia," said Dr. Maples at a press conference in Ekaterinburg. It was not just a question of her height. Anastasia had just turned seventeen at the time of the murder, and the bones of the three other daughters in the grave showed "completed growth," Maples said. Under international fire in the press, and against all objections from their

Russian colleagues, Dr. Maples and his team stuck to their conclusions: *if* the bodies in the Koptyaki forest were the Romanovs', the missing grand duchess could only be Anastasia.

The news was a major sensation in Europe and the United States, where the mystery of Anastasia and the life of Anna Anderson were far better known than in Russia. Under the Soviets, all references to and speculation about the life and death of the imperial family had been discouraged, even forbidden. Now, as Russians awoke to the prospect of democracy, it seemed to many of them — and especially to forensic specialists in Moscow — that a "Western" legend was being foisted on them, that they were being deprived of the chance to write their own history by reaching their own conclusions. Thus it was no surprise to anyone when, eventually, the Moscow scientists insisted it was Marie, not Anastasia, who was missing from the grave. This brought to four the number of women who may have been "burned

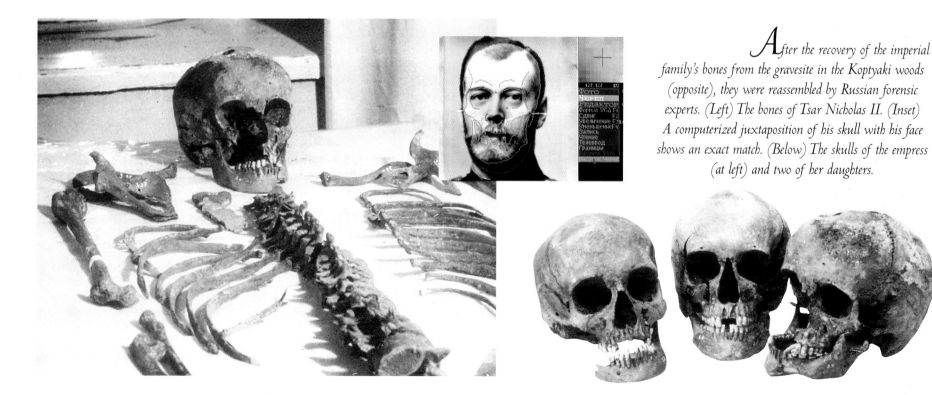

After the recovery of the imperial family's bones from the gravesite in the Koptyaki woods (opposite), they were reassembled by Russian forensic experts. (Left) The bones of Tsar Nicholas II. (Inset) A computerized juxtaposition of his skull with his face shows an exact match. (Below) The skulls of the empress (at left) and two of her daughters.

separately" on Yurovsky's mythical bonfire.

On the heels of Dr. Maples's announcement, portions of the Ekaterinburg skeletons were flown to England, where, for nearly a year, they underwent sophisticated DNA analysis under the direction of Dr. Peter Gill at the British Home Office's Forensic Science Centre at Aldermaston. Prince Philip, the duke of Edinburgh and husband of Queen Elizabeth II, is a grandson of Empress Alexandra's sister Victoria. He agreed to give blood for the tests, and in July 1993 the British verdict came in: the DNA of the female corpses in the Ekaterinburg grave matched Philip's. It took a little longer to work on the tsar, whose DNA patterns revealed an unexpected "deviation" from the norm, but Nicholas, too, was finally identified when two members of the Romanov family in exile (both of whom have remained anonymous) also agreed to give blood.

Now there remained only the question of Anna Anderson's true identity. In 1979, five years before her death, a tiny portion of her small intestine had been removed during an emergency operation. To everyone's surprise, it still existed at Martha Jefferson Hospital in Charlottesville, and when it, too, along with the carefully preserved lock of her hair, was finally flown to England, the results were entirely negative. Mrs. Anderson's DNA bore no resemblance to the genetic pattern of the skeletons at Ekaterinburg. Her identity with Anastasia was thus "totally excluded" by the laws of science. Simultaneously, her genetic profile was seen to bear a marked similarity to the family of Franziska Schanzkowska, the missing Polish factory worker with whom opponents had long hoped to identify her.

It was a verdict Mrs. Anderson's supporters refused to accept. No one who had known her (including a large number of friends and witnesses who did not believe she was Anastasia) could seriously believe that she had been born and raised in a Polish peasant hut. Even the judges sent to interview her in Germany during her endless suit for recognition emerged with the comment, strictly off the record, that she was "a *lady*." Nor was the string of surprises quite over. In 1994, at the very moment the DNA experts concluded that Mrs. Anderson was not the tsar's daughter, new forensic comparisons of her face and ears with pictures of the young Anastasia, commissioned for a television documentary in England and following routine procedures of legal identification, reached exactly the opposite conclusion. The experiment was later successfully repeated by specialists in the United States, and their conclusions, too, were delivered with "certainty" — Anna Anderson *was* Anastasia. The DNA tests have won the hour, and will probably stand as the final word on a case that has left everyone who came near it, for or against, with a sense of tragedy and persistent, nagging doubts. Mrs. Anderson herself had predicted in the 1920s that she would go down in history as "an eternal question-mark," and she was right; she will.

⁂

As this book goes to press, a state funeral for the tsar and his family has been postponed several times, partly on account of the huge controversy that still surrounds the identification of their remains (DNA or no DNA). The current Russian fascination with the tsar and his family owes less to devotion than to curiosity and a nostalgic longing for the luxury of imperial times. The writer Tatiana Tolstaya, one of the very few level-headed Russian commentators on her country's contemporary culture, insists that the members of the imperial family are beloved for the moment only because they were "glamorous," because they had "such nice clothes" and because Russians enjoy a mystery as much as anyone else.

Regardless of the reasons for the delays, the

*T*he Cathedral of Peter and Paul in St. Petersburg is the traditional resting place of the Romanov tsars. (Inset) The crypt where every Russian emperor since Peter the Great has been buried.

burial of the last tsar, his family and the small band of retainers who died with them presents a thorny problem for the international committee that is trying to arrange for the family's interment at the Cathedral of Peter and Paul in St. Petersburg. First there is the question of who is actually being buried. Is the missing girl Anastasia — or Marie, as the Russians still publicly insist? Then there is the question of whether the whole imperial family should be buried together, and if so, should they be buried — to the horror of the majority of monarchists — with the servants who died with them? Traditionally only the sovereign and his consort were given tombs in the central mausoleum of the cathedral; the children, sisters, brothers and cousins of the emperors, if they were

*"Father asks to...
remember that the
evil which is now
in the world will
become yet more
powerful,
and that it is not
evil which
conquers evil, but
only love...."*

— Grand Duchess Olga,
in a letter from
Tobolsk.

buried in Russia at all, were relegated to the so-called grand-ducal chapel farther back in the church. And servants were never buried with their masters.

The only decent solution, of course, would be to bury *all* of the Ekaterinburg victims in one place, and to let them rest together as they did for more than seventy years in their forest grave. At Ekaterinburg's new museum of "contemporary times," not far from the former site of the Ipatiev house, a dual exhibit has been mounted, half of which honors the murder of the Romanovs and the other the fate of a single Russian family — the Tariks, Vladimir and Vera, Ural mineworkers whose lives were destroyed in the Stalinist terror of the 1930s.

"Why should these victims be set above the others?" Russians want to know in regard to the tsar and his children, who after all were only the first to be slaughtered in the general nightmare of this "scientific" century. Russia being Russia, however, and with people as they are, endless quarrels have already arisen over *where* the imperial family's remains should be interred: whether at Ekaterinburg, where a church is being built on the site of the Ipatiev house (it will be called *Khram na khrovu* in Orthodox custom — "The Church on the Blood"); in St. Petersburg; or at the Feodorovsky Sobor at Tsarskoe Selo, which Nicholas and Alexandra caused to be built in 1912 and where they worshiped almost daily in the short time that remained to them. Already a bust of the tsar has been erected outside the church, and prayers are said there daily for the repose of his soul, but the statue, alas, looks like any other Bolshevik commissar, scowling and stern, and reflects none of the emperor's famous

"gentleness" and refinement in the face. There is no monument to Alexandra.

Not far from the church at Tsarskoe, five pine trees were once planted to mark the birth of each of Nicholas II's children. In the nearly eighty years since the end of Romanov rule, one of these pines has died, or at any rate disappeared. Across the park, the Alexander Palace still stands in a state of near-total decrepitude, the only one of the Romanovs' imperial residences that was not restored by the Soviets to its full and former glory.

Through all the years since the death of the Russian imperial family, two images have remained in the public mind. One is the famous formal group photograph taken during the 1913 tercentenary; in it the empress is seated next to the tsar, Alexei sits in front in his sailor suit and the four daughters, in their white silk and pearls, stand protectively behind their parents. The other is the grisly snapshot of the cellar at Ekaterinburg after the White Army had driven the Bolsheviks out of town. The photograph shows the pitted walls from which the murderers' bullets had already been dug and the floor where the victims had stood, scattered with debris. The historian Richard Pipes, in his monumental account, *The Russian Revolution*, cites the murder of the Romanovs in July 1918 as the moment when history made a turn toward genocide, when "millions of nameless beings" were placed on a list of expendables and the world entered "an entirely new moral realm." That realm is with us still. In a world grown accustomed, even inured, to the slaughter of innocents, these seven faces and this fateful room might serve as epigraphs for all the horrors the twentieth century would hold in store.

*The Feodorovsky Sobor was built by
Nicholas and Alexandra on the grounds at Tsarskoe Selo as their private house of worship. A bust of
Nicholas has recently been erected there.*

THE RUSSIAN EMPIRE

During the reign of Nicholas II

Acknowledgments

Peter Kurth would like to thank the following: Michael Barnes, Carolyn Brunton, Susan Burkhart, Julia Cort, Jamie Du Pont, Marlene Eilers, Brooke Gladstone, Maria Happe, Maggi Hayes, Robert Kenner, Greg King, Constance S. Kurth, Richard and Virginia Kurth, Kathy Layton, Irina Lomasney, Victoria Lewis, Elena Lomasney-Thompson, Suzanne Massie, Robert K. Massie, Walter Miller, David Neiweem, Raphael Sagalyn, Dick and Marina (Botkin) Schweitzer, Frank Simeone and Nancy Leeds Wynkoop.

Peter Christopher wishes to acknowledge the following: Tatyana Yermolayeva, who opened doors that were often closed; Dr. Vladimir Matveyev who pounded his desk in the Hermitage Museum every time I made another request; Victor Faybisovitch, Deputy Director of Tsarskoe Selo, who gave me his valuable time and Aleksei Guszanov, Chief Curator at Pavlosk, who did the same. I also wish to thank Oliver Weeks of Yeovil, Somerset, my translator and friend during a cold St. Petersburg February; Vladimir and Serge, who risked their licences to fly me over the Alexander Palace; and certain military personnel and old ladies in various establishments who smuggled me into out-of-bounds rooms. As well, a special thanks to Andre, my driver and protector, who played rock and roll tapes louder than I would have liked.

Madison Press Books would like to acknowledge the assistance of Dr. Mark Steinberg, who acted as the historical consultant for this book, and to thank him for his expertise and sharp eye for detail. Lynn Franklin made possible Edvard Radzinsky's introduction to the book. For their assistance in providing images thanks are due to: Aliya Barkovets, Deputy Director of the State Archive of the Russian Federation, Moscow; Bibliotheque cantonale et universitaire, Lausanne; Sondra Bierre of the Hoover Institution Archives at Stanford University; Sir David and Lady Myra Butler, who kindly permitted access to Luton Hoo's archives; Paul Byington, who generously lent photos of Grand Duchess Olga; Frank Crane, who allowed objects from his collection to be photographed; Vincent Giroud and Ellen Cordes of the Beinecke Rare Book and Manuscript Library at Yale University; Alexandra Golovina, Director of the State Archive of Film and Photographic Documents, St. Petersburg; Robert Kenner, director of the National Geographic Television film "Russia's Last Tsar"; Bryan Milton and Zena Dickinson of Luton Hoo; Sergei Mironenko, Director of the State Archive of the Russian Federation, Moscow; Howell W. Perkins of the Virginia Museum of Fine Arts; Liudmila Protsai, Curator, State Archive of Film and Photographic Documents, St. Petersburg; John Provan, for researching photos of the young Alix of Hesse; Catherine Thomas of the Forbes Magazine Collection; Lyubov Tyutunnik, Curator, State Archive of the Russian Federation, Moscow; Maria Umali of the Gilman Paper Company; Andrei Vitol, for assistance with photo research in St. Petersburg. Deserving of special mention is Alla Savranskaia, whose ingenuity, skill and patience while sourcing images proved invaluable. Thanks also to Alison Reid for proofreading the text, Catherine Marjoribanks for the index and to the trustees of the Broadlands Archive.

A Genealogy Chart

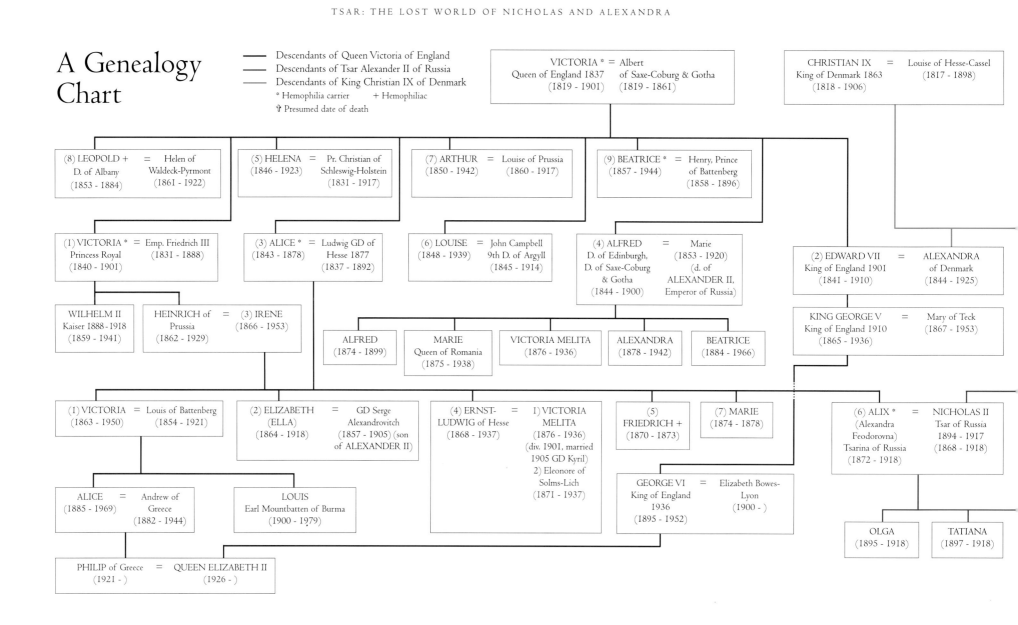

——— Descendants of Queen Victoria of England
——— Descendants of Tsar Alexander II of Russia
——— Descendants of King Christian IX of Denmark
° Hemophilia carrier   + Hemophiliac
✝ Presumed date of death

VICTORIA ° = Albert
Queen of England 1837   of Saxe-Coburg & Gotha
(1819 - 1901)   (1819 - 1861)

CHRISTIAN IX = Louise of Hesse-Cassel
King of Denmark 1863   (1817 - 1898)
(1818 - 1906)

(8) LEOPOLD +   =   Helen of
D. of Albany   Waldeck-Pyrmont
(1853 - 1884)   (1861 - 1922)

(5) HELENA   Pr. Christian of
(1846 - 1923)   Schleswig-Holstein
    (1831 - 1917)

(7) ARTHUR   =   Louise of Prussia
(1850 - 1942)   (1860 - 1917)

(9) BEATRICE °   =   Henry, Prince
(1857 - 1944)   of Battenberg
    (1858 - 1896)

(1) VICTORIA °   =   Emp. Friedrich III
Princess Royal   (1831 - 1888)
(1840 - 1901)

(3) ALICE °   =   Ludwig GD of
(1843 - 1878)   Hesse 1877
    (1837 - 1892)

(6) LOUISE   =   John Campbell
(1848 - 1939)   9th D. of Argyll
    (1845 - 1914)

(4) ALFRED   =   Marie
D. of Edinburgh,   (1853 - 1920)
D. of Saxe-Coburg   (d. of
& Gotha   ALEXANDER II,
(1844 - 1900)   Emperor of Russia)

(2) EDWARD VII   ALEXANDRA
King of England 1901   of Denmark
(1841 - 1910)   (1844 - 1925)

WILHELM II   HEINRICH of   =   (3) IRENE
Kaiser 1888-1918   Prussia   (1866 - 1953)
(1859 - 1941)   (1862 - 1929)

ALFRED   MARIE   VICTORIA MELITA   ALEXANDRA   BEATRICE
(1874 - 1899)   Queen of Romania   (1876 - 1936)   (1878 - 1942)   (1884 - 1966)
    (1875 - 1938)

KING GEORGE V   =   Mary of Teck
King of England 1910   (1867 - 1953)
(1865 - 1936)

(1) VICTORIA   =   Louis of Battenberg
(1863 - 1950)   (1854 - 1921)

(2) ELIZABETH   =   GD Serge
(ELLA)   Alexandrovitch
(1864 - 1918)   (1857 - 1905) (son
    of ALEXANDER II)

(4) ERNST-   =   1) VICTORIA
LUDWIG of Hesse   MELITA
(1868 - 1937)   (1876 - 1936)
    (div. 1901, married
    1905 GD Kyril)
    2) Eleonore of
    Solms-Lich
    (1871 - 1937)

(5)   (7) MARIE
FRIEDRICH +   (1874 - 1878)
(1870 - 1873)

(6) ALIX °   NICHOLAS II
(Alexandra   Tsar of Russia
Feodorovna)   1894 - 1917
Tsarina of Russia   (1868 - 1918)
(1872 - 1918)

ALICE   =   Andrew of
(1885 - 1969)   Greece
    (1882 - 1944)

LOUIS
Earl Mountbatten of Burma
(1900 - 1979)

GEORGE VI   =   Elizabeth Bowes-
King of England   Lyon
1936   (1900 -)
(1895 - 1952)

PHILIP of Greece   =   QUEEN ELIZABETH II
(1921 -)   (1926 -)

OLGA   TATIANA
(1895 - 1918)   (1897 - 1918)

Principal Works and Sources Consulted

❖ Alexander, Grand Duke of Russia. *Once a Grand Duke.* New York: Farrar and Rhinehart, 1932.

❖ Alexandra, Empress of Russia. *The Letters of the Tsaritsa to the Tsar.* London: Duckworth, 1923.

❖ Almedigen, E.M. *The Empress Alexandra.* London: Hutchinson, 1921.

❖ Benckendorff, Count Paul. *Last Days at Tsarskoe Selo.* London: Heinemann, 1927.

❖ Bokhanov, Alexander, Manfred Knodt, Vladimir Oustimenko, Zinaida Peregudova, and Lyubov Tyutunnik. *The Romanovs: Love, Power and Tragedy.* Italy: Keppi Productions, 1993.

❖ Botkin, Gleb. *The Real Romanovs.* New York: Fleming H. Revell, 1931.

❖ Botkin, Tatiana. *Vospominaniya o tsarskoi sem'i.* Belgrade: Stefanovich, 1921.

❖ ———. *Au temps des tsars.* Paris: Grasset, 1980.

❖ Buchanan, Meriel. *Dissolution of an Empire.* London: John Murray, 1932.

❖ Buxhoeveden, Baroness Sophie Karlovna. *The Life and Tragedy of Alexandra Feodorovna, Empress of Russia.* New York: Longmans, Green, 1928.

❖ Cowles, Virginia. *The Last Tsar.* New York: Putnam, 1977.

❖ de L'Escaille, Sidonie. *Papers relating to the Russian Imperial family.* Stanford, California: Hoover Institution on War, Revolution and Peace, Stanford University.

❖ de Grèce, Eugénie. *Le Tsarévitch: enfant martyr.* Paris: Perrin, 1990.

❖ de Jonge, Alex. *The Life and Times of Grigorii Rasputin.* New York: Coward, McCann and Geoghegan, 1982.

❖ Dehn, Lili. *The Real Tsaritsa.* Boston: Little, Brown, 1922.

❖ Grabbe, Count Alexander. *The Private World of the Last Tsar.* Edited by Paul Grabbe and Beatrice Grabbe. Boston: Little, Brown, 1984.

❖ Hough, Richard, ed. *Advice to my Grand-Daughter: Letters from Queen Victoria to Princess Victoria of Hesse.* New York: Simon & Schuster, 1969.

❖ Iroshnikov, Mikhail P., Yury B. Shilayev, and Liudmila A. Protsai. *Before the Revolution: St. Petersburg in Photographs, 1890-1914.* New York: Harry N. Abrams, 1991.

❖ ———. *The Sunset of the Romanov Dynasty.* Moscow: Terra Publishing Center, 1992.

❖ King, Greg. *The Last Empress: The Life and Times of Alexandra Feodorovna, Tsarina of Russia.* New York: Birch Lane Press, 1994.

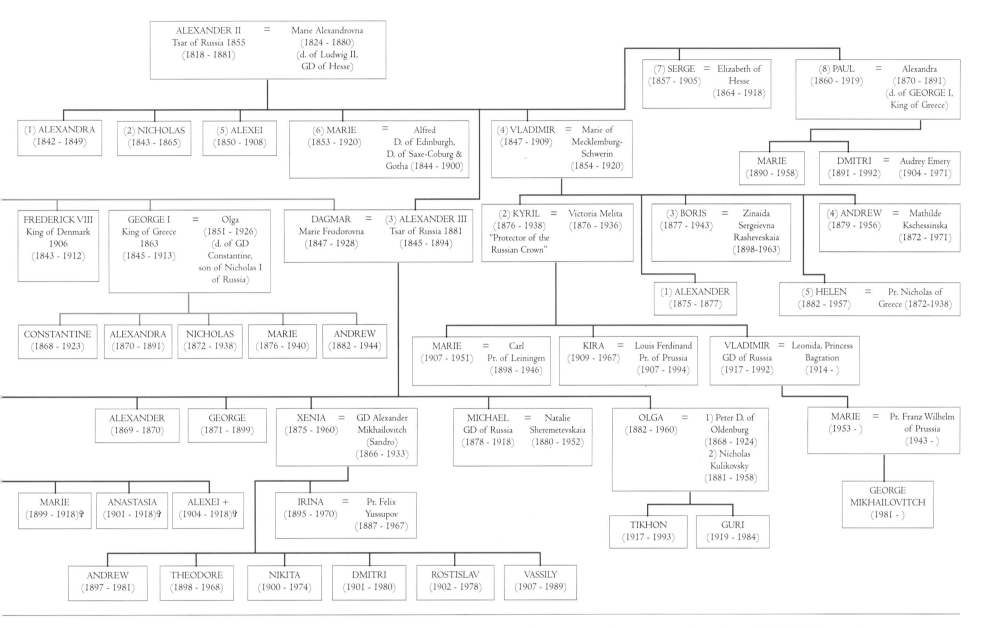

❖ Kurth, Peter. *Anastasia: The Riddle of Anna Anderson.* Boston: Little, Brown, 1983.

❖ ———. "The Mystery of the Romanov Bones." *Vanity Fair* (January 1993): 96+.

❖ Lieven, Dominic. *Nicholas II: Emperor of All the Russias.* London: John Murray, 1983.

❖ Lincoln, W. Bruce. *The Romanovs.* New York: Dial, 1981.

❖ ———. *In War's Dark Shadow.* New York: Dial, 1983.

❖ Lubov, Millar. *Grand Duchess Elizabeth of Russia: New Martyr of the Communist Yoke.* Redding, California: Kikodemos Orthodox Publication Society, 1991.

❖ Lyons, Marvin. *Nicholas II: The Last Tsar.* New York: St. Martin's Press, 1974.

❖ Maria Pavlovna, Grand Duchess of Russia. *A Princess in Exile.* New York: Viking Press, 1931.

❖ Marie, Princess of Greece. *A Romanov Diary.* New York: Atlantic International, 1988.

❖ Marie Louise, Princess of Schleswig-Holstein. *My Memories of Six Reigns.* New York: Dutton, 1957.

❖ Massie, Robert K. *Nicholas and Alexandra.* New York: Atheneum, 1967.

❖ ———. *The Romanov Family Album.* New York: The Vendome Press, 1982.

❖ Michael, Prince of Greece. *Imperial Palaces of Russia.* London: Tauris Parke Books, 1992.

❖ ———. *Nicholas and Alexandra: The Family Albums.* London: Tauris Parke Books, 1992.

❖ Mossolov, A.A. *At the Court of the Last Tsar.* London: Methuen, 1935.

❖ Moynan, Brian. *The Russian Century: A Photographic History of Russia's 100 Years.* New York: Random House, 1994.

❖ Naryshkin-Kurakin, Princess Elisabeth. *Under Three Tsars.* New York: Dutton, 1931.

❖ Oakley, Jane. *Rasputin: Rascal Master.* New York: St. Martin's Press, 1989.

❖ Pipes, Richard. *The Russian Revolution.* New York: Knopf, 1990.

❖ Radzinsky, Edvard. *The Last Tsar.* New York: Doubleday, 1992.

❖ Sokolov, Nicholas. *Enquête judiciare sur l'assassinat de la famille impériale russe.* Paris: Payot, 1924.

❖ Spiridovitch, Major General Alexander. *Les dernières années de la cour de Tsarskoïe-Selo.* Paris: Payot, 1928.

❖ Tisdall, E.E.P. *Maria Feodorovna: Empress of Russia.* New York: Day, 1958.

❖ Trewin, John. *The House of Special Purpose.* New York: Stein & Day, 1975.

❖ Vassilli, Paul [Princess Catherine Radziwill]. *Behind the Veil at the Russian Court.* London: Cassell, 1913.

❖ Viroubova, Anna. *Memories of the Russian Court.* New York: Macmillan, 1923.

❖ von Habsburg, Géza, and Marina Lopato. *Fabergé: Imperial Jeweller.* Italy: Zwemmer, 1993.

❖ Von Solodkoff, Alexander. *Masterpieces from the House of Fabergé.* New York: Harry N. Abrams, 1984.

❖ Vorres, Ivan. *The Last Grand-Duchess.* London: Hutchinson & Co., 1964.

Photograph & Illustration Credits

Every effort has been made to correctly attribute all material reproduced in this book. If any errors have unwittingly occurred, we will be happy to correct them in future editions.

All color photographs, unless otherwise designated, are by Peter Christopher © 1995.

Beinecke — Beinecke Rare Book and Manuscript Library, Yale University Library

Forbes — Forbes Magazine Collection, New York

Lausanne — Bibliothèque cantonale et universitaire, Lausanne, Fonds Gilliard, IS 1916

MEPL — Mary Evans Picture Library

Moscow — State Archive of the Russian Federation, Moscow

SP — State Archive of Film and Photographic Documents, St. Petersburg

VM — Virginia Museum of Fine Arts, Richmond, Virginia — Bequest from the Estate of Lillian Thomas Pratt

WCLH — Wernher Collection, The Luton Hoo Foundation

Front cover inset: Bettmann
Back cover (left) Moscow; (top right) Beinecke; (bottom right) Bridgeman/Art Resource
Endpapers UPI/Bettmann
3 (inset) Moscow
6–7 Moscow

CHAPTER ONE
11 SP
12 (top) Sovfoto; (bottom) Hillwood Museum, Washington, D.C.
13 SP
15 (right) Bridgeman/Art Resource; (all others) RIA-Novosti/Sovfoto
16 (all) Novosti
17 (top) WCLH; (bottom) SP
18 (top, bottom left) SP; (bottom right) Giraudon/Art Resource
19 (all) SP
20 (left) VM; (right) Hulton Deutsch Collection
22 SP
23 (inset) SP
24 (bottom) SP
25 (left, top left) Forbes — Photograph by Larry Stein; (top middle) VM; (top right) Forbes — Photograph by Peter Curran

CHAPTER TWO
26 (left) Novosti; (right) Broadlands Archive
28 (left) Beinecke; (top right, bottom right) Stadtarchiv der Stadt Darmstadt
29 (left) MEPL; (top right) Stadtarchiv der Stadt Darmstadt; (bottom right) Broadlands Archive
30 (top) Mansell Collection; (bottom) Bettmann
31 MEPL
33 (left, top right) Bettmann; (bottom right) Bunin Family Collection, Hoover Institution Archives

34 (left) VM; (top right) WCLH; (bottom right) Stadtarchiv der Stadt Darmstadt
41 Hulton Deutsch Collection
42 Moscow
43 Mansell Collection

CHAPTER THREE
44–45 Scala/Art Resource
46 (left) Moscow — Photograph by PC; (top right) Le Petit Journal, Private Collection; (bottom right) Illustrated London News, Private Collection
47 Le Petit Journal, Private Collection
48 (left) Hulton Deutsch Collection; (right) Byington Collection
49 Illustrated London News, Private Collection
50 (top right, bottom right) Illustrated London News, Private Collection
52 (top) Gilman Paper Company Collection; (bottom) Moscow
53 (bottom) SP
54 Moscow
56 Stadtarchiv der Stadt Darmstadt
57 Novosti
58 (left) Private Collection; (right) Forbes
60 (left, top right, middle right) Private Collection; (bottom left, bottom right) MEPL
61 (all) Private Collection
62 SP
63 (top) The Hundred Antiques, Sterling, Ontario; (middle, bottom) Moscow
64 (top) Moscow; (Fabergé fan) Forbes — Photograph by Larry Stein; (Dowager Empress Marie) WCLH; (all others) Woronzow-Daschkow, Hilarion Graf Collection, Hoover Institution Archives

CHAPTER FOUR
66 The State Hermitage Museum — Photograph by PC
67 Broadlands Archive
68 (left) Forbes — Photograph by Robert Forbes; (right) Gilman Paper Company Collection
69 (top) Moscow; (bottom left) RIA-Novosti/Sovfoto
70 (left) Moscow — Photograph by PC; (right) MEPL
71 SP
72 (top right) Moscow; (bottom right) Author's Collection
73 UPI/Bettmann
74 (top left) WCLH; (bottom left) Beinecke; (middle, right) Moscow
75 The State Hermitage Museum — Photograph by PC
76 Sovfoto/Eastfoto
77 (top) Gilman Paper Company Collection; (bottom left) VA/Sovfoto; (bottom 1st from left) Mansell Collection; (bottom 2nd from left) Hulton Deutsch Collection; (bottom right) UPI/Bettmann
79 (inset) Bettmann
80 (all) Hulton Deutsch Collection
81 MEPL
82 (top) MEPL; (bottom) Sovfoto/Eastfoto
83 (all) MEPL
84 SP
85 Moscow
86 Author's Collection
87 RIA-Novosti/Sovfoto
88 Moscow

89 (all) Moscow
90 (top) Lausanne; (bottom) Moscow
91 (left) Bettmann; (right) Moscow
92 (all) Beinecke
93 Moscow

CHAPTER FIVE
94 Bettmann
95 (top) Sovfoto/Eastfoto; (top and bottom left) Bettmann; (right) Moscow
96 Moscow
97 (top) SP; (bottom left) Bettmann; (bottom right) Moscow
99 (bottom left) Lausanne; (bottom middle) Hulton Deutsch Collection; (bottom right) Moscow
100 (bottom left) Beinecke
101 (top left) Beinecke; (middle left) Moscow; (bottom left) WCLH
103 (bottom left) Sovfoto; (bottom center) Beinecke; (bottom right) Mansell Collection; (all others) Moscow
104–105 (all) Moscow
107 (top left, bottom center) Beinecke; (bottom left) Bettmann; (bottom right) WCLH
108 (all) Beinecke
109 (inset left) The Bettmann Archive; (inset right) Beinecke
110 Beinecke; (inset) Moscow
111 (top right, inset left) Moscow; (bottom right, inset right, left) Beinecke

CHAPTER SIX
112 (left) Mansell Collection; (right) Moscow
114 MEPL
115 Hoover Institution Archives
117 (top) Moscow; (bottom) Lausanne
119 (inset) SP
120 (top) Hoover Institution Archives; (bottom left) SP; (bottom right) Novosti
121 (top) Hoover Institution Archives; (bottom) SP
122 (inset left) SP; (inset right) Moscow
123 (left) Pavlosk Museum — Photograph by PC; (top and bottom right) Moscow
124 Author's Collection
125 VM
126 Bettmann
127 SP
128 Moscow
129 (left) Hoover Institution Archives; (right) MEPL
130 (left) Moscow; (top right, bottom right) Lausanne
131 (top) Gilman Paper Company Collection; (bottom) Lausanne
132 (top) SP; (bottom) Beinecke
134 (inset) SP
136 Moscow
137 (left, top right) Moscow; (bottom right) Lausanne

CHAPTER SEVEN
140 WCLH
142 (all) Hulton Deutsch Collection
143 SP
144 Beinecke
147 Moscow; (inset) SP
148 Moscow
150 SP
151 WCLH

CHAPTER EIGHT
154 SP
155 Sovfoto
157 Bettmann
158 Moscow
159 (bottom left group) Moscow — Photograph by PC; (top left) Lausanne; (top right, bottom right) Moscow
160 (inset) Moscow
162 Moscow; (inset) Lausanne
163 WCLH
168 SP
169 (inset) Author's Collection
170 WCLH
171 (all) WCLH
172 (top) WCLH; (bottom) Hulton Deutsch Collection
173 (top left) The Bettmann Archive; (top right) WCLH; (bottom) WCLH — Photograph by PC
174 MEPL/Alexander Meledin Collection
175 Forbes
176 Moscow — Photograph by PC
177 (all) WCLH
178 (all) WCLH
179 WCLH
181 (inset) Author's Collection; (bottom) WCLH

CHAPTER NINE
182 WCLH; (inset) Author's Collection
184 Private Collection
185 James H. Whitehead Collection, Hoover Institution Archives
186 Lausanne
187 (bottom left) Author's Collection; (top left, right) Private Collection
189 (all) WCLH
190 WCLH
191 (left) James H. Whitehead Collection, Hoover Institution Archives; (top left) WCLH — Photograph by PC; (top right) Private Collection; (bottom right) Moscow — Photograph by PC
193 Private Collection
195 Moscow — Photograph by PC
196 (top) WCLH; (bottom left and right) Private Collection
197 MEPL

CHAPTER TEN
198 Lausanne
200 WCLH
201 James H. Whitehead Collection, Hoover Institution Archives
202–203 WCLH
203 (top, bottom left, bottom right) Private Collection; (middle right) Lausanne
204 Author's Collection
205 (all) Byington Collection
206 (all) Byington Collection
207 (all) Byington Collection
208 (left) Author's Collection; (top right, bottom right) FPG/Masterfile
209 (top) FPG/Masterfile; (bottom) Byington Collection
210 Author's Collection
211 (left, middle) Author's Collection; (right) Moscow
212 (top) Moscow; (bottom) Author's Collection
213 (all) Author's Collection
214 Private Collection
215 Private Collection
217 (all) East News/Sipa
222-223 Map by Jack McMaster

Index

❧

Design, Typography and Art Direction: Gordon Sibley Design Inc.

Editorial Director: Hugh M. Brewster

Project Editors: Rick Archbold, Mireille Majoor

Copy Editor: Shelley Tanaka

Editorial Assistant: Lloyd Davis

Production Director: Susan Barrable

Production Co-ordinator: Donna Chong

Color Separation: Colour Technologies

Printing and Binding: Sfera/Garzanti

*Today in Ekaterinburg
a cross marks the site where the
imperial family died.*

TSAR: THE LOST WORLD OF NICHOLAS AND ALEXANDRA
was produced by Madison Press Books
under the direction of of Albert E. Cummings